The Many Faces of the Church

COMPANIONS TO THE NEW TESTAMENT

The Many Faces of the Church

A Study in
New Testament Ecclesiology

RAYMOND F. COLLINS

A Herder & Herder Book
The Crossroad Publishing Company
New York

The Crossroad Publishing Company
481 Eighth Avenue, New York, NY 10001

Printed in the United States of America

Library of Congress Cataloging-in-Publication Data

Collins, Raymond F., 1935-
    The many faces of the church : a study in New Testament ecclesiology
  / Raymond F. Collins.
      p. cm.
    "A Herder & Herder book."
    Includes bibliographical references (p.   ) and index.
    ISBN 0-8245-2135-8
    1. Church—Biblical teaching. 2. Bible. N.T.—Criticism,
  interpretation, etc. I. Title.
  BS2545.C5C59 2004
  262'.009'015—dc22

                                            2003022312

1   2   3   4   5   6   7   8   9   10   07   06   05   04   03

*In Gratitude
for the People of God
throughout the World
Who Have Taught Me
What It Means to Be
the Church of God*

Contents

CHAPTER NINE

CHAPTER TEN

Preface to the Series

The Companions to the New Testament series aims to unite New Testament study with theological concerns in a clear and concise manner. Each volume:

- engages the New Testament text directly.
- focuses on the religious (theological/ethical) content of the New Testament.
- is written out of respect for the integrity of the religious tradition being studied. This means that the New Testament is studied in terms of its own time and place. It is allowed to speak in its own terms, out of its own assumptions, espousing its own values.
- involves cutting-edge research, bringing the results of scholarly discussions to the general reader
- provides resources for the reader who wishes to enter more deeply into the scholarly discussion.

The contributors to the series are established scholars who have studied and taught the New Testament for many years and who can now reap a wide-ranging harvest from the fruits of their labors. Multiple theological perspectives and denominational identities are represented. Each author is free to address the issues from his or her own social and religious location, within the parameters set for the series.

It is our hope that these small volumes will make some contribution to the recovery of the vision of the New Testament world for our time.

Charles H. Talbert
Baylor University

Preface

I have written this book at a time in my life when I am in the middle of a fifth decade of ministry in the church. At the same time I am in the middle of a fourth decade of teaching about the New Testament in the halls of academe, both here and abroad. This book comes as much from my experience of the church as it does from my probing of New Testament texts.

My life as a priest and professor has been enriched by many different experiences of church. Many of those experiences have been mediated to me by students who have not only shared with me their own experiences and expectations of church, but who have also invited me to share their experience of church by visiting the believing communities from which they themselves have come. In the summer of 2002 I was the invited guest of the Bishops' Conference of Singapore, Malaysia, and Brunei. My visit to those Asian churches gave me the opportunity to lecture on the church in the writings of Paul. My lectures were, I hope, a gift to the local churches of Singapore, Bohor Jahru, Kuala Lumpur, Penang, and Kuching. My experience of those churches was their gift to me. Once again, I had the grace to experience the profound unity and the rich diversity of the church of Christ in lands far removed from my own among people whose cultural heritages were so different from the culture in which I was raised.

Previously I had been graced to spend time in different churches in other parts of Asia, Africa, Latin America, Australia, and Europe. Each experience has been another grace, as have been the invitations to preach the word of God in the pulpit of a Christian church whose confession is somewhat different from my own. God has also allowed me to experience at once the unity and diversity of the church when I gave a lecture, preached a retreat, directed a workshop, or led Bible study among Christians who did share some of the specifics of my Roman Catholic faith.

As I look back on my years as priest and professor, I cannot help but be cognizant not only of the cultural differences among the churches implanted on the several continents of this earth but also of the different practices, beliefs, theology, and ministries that characterize believers of different Christian confessions. Culture and confession contribute immensely to the diversity of the church; so, too, does time. The church and the churches have changed so much during the years that I have been leader and lecturer. To some extent the rigid uniformity of some churches has given way to rich diversity. To some extent the isolation of some churches has yielded to an experience of unity, common understanding, and sharing. The church and the churches will surely continue to change in the decades of the millennium barely begun.

The present exegetical study seeks to foster an understanding of the different experiences of church evident in the texts of the New Testament and the variety of ecclesial expressions, of thought and practice, that are found within its pages. At the same time this study seeks to provide the church and the churches with an understanding of its roots. It will, I hope, enable those who belong to the church, especially those who study it reflectively, to touch base with its roots and see that diversity and change have been a constant concomitant of ecclesial existence from the very beginning. The church and the churches can find in the diversity of church experience to which the texts of the New Testament bear witness a paradigm and warrant for the diversity and change that they experience within the context of a profound unity which seeks ever fuller and more adequate expression.

The pages of this study were first shared with a group of students at the Catholic University of America in the fall of 2002. The group of twelve were a microcosm of the church as it exists at the present. Among the twelve were men and woman. They were leaders, laity, and would-be leaders. They came from India, Kenya, Slovakia, Sweden, Vietnam, Wales, and the United States. They were Roman Catholic, Lutheran, and Episcopalian. Such is the church as it exists at the present moment in the history of salvation, all gathered together in a single small room. I will be ever grateful to David Bird, Joseph Elamparayil, Mary-Angela Harper, Robert Harris, Kathy Ieren, Mary Elizabeth Kenel, Cosmas K'Otienoh, Kevin Offner, Peter Nguyen, Elvis Razov, Tobias Unnerstal, and Stephen Wilbricht who through their gathering and their interaction provided such a wonderful experience of church.

Among them, I am especially grateful to Mary-Angela Harper and Mary Elizabeth Kenel who so kindly read through the draft, probing the obscurities in the text and correcting its typographical errors. I must also extend a word of thanks to Ms. Joan Fricot, lecturer at Johnson and Wales University, who generously perused the final draft, using her experience as a teacher of the English language to correct the grammar and improve the quality of the text. A final word of personal thanks goes to Charles Talbert, editor of the Companions to the New Testament series. Dr. Talbert took time from his personal academic pursuits to read the manuscript and offer many valuable suggestions. To him I am ever so grateful.

Beyond these several individuals who have contributed in various ways to this study, I am grateful to so many around the world who have gifted me with an experience of church. In recent years I have been particularly blessed by the Catholic communities of St. Matthias in Lanham, Maryland, and of St. Luke in Barrington, Rhode Island. For ten and thirty years respectively, these communities have allowed me to experience the church at home. To them I shall ever be grateful for they have enriched my life and my faith.

Raymond F. Collins

Abbreviations

Pseudepigrapha

2 Bar.	2 Baruch
Jub.	Jubilees
Pss. Sol.	Psalms of Solomon
T. Abr.	Testament of Abraham
T. Naph.	Testament of Naphtali

Mishnaic and Rabbinic Literature

Names of tractates (preceded by *m.* [= Mishnah], *b.* [= Babylonian Talmud], or *y.* [= Jerusalem Talmud])

Giṭ.	Giṭṭin
Qidd.	Qiddušin
Sanh.	Sanhedrin

Other Jewish Literature

1QH	(Qumran) *Thanksgiving Hymns* (*Hodayot*)
1QM	(Qumran) *War Scroll* (*Milhamah*)
1QS	(Qumran) *Rule of the Community* (*Serek*)
1QSa	[= 1Q28a] *Rule of the Community* (Appendix a to 1QS)
Ant.	Josephus, *Jewish Antiquities*
J.W.	Josephus, *Jewish War*
CD	*Damascus Document*

Apostolic Fathers

1 Clem.	1 Clement
Did.	Didache

Herm. Vis.	*Hermas, Visions*
Herm. Sim.	*Hermas, Similitudes*
Ign. *Magn.*	Ignatius, *Letter to the Magnesians*
Ign. *Phld.*	Ignatius, *Letter to the Philadelphians*
Ign. *Pol.*	Ignatius, *Letter to Polycarp*
Ign. *Rom.*	Ignatius, *Letter to the Romans*
Ign. *Smyrn.*	Ignatius, *Letter to the Smyrnaeans*
Ign. *Trall.*	Ignatius, *Letter to the Trallians*
Pol. *Phil.*	Polycarp, *Letter to the Philippians*

Periodicals, Reference Works, and Serials

AB	Anchor Bible
ABD	*Anchor Bible Dictionary*
ABRL	Anchor Bible Reference Library
AnBib	Analecta biblica
ASNU	Acta seminarii neotestamentici upsaliensis
BETL	Bibliotheca ephemeridum theologicarum lovaniensium
BNTC	Black's New Testament Commentaries
BTB	*Biblical Theology Bulletin*
CBET	Contributions to Biblical Theology and Exegesis
CBQ	*Catholic Biblical Quarterly*
CC	Continental Commentaries
CIG	*Corpus inscriptionum graecarum.* Edited by A. Boeckh. 4 vols. Berlin, 1828-1877.
ConBNT	Conietanea biblica: New Testament Series
CP	*Classical Philology*
DRev	*Downside Review*
EBib	Etudes bibliques
EDNT	*Exegetical Dictionary of the New Testament.* Edited by H. Balz and G. Schneider. 3 vols. ET. Grand Rapids: Eerdmans, 1990-1993.
FF	Foundations and Facets
FRLANT	Forschungen zur Religion und Literatur des Alten und Neuen Testaments
GNS	Good News Studies
HTKNT	Herders theologischer Kommentar zum Neuen Testament
ICC	International Critical Commentary
IDBSup	*The Interpreter's Dictionary of the Bible: Supplementary Volume*
IG	*Inscriptiones graecae.* Editio minor. Berlin, 1924-.

IGRom	*Inscriptiones graecae ad res romanas pertinentes.* Edited by R. Cagnat et al. 4 vols. Paris, 1911-1927.
JSNTSup	Journal for the Study of the New Testament: Supplement Series
KlT	Kleine Texte für Vorlesungen und Übungen
LS	*Louvain Studies*
LSJ	H. G. Liddell, R. Scott, H. S. Jones. *A Greek-English Lexicon.* 9th ed. Oxford: Oxford University Press, 1996.
LTP	*Laval théologique et philosophique*
LTPM	Louvain Theological and Pastoral Monographs
MelT	*Melita theologica*
NewDocs	*New Documents Illustrating Early Christianity.* Edited by G. H. R. Horsley and S. Llewelyn. 9 vols. North Ride, N.S.W., 1981–.
NICNT	New International Commentary on the New Testament
NIGTC	New International Greek Commentary
NJBC	*The New Jerome Biblical Commentary.* Edited by R. E. Brown et al. Englewood Cliffs, N.J.: Prentice-Hall, 1990.
NovT	*Novum Testamentum*
NovTSup	Novum Testamentum Supplements
NTL	New Testament Library
NTS	*New Testament Studies*
OTP	*Old Testament Pseudepigrapha.* Edited by J. H. Charlesworth. 2 vols. New York: Doubleday, 1983.
PG	Patrologia graeca. Edited by J.-P. Migne, 162 vols. Paris, 1857-1886.
RB	*Revue biblique*
SBLDS	Society of Biblical Literature Dissertation Series
SBLMS	Society of Biblical Literature Monograph Series
SBLSBS	Society of Biblical Literature Sources for Biblical Study
SNTA	Studiorum Novi Testamenti Auxilia
SNTSU	Studien zum Neuen Testament und seiner Umwelt
SP	Sacra Pagina
Str-B	Strack, H. L., and P. Billerbeck, *Kommentar zum Neuen Testament aus Talmud und Midrasch.* 6 vols. Munich: Beck, 1922–61.
TBT	*The Bible Today*
TLNT	*Theological Lexicon of the New Testament.* C. Spicq. Translated by M. E. Biddle. 3 vols. Peabody, Mass.: Hendrickson, 1997.
WBC	Word Biblical Commentary
WMANT	Wissenschaftliche Monographien zun Alten und Neuen Testament
WUNT	Wissenschaftliche Untersuchungen zum Neuen Testament
ZNW	*Zeitschrift für die neutestamentliche Wissenschaft und die Kunde der älteren Kirche*

Versions of the Bible in English

AV   Authorized Version
JB   Jerusalem Bible
KJB   King James Bible [= Authorized Version]
NAB   New American Bible
NABRNT   New American Bible, Revised New Testament
NEB   New English Bible
NIV   New International Version
NJB   New Jerusalem Bible
NRSV   New Revised Standard Version
REB   Revised English Bible
RSV   Revised Standard Version

Other Abbreviations

Gos. Thom.   *Gospel of Thomas*
GNT   *The Greek New Testament*. 4th rev. ed. Edited by B. Aland et al.
               Stuttgart: Deutsche Bibelgesellschaft, 1993.
LXX   Septuagint
MT   Masoretic Text
N-A   *Novum Testamentum Graecae*. 27th rev. ed. Edited by B. Aland and
               K. Aland et al. Stuttgart: Deutsche Bibelgesellschaft, 1993.
P. Oxy.   Oxyrhynchus Papyrus

Acknowledgments

The translation of biblical texts follows the New Revised Standard Version. Translations of texts from the Dead Sea Scrolls are taken from Florentino García Martínez and Eibert J. C. Tigchelaar, eds., *The Dead Sea Scrolls*, 2 vols. (Leiden: Brill, 1997-1998). Translations of classical texts follow the editions of the Loeb Classical Library.

Chapter One

"The Church
of the Thessalonians"

In the history of the early church known as the Acts of the Apostles, Paul is said to have been in contact with churches in Jerusalem, Antioch, Lystra, Derbe, Ephesus, Syria, and Cilicia. History does not provide any clear evidence that Paul wrote to any of these churches.[1] As a matter of fact Paul's own letters never refer to any of these groups as "churches."[2]

Paul did, however, write to a number of churches. First Thessalonians[3] is the oldest of his extant letters. This letter provides the oldest attestation of the use of the word "church" to refer to a Christian group. Associating Silvanus and Timothy with himself, Paul wrote a letter to a group of believers to whom he had preached a short time previously. He identified those believers as "the church of the Thessalonians in God the Father and the Lord Jesus Christ" (1 Thess 1:1).

A Gathering

Those to whom Paul wrote were a "church" (*ekklēsia*), a duly summoned assembly. Living in a free city with some degree of local autonomy, the Thessalonians were familiar with the term that Paul used to address them. The popular assembly, *ekklēsia tou dēmou,*[4] was an essential part of their system of governance. Public assemblies were the way in which the free male populace participated in the civic life of the city.

The group to which Paul wrote was much smaller than these popular assemblies; its members came together for reasons other than political governance. Among their reasons for gathering was that the gathering

1

provided an opportunity for them to listen to the reading of the letter that Paul sent to them. Paul brought the letter to a close with a strong plea that it be read to the entire assembly (1 Thess 5:27). We do not know who convened the meeting. Most probably it was whoever was normally in charge of the group (1 Thess 5:12), but it is quite possible that the person who delivered the letter called the group together. In the Hellenistic world it was not at all unusual for a letter carrier to expand on the contents of a letter that he had delivered.

The assembly to which Paul wrote was composed of people who came together at a specific time and in a given place. The church (*ekklēsia*) to which Paul wrote was a happening, an event, whose constitutive elements were people, place, and time. The etymology of the Greek term suggests that the group was assembled as a response to a call or summons. Derived from the preposition *ek-* ("from") and the root *kal-* ("call") the word *ekklēsia* implies some kind of selection or election.[5] Paul fleshed out this implication when he described the group as an assembly of Thessalonians (*ekklēsia ek tōn Thessalonikeōn*, 1 Thess 1:1[6]). He did not write to the entire population of the capital of the Roman province of Macedonia; he wrote only to a select group of Thessalonians. The greeting of his letter is explicit in this regard. Using a partitive genitive (*Thessalonikeōn*), Paul speaks of the gathering as one that was constituted "from among the Thessalonians."[7]

Paul then described the gathering as being "in God the Father and the Lord Jesus Christ." A relationship to God and to the Lord Jesus distinguished the group to whom Paul was writing from other assemblies of Thessalonians, especially the various trade, funeral, and religious associations which existed in the city. Among the religious groups would have been an assembly of local Jews, the synagogue (*synagōgē*, a "coming together"). Paul's two-part phrase identifies the assembly to which he was writing as a religious group, one that recognizes itself as being in relationship with God the Father[8] and the Lord Jesus Christ,[9] thus, distinguishing the church from all other kinds of groups in Thessalonica.

Paul's qualifying dyad is particularly important. The deity to which the church of the Thessalonians was related was not Cabiros, Dionysis, Isis, Osiris, Serapion, or one of the other gods whose cults were celebrated in the various temples throughout the city. Rather the group to whom Paul was writing saw itself as a group of people who had a relationship with God, whom they identified as Father.[10] The designation of God as Father is so common in Paul that some commentators have claimed that Paul had only one notion of God, namely, that of God-Father. In using the word "Father," Paul identifies the assembly to which he was writing as the one God of his own Jewish tradition. God revealed himself as Father by raising Jesus, the Son, from the dead (see 1 Thess 1:10). Thus, the assembly that was related to God the Father was also related to Jesus, known in Christian tradition as the Messiah, Christ.[11] Designating Jesus Christ as "Lord," Paul implicitly professed belief that God had raised Jesus from the dead. This belief so marked Paul's understanding of God's fatherhood that he identified the church to which he wrote as an assembly related not only to the one God but also to Jesus Christ acknowledged as Lord. This christological qualification of the church of the Thessalonians distinguished the assembly from an assembly of Jews who acknowledged the one God but did not accept Jesus as Messiah and Lord.

The way that Paul identified the Thessalonians in the salutation of the letter is unpacked in the thanksgiving that immediately follows the opening greeting (1 Thess 1:2–2:13). Among Paul's cherished memories of the Thessalonians was his knowledge that they had been chosen by God. He is aware of their election (*tēn ekklogēn*[12] *hymōn*).[13] The idea of election is a key feature of his thoughts about them.[14] The members of the church are beloved by God; they are God's chosen ones. God who loved and has chosen them has also called them (see 1 Thess 1:1; 5:24) and taught them (1 Thess 4:9).

The Thessalonians had been called to be God's own people. Their calling set them apart from people who do not know God (see 1 Thess 4:5). In Paul's simple sociology there are but two kinds of people: those who know God and those who do not. The two groups are radically different from each other. The members of the church to whom Paul was writing had abandoned their previous devotion to one or another idol. They embraced the one God in whom they placed their trust (1 Thess 1:8). They committed themselves to the service of this one God (1 Thess 1:9). Thus, the Thessalonians became members of the chosen people.

Reflecting on their election, Paul declared that he knew that the Thessalonians had been chosen by God because his preaching of the word of God among them had been effective (1 Thess 1:4-5).[15] In his preaching, God's powerful word was at work among the Thessalonians with the result that they became believers (1 Thess 2:13). They received the word of God with "inspirited" joy (1 Thess 1:6). Their joy was an indication that they now existed in the presence of God.

The immediate effect of Paul's proclamation of the gospel was that the Thessalonians who received his message abandoned their worship of idols and began to serve the living and true God (1 Thess 1:9). Their service bespeaks their allegiance to the one God; they became servants of the deity who alone can be called the living and true God. Had the God whom they now acknowledged not been the one God, there would have been no need for the Thessalonians to abandon their worship of idols. Located in the heart of the empire, the Roman Pantheon was a temple dedicated to all the gods. Service to the living and true God required, however, that those who were loved and chosen by him turn from the idols to whom they previously had been devoted.

Service of the God who broached no worship of idols was service to the "living and true God." Paul's two-word description highlights two of God's primary traits. The living God was not only the active God; God was also a life-giving God, God the creator. The true God was not only authentically god, God to whom the word "god" was applicable in a way that it was to no other reality; God was also a faithful God, true to his promise, the God who had chosen his people. Creation and election were the focal points of Paul's pregnant description of the God to whom the chosen Thessalonians had turned. They knew the living God (cf. 1 Thess 4:5); they had been loved, chosen, and taught (1 Thess 4:9) by the God who remains faithful to them (1 Thess 5:24).

Having prayed for an increase in their love, Paul encouraged and urged them to grow in their love for one another.

Marks of the Church

Paul's recollection of this beloved assembly focused on its life in the presence of God. They were a group of people characterized by dynamic faith, active love, and steadfast hope in the Lord Jesus Christ (1 Thess 1:3). These three qualities were the marks of the church of the Thessalonians; they were its characteristic and identifying traits.

The assembly's relationship with God, the relationship of trust that came to be known as "faith," made an impact on their lives. Their faith was a dynamic faith. Not only did their faith lead them to embrace the living and true God; their faith was so dynamic that the word of God spread from the Thessalonians throughout the province of Macedonia and as far south as the province of Achaia (1 Thess 1:7). The example of the Thessalonians' faith sustained the faith of believers in Macedonia and Achaia.

Active love was a second hallmark of the Thessalonian church. Paul wrote about their "labor of love," implying that their love was not merely a matter of kind dispositions or feelings of good will. Rather, their love required effort on their part. Demanding effort and energy, their love could tire them out. Later in the letter, Paul wrote that Timothy had returned from a visit to Thessalonica with good news about the love of this church (1 Thess 3:6). Timothy's report confirmed the impression that Paul remembered. The church of the Thessalonians was a community of people whose love for one another was one of their most characteristic traits.

In his prayer, Paul mentioned their love for one another and for all (*eis allēlous kai eis pantas*, 1 Thess 3:12). He prayed not only that the members of the church be preserved blameless until the coming of the Lord Jesus Christ (1 Thess 3:13; 5:23) but also that their love might grow and abound. He desired that this defining trait be intensified and that the parameters of its outreach be extended. Having prayed for an increase in their love, Paul encouraged and urged them to grow in their love for one another.

Such was the love of the Thessalonians for one another that Paul could say that he really had no need to mention it (1 Thess 4:9). His disclaimer was a subtle way of drawing attention to the quality of their love. Paul described their love as *philadelphia*, love among siblings. Their love for one another was similar to the kind of love that ought to characterize the members of a family, a love for one's brothers and sisters.

Their love was a given; yet for all its reality it could be intensified and expanded. Paul described the Thessalonians' sibling love as a love for one another that extended to all their brothers and sisters in faith throughout Macedonia. The expansive love of the Thessalonian church reached beyond the confines of their own assembly to embrace fellow Christians throughout the province. Paul prayed that their love would reach out beyond their fellow believers to everyone (1 Thess 3:12).

As the working love remembered by Paul (1 Thess 1:3), the Thessalonians' love for one another was directed to other members of their own church in a way that could not be extended to all Macedonian believers and beyond them to everyone. Urging them to increase their love (*perisseuein mallon*, 1 Thess 4:10), Paul spelled out what their labor of love entailed: "Aspire to live quietly, to mind your own affairs, and to work with your

hands . . . so that you may behave properly toward outsiders and be dependent on no one" (1 Thess 4:11-12). Paul was not promoting quietism or
withdrawal from life in the city; rather, he urged believers to take care of
their own affairs and engage in the manual labor that would enable them
to be a group of people that was more or less self-sufficient. They were
expected to find among themselves the kind of resources that would obvi-
ate any need (*chreian*) for assistance from people outside the community.
Doing so, believers in Thessalonica would be able to live the kind of peaceful life to which people in the Greco-Roman world aspired (see 1 Tim 2:2).
They could treat others properly, gaining respectability as they did so.

Identifying these other people as "outsiders" (*tous exō*, 1 Thess 4:12),
Paul shows that he considered the church of the Thessalonians to be iden-
tifiably distinct from others. The distinction in 1 Thessalonians between
insiders and outsiders is only one among several textual indications that
the church of Thessalonians was a discrete group of people. The difference
between them and others was implicit in the way that Paul described the
assembly in 1 Thess 1:1 and his reference to their having been chosen by
God. They were a select group. They were distinct from those who did not
know God (*ta ethnē ta mē eidota ton theon*, 1 Thess 4:5). They were different from those who have no hope (*hoi loipoi hoi mē echontes elpida*, 1 Thess
4:13). These people were the outsiders on whom the Thessalonian Christians were expected to make a favorable impression.

Identifying a lack of hope as an outsiders' trait, Paul reinforced the
view that hope is a trait that ought to characterize the assembly of believers. Hence, Paul identified steadfastness of hope in our Lord Jesus Christ
as a third defining quality of the Thessalonian assembly, so fondly remembered by Paul (1 Thess 1:3). As its faith was dynamic and their love a real
effort, so their hope was one that persisted in spite of difficulties.

Paul does not mention the difficulties[16] that may have confronted
their hope during the time of his visit to Thessalonica. When Timothy
returned from Thessalonica, Paul learned from him that there was something missing in the Thessalonians' faith (1 Thess 3:10). Timothy returned
from his visit to Thessalonica with news about their faith and love (1 Thess
3:6), but nothing was said about their hope. The report that Timothy
brought to Paul about the church at Thessalonica seems not to have been
as favorable with regard to hope as it was with regard to their love. Something was missing in their faith: the missing element was the hope that
should have flowed from their trust in God. The hope that at one time had

been steadfast was now shaky. The deaths of some members of the community, perhaps at the hand of a few fellow citizens (1 Thess 2:14-16), seems to have shaken the faith of this new church.

Paul's letter to the Thessalonians was intended to strengthen their hope, thereby supplying what was lacking in their faith. The object of their hope was the Lord Jesus Christ (1 Thess 1:3). Thessalonian believers were waiting for the appearance of the Son from heaven, Jesus, whom God had raised from the dead (1 Thess 1:10). Their salvation was to consist of their being with the Lord forever (1 Thess 4:17). But Paul's Thessalonians were worried. Their hope was shaken by the reality that some of them died before the parousia. Paul's response was that they ought not to grieve, as outsiders do. Just as Jesus had been raised from the dead by God, so those who died in Christ will be raised from the dead (1 Thess 4:14-16). With regard to ultimate salvation, the eschatological situation will be one of parity. The living will have no advantage over the dead because God will bring with Jesus those who have died in him. Hope that all who have gathered will live with the Lord distinguishes the members of this gathering from all other gatherings in Thessalonica.

Paul could and did pray that those who gathered in Thessalonica, listening to the reading of his letter (1 Thess 5:27), would be preserved blameless until the coming of the Lord Jesus (1 Thess 3:13; see 5:23). Ultimate salvation could not be taken for granted. The Thessalonians had no need for him to write about the time of the Day of the Lord (1 Thess 5:1-2). It was inevitable and would come when least expected. While waiting, the Thessalonians were to arm themselves for the struggle of life. Using a scriptural image (see Isa 59:17), Paul urged them to put on the breastplate of faith and love (1 Thess 5:8).

Paul recalled that faith and love characterized the community that he remembered (1 Thess 1:3). He had received encouraging news that they had persevered in faith and love (1 Thess 3:6). Now, as his letter draws to its close (1 Thess 5:8), he urges the Thessalonians to continue in the two dimensions of righteousness, right relationship with God (faith) and right relationships with others (love). In his epistolary thanksgiving, Paul had recalled, to the Thessalonians' own benefit, that their faith was dynamic and their love was demanding. Using the military metaphor of armor, Paul subtly reminded the Thessalonians that life is a struggle and that the dyad of active faith and love equips them for life in the real world. He then complemented his description of their being clothed for battle with a reference to hope: the

Thessalonians were to put on the hope of salvation as if it were a helmet. Their hope, as well as their faith and love, should sustain them as they struggle to be vigilantly alert in the journey of life.

Internal Bonds

If the realities of faith, love, and hope characterized the assembly, helping to distinguish it from various groups of outsiders, internal bonds united the members of the assembly with one another. The ties that bound them together were manifest in their active love for one another. Their love was such that Paul identifies it as sibling love (*philadelphia*).[17] Kinship language is the "language of belonging."[18] Such language strengthens the bonds that tie people together, imparting a sense of identity that distinguishes them from outsiders.

The Thessalonians' active love for one another is a manifestation of these kinship ties. Their active love held this fictive family together. They were expected to live in peace with one another, encourage one another, admonish the unruly, exhort the fainthearted, help the weak, and be patient with everyone (1 Thess 5:13-14). Paul urged them to work with their hands so that their family would not need to rely on outsiders (1 Thess 4:11-12). Commenting on this passage, Mikael Tellbe observes that in this way Paul reinforces the church's identity as a "court of reputation" and strengthens their self-understanding.[19]

Having once preached the word of God to those who were then assembled in Thessalonica, Paul likened himself to a parent, a mother or a father (1 Thess 2:7, 11). He addressed them as his siblings (*adelphoi*). At the beginning of his letter he addressed them as siblings chosen by God (1 Thess 1:4). At the end of his letter, he addressed them as his brothers and sisters, asking them to pray for his companions and himself (1 Thess 5:25). All told, this relatively short letter appealed fourteen times to those who gathered to listen to it as Paul's siblings, members of his family.[20] Among Paul's extant letters, only the much longer 1 Corinthians exceeds 1 Thessalonians in the number of times that Paul appeals to his addressees as members of his own family.[21] The intensity of Paul's language is a reflection of his desire to knit them together as a distinct and cohesive group.[22]

Family ties extended beyond the small group that assembled in Thessalonica. Not only did Paul consider himself their brother; he also considered Timothy (1 Thess 3:2) to be their brother as well. Presumably, Silvanus would also have been a member of their extended family. Beyond this trio of apostles sent to the Thessalonians (1 Thess 2:7), the Thessalonians' kinship and love extended to other Christians throughout Macedonia. These probably included the Philippians, who lived a scant hundred miles from Thessalonica. This extended family may have included other people in the province who had been in Thessalonica during the time of Paul's visit and had been able to listen to his preaching on the occasion. In any event, it is certain that word of the Thessalonians' faith went beyond the provincial capital's city limits (1 Thess 1:8).

The Holy Spirit

In his initial characterization of the gathering at Thessalonica as an assembly "in God the Father and the Lord Jesus Christ" (1 Thess 1:1), Paul made no mention of the Spirit. His silence in that regard did not at all suggest that he looked upon the church of the Thessalonians as unrelated to the Spirit. Far from it. All three references to the Holy Spirit in the letter to the Thessalonians are related to the church.

Paul first mentioned the Spirit in his initial thanksgiving (1:2–2:12). He said that the Thessalonians were chosen by God whose Holy Spirit was at work as Paul preached the gospel among them. He told the Thessalonians: "our message of the gospel came to you not in word only, but also in power and in the Holy Spirit (*en pneumati hagiō*) and with full conviction"[23] (1 Thess 1:5). This rhetorical contrast emphasizes the fact that the power of the gospel resided not in the rhetorical appeal of Paul's own words; rather it derived from the power of the Holy Spirit at work in the proclamation of the gospel. Paul reiterated this same idea in 1 Corinthians, where he wrote: "My speech and my proclamation were not with plausible words of wisdom, but with a demonstration of the Spirit and of power (*en apodeixei pneumatos kai dynameōs*)" (1 Cor 2:4).

The Holy Spirit is God's power at work. For Paul the preaching of the gospel was as much a manifestation of the Spirit as were the mighty works (*dynamesin*) that he considered to be the signs of his apostolate (see 2 Cor 12:12). Later in his life, commenting on the preaching of the gospel, Paul used the same words that he had written to the Thessalonians: "By word and deed, by the power of signs and wonders, by the power of the Spirit (*en dynamei pneumatos*) of God . . . I have fully proclaimed the good news (*to euangelion*) of Christ" (Rom 15:19). In the Letter to the Romans, Paul described the gospel as "the power of God for salvation to everyone who has faith" (Rom 1:16).

For Paul the power of the Spirit was at work not only in his preaching of the gospel but also in the Thessalonians' reception of his word. They received it not as a merely human message but as the word of God at work among them (1 Thess 2:13). They had received the word of God with a joy that comes from the Spirit of God (1 Thess 1:6). In the Letter to the Romans, Paul wrote about the power of the Holy Spirit, which produces not only joy but also hope among those who believe (see Rom 15:13).

The Holy Spirit was at work in the very foundation of the church of the Thessalonians in Paul's preaching to them and in their reception of the gospel for what it was, namely, God's word at work. Subsequently the Holy Spirit continued to work among the chosen Thessalonians. The Holy Spirit was God's abiding gift to them (1 Thess 4:8). The way that Paul speaks about this gift in 1 Thess 4:3-8 indicates that the Spirit is the operative Spirit of holiness in the community. It is the Spirit, God's active power at work, that constitutes the chosen Thessalonians as God's holy people. God's will for them is their sanctification; the Holy Spirit sanctifies them, making them God's holy people, people who belong to God. They are set apart from people who do not know God (1 Thess 4:5).[24] The Thessalonians who accepted Paul's preaching of the gospel are God's chosen ones, God's holy people.

> *The community could not exist without the power of the Spirit at work among those who spoke the word of God to them.*

Later in his letter, Paul urged the Thessalonians not to quench the Spirit (1 Thess 5:19). The powerful metaphor was common in Greek literature.[25] It evokes the image of a fire that must not be extinguished. As humans need fire for warmth and light, so the Thessalonian community needed the Spirit. They are not to let the Spirit disappear from their midst, nor should they attempt to control the Spirit.

Paul issued this exhortation as one of the last things that he said to them before offering a final prayer and expressing his farewell greetings. The exhortation introduces additional hortatory remarks on prophecy and the discernment of good and evil (1 Thess 5:20-22). Although the gospel had been preached to those who gathered to read Paul's letter just a few months before, Paul urged them not to despise prophetic utterances, the words of prophets (*prophēteias*). His understatement was a subtle reminder that the community could not exist without the power of the Spirit at work among those who spoke the word of God to them.

This does not mean that everything spoken by a prophet is a prophetic utterance. Paul's final exhortation urged the Thessalonians to use discretion, to make a judicious distinction between good and evil, to separate the authentic from the unauthentic. In this first of his letters Paul did not write about charisms, spiritual gifts, as he would in 1 Corinthians. In 1 Thessalonians Paul did not explicitly describe prophecy as a gift of the Spirit nor did he identify the discernment of spirits as a charism.[26] Paul was, nonetheless, already thinking along the lines that would eventually lead him to write about the charismatic nature of the church.[27] For the moment, Paul simply reminded the Thessalonians (1) that the Holy Spirit was operative in the foundation of the church in the preaching and reception of the gospel, (2) that the Holy Spirit continued to be active in the church sanctifying the members of the assembly and making them God's holy people, and (3) that the Holy Spirit would at least on occasion manifest itself in the word of God spoken among them.

Care of the Church

On any reading of Paul's letter to the Thessalonians, it is apparent that Paul did not abandon the Thessalonians. He spoke of the pain of separation, comparing it to that of the orphan (1 Thess 2:17), and of his desire to see them again. A burning desire to visit the Thessalonians was a focus of his prayer (1 Thess 3:10-11). Unable to make the visit for which he yearned, Paul sent Timothy in his stead. Later, he reached out to them in the form of a letter that has providentially been preserved to the present day. The letter is an expression of Paul's pastoral care[28] for the church at Thessalonica.

Any cohesive group of people needs, however, some form of on-site leadership. Paul wrote about leadership among the Thessalonians in an exhortation summarizing the responsibilities of the leaders of the community and speaking about the consideration that members of the assembly were expected to extend to their leaders: "We appeal to you, brothers and sisters, to respect[29] those who labor among you, and have charge of you in the Lord and admonish you; esteem them very highly in love because of their work" (1 Thess 5:12-13). Paul urged the assembly to recognize these people as their leaders, to perceive them as leaders and really experience their leadership. Because of their work, the leaders of the church were to be held in high esteem and treated with a superabundant kind of love.

Paul's exhortation was right at home in a letter written to an assembly of Thessalonians. Civic leadership of their city was provided by a group of "politarchs."[30] These office-holders were chosen from among the Thessalonians themselves for a one-year period of time during which they were responsible both to the citizenry and to the imperial authorities for just about every aspect of civic life. Similarly, the leaders commended by Paul were members of the assembly to which Paul was writing.[31] As the politarchs were chosen from among the city's wealthier citizens,[32] it is likely that the leaders of the assembly were those whose homes were large enough to host such a gathering.[33] Responsible to the Lord (1 Thess 5:12), these leaders were presumably responsible for and to the assembly.

Paul's exhortation that the assembly respect its leaders served to remind the leaders themselves of their responsibilities. As he often did, Paul used a group of three words to describe the leaders' tasks: they were to labor, to be in charge, and to admonish (*nouthetountas*). Clearly the role of these leaders was to serve the gospel, but it is difficult to determine precisely what their responsibilities were. Paul referred to what they did as "labor" (*kopiōntas*);[34] time, effort, and energy were demanded of them.

The task at hand was leadership in the Lord. The verb "be in charge" (*proïstamenous*), literally "to stand in front of," was commonly used to describe those who exercised civic leadership, particularly those who were leaders of a people or a city.[35] When he wrote to the Romans, Paul used this same expression (Rom 12:8) to describe the role of those who had a leadership function among God's beloved saints in Rome.[36] Qualifying leadership as leadership "in the Lord" (cf. Luke 22:25-27), Paul reminded both the leaders of the assembly and those who gathered in Thessalonica that the Lord was the source of the leaders' authority. Leaders were responsible to the Lord just as the politarchs were responsible to their *kyrios*, the Roman emperor.

All the members of the gathering were expected to admonish those who needed admonishing (1 Thess 5:14), but a special responsibility in this regard fell to the leaders of the assembly. Pseudo-Demitrius tells us what people in those times meant when they talked about admonishing someone. He writes: "Admonition (*nouthetein*) is the instilling of sense in the person who is admonished, and teaching him what should and should not be done."[37] Understood in this sense, admonishment is clearly the task of those who exercise leadership within a group.

Activities of the Church

Paul told the Thessalonians that he expected that his letter would be read to the entire assembly (1 Thess 5:27). He did not tell us where they met nor did he tell us what they might have done when they came together. He urged them to pray and give thanks (1 Thess 5:17-18) but gave no indication that these activities were communal activities. In fact, the exhortation that they should pray without ceasing and should give thanks in all circumstances indicates that prayer and thanksgiving were to pervade their lives rather than being restricted to occasional "liturgical" gatherings.[38] His reflection that they have been "taught by God" (*theodidaktoi*) to love one another was probably a reference to baptismal catechesis. In the context of the letter, the phrase primarily indicates that the Thessalonians are not self-taught, as some philosophers claimed to be. Rather, the Thessalonians have been taught by God in whose name they gathered.

Discussion and Study Questions

1. Why is the idea of election so important in Paul's understanding of the church?

2. What is the gift of prophecy? What does it mean for the church? Does it still exist at the present time?

3. What do most people consider to be the essential qualities of the church, "the marks of the church"?

4. What can we do to make our parish church more of a "gathering," a real church?

Chapter Two

"The Church in Your House"

When he wrote what is presumably his first letter, Paul addressed those who came together to listen to it being read as a gathering (*ekklēsia*, 1 Thess 1:1). Gatherings require people, a time to gather, and a place in which to gather. In that first letter Paul did not indicate the place where the audience gathered to listen to his message (1 Thess 5:27). Paul's frequent use of kinship language, especially the familiar form of his addressing those to whom he was writing as his brothers and sisters (1 Thess 1:4; 2:1, 9, 14, 17; 3:2, 7; 4:1, 6, 10 [2x], 13; 5:1, 4, 12, 14, 25, 26, 27), not only evokes the warm regard in which Paul held the Thessalonians but also suggests that Paul's audience gathered in a locale in which kinship language was properly "at home."[1]

When the situation of the Thessalonians is taken into consideration, it becomes even more likely that the Thessalonians gathered in the home of a member of their community. Paul's letter gives ample indication that the Christians of Thessalonica were under duress (1 Thess 1:3, 6; 2:2, 14-16; 3:3-5; 4:18; 5:11). It may even be that those considered to have died prematurely did so as a result of the physical suffering they had endured at the hands of hired ruffians (see Acts 17:5-9). The hostile situation makes it likely that Thessalonian Christians gathered in a private venue rather than in some public place where they could be readily noticed and easily set upon. Luke provides an account of a man named Jason who was dragged before the city's politarchs on the accusation that he had harbored seditionists, when all he had done was provide hospitality in his home for Paul and his companions.

Kinship Language

The shortest of Paul's letters provides further indication that those whom Paul evangelized did indeed meet in people's homes. This short letter is addressed "to Philemon our dear friend and coworker, to Apphia our sister, to Archippus our fellow soldier, and to the church in your house" (*tē kat'oikon sou ekklēsia*, Phlm 1b-2). In Greek, the word *oikos* and its synonym *oikia*, both of which are used in the New Testament, meant house, home, or dwelling place. Sometimes the words connoted household, family, or (reigning) house. Rarely were the words distinguished from one another;[2] in some texts they are used interchangeably. In the New Testament the root *oik-* is also found in a number of related terms, such as the verb *oikeō*, which means "dwell," and the noun *oikodespotēs*, which means "master of a household" or "head of a family."

When Paul, accompanied by Timothy, wrote "to the church" in Philemon's house, he was writing to those who gathered in Philemon's home. Paul used this social setting to good rhetorical advantage. The letter, most likely written in the mid-fifties,[3] was drafted as a plea for Onesimus, a slave who sought Paul's help. Roman jurisprudence allowed slaves who believed that they were being mistreated to appeal to one of their master's friends or acquaintances, an *amicus domini*, to intervene on their behalf. Paul addressed Philemon as his beloved friend, all the while acknowledging that he himself was in prison (Phlm 1, 9, 10, 13).

In Jewish tradition the faithful transmission of traditional lore from father to son was the responsibility of a true father.

During his imprisonment, Paul evangelized Onesimus. In sending Onesimus back to Philemon with this short personal note, Paul asked that "[Philemon] have him back forever, no longer as a slave but more than a slave, a beloved brother (*adelphon agapēton*)" (Phlm 15-16). This is the very language that Paul used in regard to Philemon himself (Phlm 1).

Paul appealed to Philemon's ego, describing him as a brother whose love he remembered (Phlm 7), before making his plea, "Brother, let me have this benefit from you in the Lord! Refresh my heart in Christ" (Phlm 20). From the outset of the letter Paul set the scene in the home; he talked about the members of his fictive family. He called Timothy "brother" and Apphia "sister" (Phlm 1-2). His appeal was based on the family ties that bound the two men together as brothers. These were the kind of family ties, sibling love (*philadelphia*), about which Paul had written in the Letter to the Thessalonians (1 Thess 4:9-12). The kind of behavior that Paul expects Philemon to demonstrate is sibling love at work, albeit in less than usual circumstances.

Sibling Love at Work

Why was it that Paul considered Onesimus to be a member of the fictive family that met in Philemon's home? The answer is to be found in Paul's formal plea to Philemon, "I am appealing to you for my child, Onesimus, whose father I have become during my imprisonment" (Phlm 10). Paul's appeal to Philemon surely did not arise from Paul's having become a biological father while in prison; rather it stems from the fact that Paul had preached the gospel to Onesimus, leading Philemon's slave to embrace the Christian faith.

In Jewish tradition the faithful transmission of traditional lore from father to son was the responsibility of a true father. Thus the Talmud says: "The father is bound in respect of his son, to circumcise, redeem, teach him Torah, take a wife for him, and teach him a craft" (*b. Qidd.* 22a). Accordingly, if a man taught the Torah to another's child, it was as if he had begotten that child (see *b. Sanh.* 19b). Through instruction, the child had become a son to him. Replacing the Torah with the gospel as a way of becoming a father (see 1 Cor 4:15, 17), Paul shared this Jewish understanding of paternity. Evangelizing Onesimus as he did, Paul was considered to be Onesimus's father; Onesimus was his child.

How could Philemon, Paul's brother, and Apphia, his sister, not embrace Paul's own child as a member of their own family? Humanly speaking, they would not have been able to do so. Thus, Paul was confident that they would heed his plea when he appealed to Philemon to accept Onesimus as a member of the family (Phlm 21). He had begged Philemon to give an example of that sibling love which should characterize the true Christian.

If the home was the locale in which sibling love had its real place, the home was also a place where a visitor could expect hospitality (see 1 Tim

3:2; Titus 1:8; 1 Pet 4:9; 2 John 10; 3 John 5-6). Confident that he would soon be released from his imprisonment, Paul had another request to make of Philemon. Paul asked Philemon to prepare a guest room for him (*zenian*, Phlm 22). Among Jews, hospitality was an important virtue. Hospitality was an expression of the covenant relationship that bound members of the chosen people to one another. Among Christians, hospitality was an expression of the love that bound them together; but it was also an important means of evangelization. For a start, the gospel was preached within the home. The reading of Paul's letter to those who gathered in Philemon's house was a way in which the gospel was preached.

Prisca and Aquila

In addressing the gathering in Philemon's house, Paul used the expression "the church in your house." He also used this expression in the final greetings of his longest letters, Romans and 1 Corinthians. Writing to the Romans, Paul asked his addressees to greet "the church in the house" of Prisca and Aquila (Rom 16:5).[4] Writing to the Corinthians, Paul sent greetings on behalf of Aquila and Prisca, together with "the church in their house" (1 Cor 16:19).

The Epistle to the Colossians likewise has this kind of second-person greeting among the letter's final greetings: "Give my greetings[5] to the brothers and sisters in Laodicea and to Nympha and the church in her house" (Col 4:15). Nympha, probably a widow, is not otherwise mentioned in the New Testament. Colossians appears to be a letter written by Paul. It is, however, quite likely that the epistle was written to adapt Paul's message for an Asian church some few years after the apostle's death.[6] That its pseudonymous author mentioned the assembly that gathered in Nympha's house in Laodicea indicates that house churches continued to exist in the areas evangelized by Paul even after his death. Nympha's gender did not preclude her being the head of a household and of the church that gathered in her house.[7]

Were one to express Paul's greetings in contemporary language, that person would probably write something like "say hello to" or "remember me to" the church in the house of Prisca and Aquila. For Paul's third-person greetings, he or she would write that those gathered in the house of Aquila and Prisca "say hello" or "want to be remembered to you." Aquila was a Jew who, together with his wife Prisca,[8] was expelled from Rome because of a decree of the Emperor Claudius.[9] After their expulsion from Rome in 49 c.e., the couple made their way to Corinth, then moved on to Ephesus before finally returning to Rome.[10] Paul praised this married couple because they had worked with Paul in the mission of evangelization and had risked their lives for him (Rom 16:3-4). This was enough to merit an expression of Paul's personal thanks, as well as the gratitude of various Gentile churches.

Luke tells us that during their stay in Corinth Prisca and Aquila were visited by Paul (Acts 18:1-5). They offered him hospitality and a venue in which to ply his trade and earn a living for himself. This example illustrates well the importance of the house in the early church's work of evangelization. Traveling missionaries like Paul needed both a place to stay and a place in which to preach the gospel. When they departed, their hosts would be expected to provide them with provisions for their journey.[11] In Paul's case, Prisca and Aquila's leather-worker's shop was a convenient location for him to preach the gospel as he worked the leather.[12] When the couple moved on to Ephesus, they instructed Apollos, bringing him to a fuller understanding of the gospel (Acts 18:26).[13]

Baptism of the Entire Household

Luke offers several examples of Paul himself using a house as a locus for evangelization. He tells the story of Lydia, the God-fearing trader, who had heard Paul speak in a place of prayer on the outskirts of the city of Philippi (Acts 16:11-15). She opened her heart to the gospel and her home to Paul.[14] Lydia and her household were baptized. When Paul was later miraculously released from imprisonment in Philippi, the jailer was so impressed by what had happened that he asked Paul and Silas what had to be done in order that he might achieve salvation (Acts 16:26-34). Paul preached the word of God to him and the members of his household, after which they were immediately baptized. Then the jailer offered the missionaries hospitality and a meal.

Paul's journey would eventually bring him south to the Achaian capital of Corinth. There, says Luke, Paul encountered difficulties in the synagogue, so he went to the nearby house of Titius Justus (Acts 18:7-8). Despite having to leave the synagogue, Paul was able to evangelize a synagogue official named Crispus, who became a believer in the Lord and was baptized together with all his household. Writing to the Corinthians, Paul mentioned that he had baptized Crispus. He also baptized Gaius and the household of Stephanas (1 Cor 1:14, 16). So eager was Paul to affirm that his own ministry was one of evangelization rather than of baptizing that he almost forgot to mention that he had also baptized Stephanas and his household—this despite the fact that the conversion of the household of Stephanas was the firstfruits of Paul's mission in Achaia (1 Cor 16:15).

Baptism seems to have followed immediately upon a profession of faith in the risen Lord. Whole households were evangelized; whole households were baptized.[15] In the Greco-Roman world the household normally adopted the religion of the paterfamilias. When the head of a household became a believer, it was normal for the entire household to go along with him—or her, in Lydia's case—in the new belief. The baptism of an entire household was a foundational element of the church in someone's house.

Rome and Corinth

Philemon lived in the city of Colossae or at least in the area thereabouts. As an owner of slaves and a man who had a house large enough to have a guest room, he might have been able to have a relatively large number of people gather together as the church in his house. Other Christians might not have been as well-off. Since even a relatively large villa could accommodate only thirty to forty persons for a gathering,[16] the typical church in someone's home would have probably been a much smaller gathering.

In the larger cities of the empire, there may well have been several house churches. This would seem to have been the case in both Rome, the capital of the empire, and Corinth, the capital of the province of Achaia. The long series of greetings appended to the Letter to the Romans includes not only greetings to the church in the house of Prisca and Aquila (Rom 16:5) but also greetings to those who belonged to the family of Aristobulus (*tous ek tōn Aristoboulou*, Rom 16:10) and those in the Lord who belong to the family of Narcissus (*tous ek tōn Narkissou tous ontas en Kyriō*, Rom 16:11). Paul would also greet Asyncritus, Phlegon, Hermes, Patrobas, Hermas, and the brothers and sisters with them (*tous syn autois adelphois*, Rom 16:14) as well as Philologus, Julia, Nereus, and his sister, and Olympas, and all the saints who are with them (*tous syn autois pantas hagious*, Rom 16:15). The way in which Paul greeted these people seems to indicate that he was aware of the existence of at least five house churches[17] in the imperial capital.

Some estimate that the population of Rome during Paul's lifetime was about a million people. Perhaps some fifty thousand were Jews who gathered in various synagogues. Corinth, situated as a commercial center at the juncture of a north-south land route traversing Macedonia and the Pelopennesian peninsula and the east-west sea route to which Corinth had access via the ports of Cenchreae on the east and Lechaeum on the west, was a smaller city with a population of perhaps a quarter of a million people. As was the case in Rome, there was more than one house church in the city of Corinth. It is likely that the house of Stephanas was one such church (1 Cor 1:16) and that the house of Crispus was another (Acts 18:8). It is quite likely that Prisca and Aquila also hosted a church in Corinth just as they did in Rome and in Ephesus.

The Corinthian house churches came together from time to time. This larger gathering was the "whole[18] church" (*holēs tēs ekklēsias*) mentioned by Paul at the end of the Letter to the Romans. The gathering was hosted by Gaius, who had been baptized by Paul (1 Cor 1:14). Capitalizing on the fact that there were at least fourteen male believers in Corinth, all of whom would presumably have been married, Murphy-O'Connor suggests that the gathering of the whole church in Gaius's house included at least fifty people.[19] Such a gathering would have required a very large home.

Coming Together as a Church

When such a large group of people come together, it is almost inevitable that there be some tension among them. Differences of opinion and boorish behavior are easily noticed. Such was the case in Corinth. When the believing Christians of Corinth came together as a whole church,[20] the differences among them were readily apparent. For Paul, this was an intolerable situation. He wrote:

I do not commend you because when you come together it is not for the better but for the worse. For, to begin with, when you come together as a church (*synerchomenōn hymōn en ekklēsia*), I hear that there are divisions among you; and to some extent I believe it. Indeed, there have to be factions among you, for only so will it become clear who among you are genuine. (1 Cor 11:17-19)

Paul made his point by describing what happened when the Corinthian believers came together[21] for a potluck supper. Meals such as these were a common feature of life in the Hellenistic world, where they were called *eranoi*. Everyone contributed something.[22] In the *Odyssey* (1.226) Homer wrote about such a meal. Authors like Plato (*Symposium* 174A) and Martial (*Epigrams* 10.48; 11.52) mentioned some rules of etiquette that people were to follow when they gathered for such a meal. Reciprocity, sharing, and equality[23] were the hallmarks of a true *eranos*. Xenophon described how the meal was to take place:

> Whenever some of those who came together for dinner brought more meat and fish than others Socrates would tell the waiter either to put the small contributions into the common stock or to portion them out equally among the diners. So the ones who brought a lot felt obliged not only to take their share of the pool, but to pool their own supplies in return; and so they put their own food also into the common stock. Thus, they got no more than those who brought little with them. (*Memorabilia* 3.14.1)

The eucharist had already become a fixed tradition in the church at this early stage of its history, just a quarter of a century after Jesus' death and resurrection.

Reciprocity, sharing, and equality were missing when the Christians of Corinth came together: "Each of you," Paul wrote, "goes ahead with your own supper, and one goes hungry, and another becomes drunk" (1 Cor 11:21). Communal sharing was not a feature of their assembly. Paul's condemnation of the situation was quite severe. He said that when the Corinthians gave evidence of such blatant individualism and selfishness, they were showing contempt for the church of God (1 Cor 11:22c). They humiliated those who were less well-off (1 Cor 11:22d). What they were doing was not under the patronage of the Lord. It was not, said Paul, the Lord's Supper (*kyriakon deipnon*, 1 Cor 11:20).

To make his point, good rhetorician that he was, Paul gave an example. He cited a traditional etiological narrative:

> For I received from the Lord what I also handed on to you, that the Lord Jesus on the night when he was betrayed took a loaf of bread, and when he had given thanks, he broke it and said, "This is my body that is for you. Do this in remembrance of me." In the same way he took the cup also, after supper, saying, "This cup is the new covenant in my blood. Do this, as often as you drink it, in remembrance of me." For as often as you eat this bread and drink the cup, you proclaim the Lord's death until he comes. (1 Cor 11:23-26)

From Paul's poignant rejoinder to the Corinthians (1 Cor 11:17-34), the church has received not only the name for its celebration of the eucharist, which it calls the "Lord's Supper," but also the oldest written account of the institution of the eucharist. The language that Paul used to introduce the narrative shows that it had already become a fixed tradition in the church at this early stage of its history, just a quarter of a century after Jesus' death and resurrection. Paul wrote about "receiving" the narrative and "handing it on," language that reflects the technical jargon used by rabbis to speak of the oral tradition which they had learned from their own masters and were now passing along to their students.

Paul said that he had previously passed the tradition on to the Corinthians. They were already familiar with it. Undoubtedly they told the stylized story when they came together as a whole church. Their custom was similar to the practice of Hellenistic religious, trade, and funeral associations. By definition, religious associations were devoted to one or another deity; trade and funeral associations generally met under the patronage of a god or goddess. When these groups came together and had a meal—one of those potluck dinners known as *eranoi*—a libation was offered to the deity. The libation took place after the meal and preceded whatever after-dinner speech was to follow. The celebration that Paul described in 1 Corinthians 11 seems to have followed the same pattern, with one notable exception, namely, that the narrative of the institution of the eucharist replaced the customary libation to the deity. Retold in stylized fashion, the narrative explained the meaning and origin of the Christian ritual, a sharing of broken bread and of a cup of blessing (1 Cor 10:16).

Analyzing the ritual narrative, scholars frequently make a minute

comparison of Paul's version of the story with those found in the Synoptic Gospels (Matt 26:26-29; Mark 14:22-24; Luke 22:19-20). It is, however,
important to realize that Paul recounted the narrative for a very different
reason from the reasons that inspired the Synoptists to write about the
eucharist. Paul's emphasis called on the Corinthians to take cognizance of
the meaning of the ritual that they performed.

Among the evangelists who told the story of the institution of the
eucharist, only Paul twice mentioned the fact that the ritual gesture was to
be performed in remembrance of Jesus (1 Cor 11:24-25; cf. Luke 22:19).
Mention of the remembrance confirms the etiological character of the
narrative. Paul's insistence on the fact that ritual is performed as a remembrance served to remind the Corinthians that they were to remember Jesus
as they performed the ritual.

Two additional traits of Paul's account distinguish it from the Synoptists' accounts of the institution and serve Paul's rhetorical purpose. He
had written about the "Lord's Supper." In the Greco-Roman empire,
"Lord" (*kyrios*) was a title whose connotation evoked supreme authority.
In that society a lord was not to be confronted; his authority was not to be
contravened. In that society, this was often a matter of life or death. In
Paul's short account of the institution of the eucharist, the title "Lord"
appears five times in just five verses, all but once without the use of even
Jesus' proper name (1 Cor 11:23-27). Two of these occur in the paraenetic
inference that Paul draws from the tradition: "Whoever, therefore, eats the
bread or drinks the cup of the Lord in an unworthy manner will be answerable for the body and blood of the Lord" (1 Cor 11:27). The Corinthians
could not help but understand that ultimately what was at issue was the
reality of Jesus' lordship. Jesus was the Lord whom they acclaimed (1 Cor
12:3) and to whom they were expected to pay heed.

In addition to his emphasis on the dominion of the Lord Jesus, Paul
was more explicit than were the Synoptic authors in the emphasis that he
placed on the death of the Lord Jesus. While references to the death of Jesus
can be gleaned from references in the Synoptic Gospels to the blood of the
covenant and Jesus not drinking of the fruit of the vine until entering into
the Kingdom of God (Matt 26:28-29; Mark 14:24-25),[24] the link between
the eucharist and the death of Jesus is primarily established by the setting
of the narrative of the passion and death of Jesus. Not so with Paul.

Paul begins his narrative by situating the institution of the eucharist
"on the night when he [the Lord Jesus] was betrayed" (1 Cor 11:23). He

concludes the narrative by interpreting[25] the celebration of the ritual as a proclamation of the gospel: "For as often as you eat this bread and drink the cup, you proclaim (*kataggellete*) the Lord's death until he comes" (1 Cor 11:26). The celebration of the ritual, said Paul, is itself a proclamation of the kerygma whose core is the death and resurrection of Jesus.[26]

According to Paul, the celebration of the eucharistic ritual is an interim reality, recalling the death of Jesus, anticipating the parousia: it is to be celebrated "until he comes." Believers are expected to look to the parousia as the completion of the salvific event begun with Jesus' death and resurrection. Paul, however, forcefully reminded the Corinthians that "whoever eats the bread or drinks the cup of the Lord in an unworthy manner will be answerable for the body and blood of the Lord" (1 Cor 11:27). Eating and drinking unworthily is to eat and drink in such a way that the divisions within the community are apparent. Eating and drinking in this way makes a person somehow responsible for the death of Jesus.

Paul's exhortation (1 Cor 11:27-32) is full of the language of the courtroom, the language of judgment. He wrote about scrutinizing oneself (*dokimazetō*) and about unworthiness (*anaxiōs*, v. 27). Three times he spoke about judging, using three different verbs (*diekrinomen, ekrinometha, krinomenoi*,[27] vv. 31-32). Paul also wrote about judgment (*krima*, v. 29). He spoke about the consequences of one's actions (*dia touto*, v. 30), of chastisement (*paideuometha*, v. 32), and of condemnation (*katakrithōmen*, v. 32). Who would judge these Corinthians? None other than the Lord, whose supper they claimed to eat, all the while making a mockery of it.

In the peroration of his eucharistic discourse, Paul again brought up the subject of condemnation: "So then, my brothers and sisters, when you come together (*synerchomenoi*) to eat, wait for one another. If you are hungry, eat at home, so that when you come together (*synerchēsthe*), it will not be for your condemnation (*krima*)" (1 Cor 11:33-34a). When the Corinthians came together as a whole church, they had a choice. Were they to come together to celebrate the Lord's Supper? Or were they to come together for their own condemnation?

Whence Division?

When the Corinthians came together as the whole church, the divisions among them were credible and clear (1 Cor 11:18-19). For Paul, such divisions were a blatant manifestation of contempt for the church of God (1 Cor 11:22). The way that the Corinthians were eating the *eranos* humiliated the have-nots among them. When the whole church assembled to eat its meal, the class divisions among those who gathered became apparent, much to Paul's dismay.[28]

In the beginning of the letter, Paul had asked the Corinthians to consider their social status at the time of their call (1 Cor 1:26-29). In chapter 7, Paul spoke about the paradox of slaves and free people within the church (1 Cor 7:21-24). Paul's description of the Corinthians' potluck supper mentioned those who arrived first,[29] partook of their own meal, and drank so much that they became drunk[30] (1 Cor 11:21). Since Paul described those who were humiliated by this behavior as "those who have nothing" (1 Cor 11:22d), it would seem that the latecomers were the poor and the slaves.

The former would not have lived in neighborhoods with houses large enough to host a gathering of fifty or so people. The latter would have had to attend to their master's needs and wishes before going to the gathering of the whole church; their time was not their own. When the poor and slaves were left to eat the crumbs and drink the dregs, as it were, the meal that was eaten could not be called the "Lord's Supper."[31] The eucharistic ritual proclaimed the death of the Lord (1 Cor 11:26). Paul had reminded the Corinthians that the Lord died for those who were weak (1 Cor 8:11). When the Corinthians neglected and humiliated the have-nots in the church as they did, they were not paying attention to the Lord's death. As a result, they were answerable for the body and blood of the Lord (1 Cor 11:27).

It is not unlikely that another source of division that became apparent when the Corinthians came together as the whole church was the different house churches themselves. Power struggles are almost inevitable when different groups come together. At the beginning of his letter Paul had addressed the issue of factions within the community. He spoke of himself, Apollos, Cephas, and Christ as invoked in the rallying cry of these different groups (1 Cor 1:12; cf. 3:22-23). Probably these names were ciphers for the real names of the leaders around whom the various factions rallied.[32] They were probably the leaders of the different house churches who came together "as the whole church" in a single place in Corinth.

Several Churches

Paul's First Letter to the Corinthians and his Letter to the Romans provide clear evidence of the co-existence of several house churches in two of the larger cities of the Roman Empire. The New Testament does not explicitly attest to the simultaneous existence of house churches in other cities, but it is quite likely that more than one such church existed in Philippi (Acts 16:15, 33-34) and Ephesus, where Paul stayed for more than two years (Acts 19:10). Perhaps there was more than one house church in Jerusalem, where the divisions between Hellenists and Hebrews were to become apparent (Acts 6:1). Certainly there were several house churches in Judea (1 Thess 2:14) and Galatia (Gal 1:2).[33]

Paul's First Letter to the Corinthians indicates that at least in that city Christians came together for a common meal on which occasion they recalled and celebrated the institution of the eucharist. As a group of siblings, Christians who came together for such a meal ought to have treated one another as brothers and sisters (1 Cor 11:33). Fictive kinship relationships extended beyond an individual house church (1 Thess 4:10). Various house churches knew about one another (1 Thess 1:8-9); they could learn from one another (1 Cor 11:16; 16:1; 2 Cor 9:2) and even be inspired by one another (1 Thess 1:7; 2:14). The third-person greetings appended to several of Paul's letters bear witness to the relationship between some of these churches and other churches (Rom 16:16; 1 Cor 16:19; Phil 4:22).

The fact that Paul wrote his Letter to the Galatians "to the churches of Galatia" (Gal 1:2) indicates that there was some relationship among the churches of the area.[34] The Galatian region[35] was so large as to make it unlikely that all of the churches in the area came together as a whole church. Paul's letter was a circular letter[36] intended to be read to several churches in turn. This raises the issue of the nature of the relationship among the various churches of an area.

The churches certainly knew that other churches existed (see Rom 16:16; 1 Cor 16:19-20; 2 Cor 12:13; Phil 4:21-22; 1 Thess 1:7-8; 2:14). Was the relationship among them merely one of kindred spirits, siblings united in some sort of extended family relationship?[37] Or did some organizational relationship exist among the churches of an area?[38] No sure answer can be given to these questions, but it is clear that Paul expected his own ecclesial foundations to abide by the same rule of life (1 Cor 7:17).

Paul also expected his churches to acknowledge their indebtedness to the church in Jerusalem (1 Cor 16:1-3). The collection for the saints in Jerusalem was one of the most important signs of unity among the early churches (Rom 15:25-28; 1 Cor 16:1-4; 2 Corinthians 8–9; Gal 2:10; cf. Acts 11:29-30). Paul considered this collection, whose beneficiaries were the poor in the church of Jerusalem, to be a service to God's holy people, a ministry to the saints (Rom 15:25; 2 Cor 8:4; 9:1), and a proof of love (2 Cor 8:8). As Philemon's acceptance of Onesimus was a sign of sibling love, so the collection that was made in the churches of Achaia, Galatia, and Macedonia for the benefit of Jerusalem Christians was *philadelphia* in action.

The collection for the saints was truly a labor of love (see 1 Thess 1:3). Most of the members of Paul's churches were probably free artisans, small traders, or slaves.[39] Their material resources would have been quite limited. Contributions were voluntary (Rom 15:26-27; 2 Cor 8:2-3), but each member of the church was expected to contribute according to one's means (1 Cor 16:2; 2 Cor 8:12-14). Paul gave directions as to what the Corinthians should do in order to make their support for the poor in Jerusalem substantial. He asked that each member of the community set aside some money, putting it into the common purse when they gathered on the first day of the week.[40]

The ecclesial sense of the collection was important. The collection was a sign of social outreach, an expression of concern for the poor, and a manifestation of the sibling love that served as a mark of the church. Most significantly, however, the collection was an expression of gratitude for the spiritual benefits that Christians in the Diaspora had received from the mother church in Jerusalem, the first Christian "church of God," the one whose members were first called God's "holy ones." Paul expected the collection to elicit prayers of thanksgiving on the part of the saints in Jerusalem, leading them to a sense of their unity with Gentile Christians (2 Cor 9:12-15). In this way the collection was an expression of Paul's eschatological vision in which Jew and Gentile are united in the one body of Christ (Gal 3:28; 1 Cor 12:13), a vision marvelously exploited in the Epistle to the Ephesians, which was written by a disciple of Paul.

In Paul's eyes the collection was so important that he was willing to interrupt his missionary travels in order to bring the proceeds of the collection to Jerusalem (1 Cor 16:4). This seems to have happened; Paul told the Romans: "At present I am going to Jerusalem in a ministry to the saints; for Macedonia and Achaia have been pleased to share their resources with the poor among the saints at Jerusalem" (Rom 15:25-26). Chapters 8 and 9 of 2 Corinthians are devoted to the collection. They give the theological rationale for the collection and designate Titus as chief agent for the collection. It may be that these two chapters were originally administrative letters composed for this purpose.[41]

Summing Up

Paul's letters give ample evidence that the communities which emerged as a result of his preaching the gospel were organized into household units. The home with its expressive kinship language was the basic unit of Pauline foundations. Communication and kinship relationship bound the churches together. In some cities there were several house churches. In Corinth members of different house churches came together as a "whole church" for a potluck dinner, the traditional *eranos*, and the eucharistic ritual. Some house churches existed independently of Paul's evangelization. There were, for example, house churches in Rome and Jerusalem.

Paul asked that each member of the community set aside some money, putting it into the common purse when they gathered on the first day of the week.

The house church was essential to the vitality of the first-century church. The church met as an assembly of believers in the home of a member of the community. Baptism of entire households was frequently the practice; these households served as the foundation of the church in a given area. The house church served the gospel as a venue for catechesis and as a source of welcome hospitality for traveling evangelists. It was the locus where *philadelphia*, the sibling love characteristic of the believer, was practiced. Finally, the eucharist was celebrated when believers came together as church in a particular place, the home of one of them.

Discussion and Study Questions

1. How can and how do married couples, as couples, participate in the life of the church today?

2. What are the social implications of the celebration of the eucharist?

3. How is real sibling love expressed in your parish community? How can it be expressed?

4. Are small groups—house churches—as essential to the life of the church today as they were at the time of Paul? Why or why not?

Chapter Three

"The Body of Christ"

In 1 Corinthians, Paul tells us that he learned about divisions in the Christian community at Corinth from some of Chloe's people who came to him (1 Cor 1:11). This group of Christian slaves may have been sent to Paul for this specific purpose, but it is more likely that they had been sent on a commercial mission to buy, sell, or trade merchandise in Ephesus. They seized the opportunity to meet with Paul and tell him about the situation in Corinth. To respond to the situation, Paul wrote a letter to the Corinthians. He stated his purpose very clearly: "Now I appeal to you, brothers and sisters, by the name of our Lord Jesus Christ, that all of you be in agreement and that there be no divisions among you, but that you be united in the same mind and the same purpose" (1 Cor 1:10).

The Church of God at Corinth

Paul customarily used the *intitulatio* of the epistolary address to prepare the argument that he was about to develop in his letter.[1] So, he wrote:

> To the church of God that is in Corinth, to those who are sanctified in Christ Jesus, called to be saints, together with all those who in every place call on the name of our Lord Jesus Christ, both their Lord and ours. (1 Cor 1:2)

The ecclesiology expressed in this passage is the richest to be found in the salutation of any of Paul's extant letters. Paul began by immediately designating his addressees as "the church of God that is in Corinth" (*tē ekklēsia*

31

tou theou tē ousia en Korinthō),[2] an epithet that Paul used again in the address of 2 Corinthians. The location of this church in the bustling capital of the province of Achaia is an indication of Paul's missionary strategy: he visited the principal cities along the major trade routes of the Roman Empire.

The theological term with which Paul qualifies the church in Corinth is "of God" (*tou theou*). Paul used this qualifier some time previously when he recalled that the Thessalonian church had imitated "the churches of God [in Christ Jesus] that are in Judea" (*tōn ekklēsiōn tou theou tōn ousōn en Ioudaia*) (1 Thess 2:14). In 1 Thessalonians Paul used the expression in the plural; most likely, the term "church of God" was first used as a self-designation by the early church in Jerusalem.[3] A popular understanding of this expression locates its Christian origins in the Greek Bible, where the term *ekklēsia tou kyriou* ("assembly of the Lord") was used to designate the people of God who assembled to hear the word of God from Moses at the time of the Exodus.[4]

> *Holiness was their status and their vocation: they are called saints; they are called to be saints.*

The Dead Sea Scrolls shed more light on the origins of the Christian use of the term. Two of these scrolls use the Hebrew expression *qahal ʾel* ("assembly of God") to designate the apocalyptic assembly. Thus, an appendix to the *Manual of Discipline* states that no man who suffers from one of the uncleannesses that affect humanity shall enter "God's assembly" (1QSa 2:4). The *War Scroll* identifies "God's assembly" as a slogan on the sixth of the eight banners prepared for the final battle (1QM 4:10). The meaning of the expression is clear: it designates the eschatological people of the covenant. Early Christians who gathered in Jerusalem awaiting the parousia (cf. 1 Thess 1:10) applied similar nomenclature to themselves.

From Jerusalem the term could be applied to other Judean communities of Christians, as Paul did in 1 Thess 2:14. Paul also used the term to speak of the church that he himself had persecuted (1 Cor 15:9; Gal 1:13). In addition, Paul knew and wrote about the customs of "the churches of God" (1 Cor 11:16). Nonetheless, the only church that Paul formally addressed as "the church of God" is the church of God at Corinth (1 Cor

1:2; 2 Cor 1:1), a designation that Paul used to good advantage in taking the Corinthians to task for their sordid way of having an *eranos* and recalling the institution of the eucharist as he did so (1 Cor 11:17-34).

In addition to describing his addressees as "the church of God"—a corporate epithet—Paul identified them as "those who are sanctified in Christ Jesus, called to be saints" (1 Cor 1:2). The church of God is composed of God's holy ones, people who belong to God. The group of holy people in Corinth belong to God because of their relationship with Christ Jesus. The implications of the relationship will be spelled out in the rest of the letter. In the meantime, Paul reminded the Corinthians that holiness was their status and their vocation: they are called saints; they are called to be saints.[5]

As the church of God, the saints of Corinth did not stand alone in their status and vocation. They were a community of holy people "together with all those who in every place call on the name of our Lord Jesus Christ, both their Lord and ours." Paul does not specify the nature of the relationship between the church of God and these others, but his language suggests that some bond of unity exists. At a minimum, they had one and the same Lord.

Both they and the Corinthians call on the name of our Lord Jesus Christ (*epikaloumenois to onoma tou kyriou hēmōn Iēsou Christou*). The formula evokes cultic activity. In Hellenistic society the verb *epikaleō* was used to summon a god to a sacrifice or call upon a deity as a witness to an oath. The members of the church of God at Corinth invoked the name of "our Lord Jesus Christ." The dominant idea in this christological title is "our Lord," who is then identified as "Jesus Christ."[6]

A Field and a Building

The communities of believers that resulted from Paul's preaching of the gospel bore witness to the fact that the Spirit and the word of God were at work among them. The existence of these communities also proved that, despite his demurrer (1 Cor 2:1-5), Paul was a skilled orator. People, as Aristotle noted, commonly use metaphors to make their point (see *Rhetoric* 3.2.6). Aristotle went on to say that metaphors set things before the eyes (*Rhetoric* 3.11.1). Metaphors provide perspicuity and pleasure in a person's argument (*Rhetoric* 3.2.8).[7] Trying to persuade the saints at

Corinth to heed his plea for unity among themselves, Paul, a skilled rhetorician, employed two metaphors drawn from everyday experience, a field and a building (1 Cor 3:9).

The apostle was not alone in pairing these images from everyday experience. Biblical authors[8] and philosophers[9] had done so before him; his contemporaries did so as well. The two metaphors were also paired together in the description of the community in the Dead Sea Scrolls. In the *Manual of Discipline*, the community is described as "an everlasting plantation, a holy house" (1QS 8:5); it was "a foundation of the building of holiness to be an everlasting plantation throughout all future ages" (1QS 11:8-9).

Paul combined an agricultural image with a construction image in 1 Cor 3:9 where he segued from one to the other: "You are God's field, God's building." The first metaphor serves Paul's rhetorical purpose insofar as he uses the imagery to teach the Corinthians a lesson about cooperative leadership in community. A man whose apostolic journeys led him along the major trade routes of the empire with stops in the most important cities, Paul did not often employ agricultural imagery.[10] Nevertheless, he used the imagery in 1 Cor 3:5-9 to speak about the respective roles of Apollos and himself in the cultivation of the field. The pair of rhetorical questions with which he introduced the image, "What then is Apollos? What is Paul?" (1 Cor 3:5), drew attention to their respective roles[11] even before the image was identified. The role of Paul and Apollos is that of servants to whom God has assigned particular functions.[12] He and Apollos are only servants whose tasks are to fulfill the respective functions that God has assigned.

To make his point clearly and forcefully, Paul uses the image of a field in which each worker has a role to play. The first role is Paul's own role: he is the planter. The mere planting of seeds produces nothing unless there is water. Paul, the planter, needs the work of Apollos, who does the watering. Theirs is a common purpose (v. 8), yet their work counts for nothing unless God provides fruit. Unless the field is ultimately nurtured by God, it is nonproductive. So, Paul affirmed that it is God who gives the growth.

To conclude his exposition of the image, Paul answered the rhetorical question with which he began (see v. 5c). What are Paul and Apollos? They are "God's fellow workers" (*theou . . . synergoi*, v. 9).[13] This self-designation underscores the idea that Paul and Apollos are doing God's work; they worked together to produce the crop; God cooperated by making it happen.[14] Where did this happen? In Corinth, for the Corinthians are "God's field" (*theou geōrgion*, v. 9b).

The identification served as a transition to the next image, "God's building" (*theou oikodomē*[15]).[16] In constructing the image (1 Cor 3:10-17), Paul began with himself. His role in the construction of the building is like that of a "master builder" (*sophos*[17] *architektōn*) who lays the foundation. This classic simile[18] emphasizes Paul's foundational role in the church at Corinth. He was deputized[19] and empowered by the grace of God (*tēn charin tou theou*, v. 10) to preach the gospel to the Corinthians. Hence, he was apostle to them (1 Cor 9:2).[20] Paul's foundational role—mother (1 Cor 3:1-2),[21] planter (v. 6), and master builder (v. 10)—was accomplished by preaching the gospel to the Corinthians.

Doing so, Paul laid the foundation of the building, which is Jesus Christ. Paul subsequently developed the image of the building by talking about the role of the different builders. There is only one foundation, Christ Jesus. Workers must build on this single foundation. They must be careful how they work. Whether they work in gold or silver or with gems, wood, hay, or straw, the quality of their craftsmanship will be readily apparent. Paul's point is obvious. Anyone who looks at various parts of any building can see how well the building has been constructed.

Paul did not specifically state that among the construction workers are goldsmiths, silversmiths, jewelers, carpenters, and bricklayers, but this may be inferred from the way that he crafts his complex image. Different building materials require that those who use them have different skills from those who work with other materials. The apostle's principal point is that there are many builders, but a single person lays the foundation. There is only one foundation; many materials are used in the construction erected on the foundation.

Paul did not stress the notion of the one and the many in his use of the construction imagery; he left that notion to be developed in a later part of his letter (1 Corinthians 12). In 1 Corinthians 3, his principal concern was paraenetic. He strove to encourage the various builders to work on a common construction project, carefully discerning the quality of their own work (v. 10, cf. v. 13). Not only will that work be visible; it will also be subject to a process of quality control.

Paul's language was similar to that of a fourth-century b.c.e. Arcadian epigraph[22] describing the building and repair of a temple of Athena. Different workers, more or less comparable to modern-day subcontractors, were involved in various phases of the construction. Each had a specific task to perform. The inscription repeatedly mentions their "work" (*ergon*; see vv. 13, 14, 15). It refers to the penalties to be meted out to contractors for various infractions, such as delaying the construction by failing to finish their work on time, harming workers, and damaging property. In similar fashion, Paul made a distinction between those whose craftsmanship was satisfactory, having been built on the foundation (*epoikodomēsen*) and who were paid their wages,[23] and those who suffered a loss because their work did not pass inspection (vv. 14-15).

In Paul's construction image, fire is a polyvalent element. On the one hand, fire appears to be associated with day and with light (v. 13b); on the other hand, fire appears to be the means of quality control (v. 13c). Then again, fire appears as a means of salvation (v. 15). In terms of quality control, the use of fire in the process of assaying and refining metal[24] was well known to biblical and classical authors. Similarly, it is common knowledge that hay and straw burn quite readily,[25] while gold and silver are resistant to fire, even if they should lose their shape in the heat of an intense fire.

The reader should not interpret Paul's metaphor as if it were an allegory,[26] despite his identification of himself as the master builder and of Jesus Christ as the foundation (vv. 10-11). With paraenetic intent, Paul's focus is on wages (vv. 8, 14) and quality control: workers should be careful about the quality of their work (v. 10); at the end it will be tested (v. 13). Given Paul's hortatory purpose and the reference to eschatological destruction in verse 17, it is all but certain that fire is a symbol of punishment and is to be associated with the coming of "the Day," the eschatological Day of the Lord. A similar reference to fire appears in the *Testament of Abraham*:

> He [God] tests the work of men through fire. And if the fire burns up the work of anyone, immediately the angel of judgment takes him and carries him away to the place of sinners, a most bitter place of punishment. But if *the fire tests the work of anyone* and does not touch it, this person is justified and the angel of righteousness takes him and carries him up to be saved in the lot of the righteous. And thus, most righteous Abraham, all things in all people are tested by fire and balance. (*T. Abr.* 13:11-14; translation by E. P. Sanders)

Paul's own well-crafted image moved through three stages of building: the laying of the foundation (vv. 10-11), construction on this foundation (vv. 10b, 12-15), and inhabitation (v. 16). The Holy Spirit is the inhabitant: "God's Spirit dwells (*oikei*) in you" (v. 16b). This indwelling of the Spirit makes of the construction a temple of God. Hence, Paul could say: "you are God's temple." God's building in verse 9 is now identified as the temple of God. God owns and works the field; God dwells in the temple built by human hands.[27] The church at Corinth is the temple of God.[28]

If anyone destroys God's temple, that person will be destroyed. This is the ultimate tit for tat.[29] Paul's words could not have been more forceful. Lest the Corinthians miss the thrust of his message, Paul brought the construction image to a close, recalling a theme that he had first used in his initial greeting: "God's temple is holy, and you are that temple" (1 Cor 3:17; see 1 Cor 1:2).

Construction imagery recurs in 1 Peter, a text that appears to have been influenced by Paul's letters. The anonymous author of this letter employs the theme in a passage (1 Pet 2:4-10) whose principal thrust is the elect and holy character of the eschatological covenant community.[30] To speak of Christ, the author employs the biblical image of the cornerstone (1 Pet 2:6, 7; Isa 28:16). The community in which the Spirit is found is identified as a spiritual house (*oikos pneumatikos*), an image that suggests the temple motif, even though the author's emphasis lies on the idea of a spiritual household since he qualifies the phrase with a reference to a holy priesthood (*eis hierateuma hagion*; cf. 1 Pet 2:9). The qualifying phrase is telic, suggesting that believers are formed into a spiritual household so that as a corporate priesthood[31] they can offer acceptable sacrifice to God. Later in 1 Peter, the church is identified as "the household of God" (*tou oikou tou theou*),[32] the initial focus of final judgment.

Gifts of the Spirit

Having described the church at Corinth as the temple in which God dwells, Paul returned to the topic of God's Spirit in chapters 12–14. The issue that prompted Paul to focus on the Spirit in these chapters was the claim by some members of the church at Corinth that they possessed "spiritual gifts" (*pneumatika*). The root of this Greek word places the emphasis on "spiritual." Apparently, the problem was that some in the church thought more highly of themselves than of others because they personally enjoyed some sort of "spiritual" or "ecstatic" experience. As Paul developed his argument, it is clear that the real problem was not so much spiritual gifts in general as it is the fact that some members of the community had an inflated view of themselves because they were able to speak "in tongues," the focus of chapter 14.[33]

Paul began his consideration of the issue by identifying the topic and setting up the parameters of his discussion (1 Cor 12:1-3). He wrote that those who were able to speak in tongues enjoyed this gift even before they became Christian. Ironically, those who were enticed by the experience worshiped idols who were not even able to speak. Their experience exalted them above the very idols whom they worshiped. Having suggested that the mere ability to enjoy an ecstatic phenomenon does not mean that a person has received the Spirit of God, Paul offered a two-part rule of thumb pertaining to speaking by the power of the Spirit of God: "No one speaking by the Spirit of God ever says 'Let Jesus be cursed!' and no one can say 'Jesus is Lord' except by the Holy Spirit" (1 Cor 12:3).

The first sign of the presence of the Spirit in a person is the ability to proclaim and acclaim that "Jesus is Lord" and really mean it. The confession of Jesus as Lord means that a person believes that Jesus has been raised from the dead[34] and that he or she acknowledges the Risen One to be the lord of one's own life. Those who proclaim that Jesus is Lord acknowledge that they are ready to serve, that Jesus the Lord is *the* authority in their lives.

With that understanding as an introduction, Paul began to talk about the topic at hand. Instead of talking about spiritual gifts (*pneumatika*), he chose to write about "gifts" or "charisms" (*charismata*). He used a neologism, whose root places the emphasis on "gift" (*charis*), as a critique of the Corinthians' use of *pneumatika,* with its emphasis on the "spiritual" and "ecstatic." For Paul the extraordinary is not what matters; it is the gift of the Spirit that matters. Thus, he wrote:

> Now there are varieties of gifts, but the same Spirit; and there are varieties of services, but the same Lord; and there are varieties of activities, but it is the same God who activates all of them in everyone. (1 Cor 12:4-6)

According to Paul, there are many different gifts but there is only one Spirit. To understand the gifts of the Spirit, it is necessary to recognize both the diversity of the Spirit's gifts and the unicity of the source of gifts: there are many different gifts but only one giver of gifts. Those who receive gifts receive them in order to serve. Charisms are not given so that the recipient can boast of his or her gifts; rather they are given so that those who receive them can serve the Lord. Moreover, since the Spirit is the power of God at work in the world, the gifts of the Spirit are sources of empowerment: they are a means by which God acts in the world. God's "energy" is at work in the gifts of the Spirit: the one God, as Paul said, "activates all of them in everyone" (*ho energōn ta panta en pasin*).

The point is well made. The charisms are gifts given for service. They are given so that people who confess Jesus as Lord can serve him. The gifts of the Spirit come in different varieties. Three times Paul mentioned the varieties of gifts. He spoke of the uniqueness of the source of these gifts and concluded with the idea that gifts are given to everyone. Paul illustrated the variety of the gifts given by the Spirit in 1 Cor 12:8-10. Using paronomasia, Paul so constructed his argument that the word "Spirit" echoed throughout the pericope.[35]

Among the Spirit's gifts are the utterance of wisdom, the utterance of knowledge, faith, healing, the working of miracles, prophecy, the discernment of spirits, various kinds of tongues, and the interpretation of tongues. Nine different gifts are mentioned. The gift of tongues is next to last on Paul's list. The gift of tongues would have been last on the list were it not for the fact that Paul wanted those who possessed this gift to realize that it was not really serviceable unless it was accompanied by another gift, the gift of the interpretation of tongues (see 1 Cor 14:5, 13).

As much as Paul wanted to put the gift of tongues in its proper place amid the array of the Spirit's gifts, he also wanted the members of the church at Corinth to know that each and every one of them was gifted. He emphasized this important idea by creating a literary ring construction:[36] "To each is given the manifestation of the Spirit for the common good. . . . All these are activated by one and the same Spirit (*to hen kai to auto pneuma*), who allots to each one individually just as the Spirit chooses (*kathēs bouletai*)" (1 Cor 12:7, 11).

"To each his [her] own" is the Spirit's operative principle. There is no such thing as a noncharismatic believer; the Spirit of God endows each member of the church with gifts (1 Cor 12:6). The gifts are allotted not as the members of the church might wish; rather they are allotted as the Spirit of God wills. Since it is one and the same Spirit (1 Cor 12:4, 11) who allots these gifts, any boasting about the relative importance of gifts is a sin against the Holy Spirit.

Laying the ground for the discussion of the real gifts of the Holy Spirit, Paul said that the different gifts were "varieties of services" (*diareseis diakoniōn*) (1 Cor 12:5). This raised the issue of the purpose of the gifts that have been given. Paul reminded the Corinthians that there is but one Lord. The gifts that are given are given so that the members of the church of God might serve this one Lord. In common parlance, "lord" is a relational term; a lord is lord over an individual or a group of people. In the biblical tradition, the Lord is the Lord of his people. The Lord of Jewish and Christian revelation is a Lord whose people are servants. From the perspective of Paul writing the letter to the Corinthians, the church of God at Corinth was the group of people who belong to the Lord (1 Cor 1:2). In turn, they acclaimed Jesus as Lord (1 Cor 12:3).

What then about the gifts as service? Gifts of the Spirit were given for the "common good" (*pros to sympheron*, 1 Cor 12:7). In Greek, "common good" is a participial form of the verb "*sympherō*" ("to bring together"). The purpose of the gifts as manifestations of the Spirit is that the members of the church of God might be brought together. The term, used in the sense of "advantage" or "one's own interest," was a classic topos in Hellenistic rhetoric.[37] Paul has subtly argued that the use of the Spirit's gift for the sake of unity is to the advantage of the church of God at Corinth.

In the third section of his three-part exposition on the charisms, Paul was more specific. He stated that building up the church is the purpose for which charisms are given. He urged the members of the church of God to be eager for the gifts, striving to "excel in them for building up the church" (*pros tēn oikodomēn*[38] *tēs ekklēsias*) (1 Cor 14:12; cf. 14:5). "Let all things be done," he said, "for building up" (*pros oikodomēn*) (1 Cor 14:26). Charisms are given so that those who use them may build one another up (1 Cor 14:3, 17) rather than build themselves up (1 Cor 14:4). Those who thus use the gifts serve the Lord and his people.

The Body of Christ

To make his point even more clearly, Paul made a rhetorical digression to speak about the body of Christ (1 Cor 12:12-26).[39] Hellenistic rhetoricians highly valued the use of examples[40] to make a point and clarify an issue. The example of the body was a classic topos. Paul's contemporary Dio Chrysostom (ca. 40/50-110 C.E.) said that Aesop, the legendary fabulist, had used this metaphor (*Discourses* 33.16). Dio himself used the metaphor so often in his speeches on community harmony that it almost became tiresome (*Discourses* 9.2; 33.44; 34.32; 39.5; 40.21; 41.9; 50.3). Cicero, too, spoke of the body in his political discourse (*On Duties* 3.5.22-23; 3.6.26-27), as did Seneca in his moral discourse (*Anger* 2.31.7). Perhaps the best-known use of the body image in antiquity is found in a story attributed to the Roman senator Menenius Agrippa. Urging the people of Rome to work together, Menenius told a story about the hands, mouth, and teeth revolting against the belly, with the result that the whole body was impaired (see Livy, *History of Rome* 2.32.7–33.1).

Using the image in much the same way as did many of his contemporaries, Paul introduced the metaphor into the letter in order to make a plea for the unity of the community. The image of the body was particularly germane to Paul's purpose in writing the letter (1 Cor 1:10) since some members of the community were extolling their personal spiritual experiences to the disadvantage of others. The body is a vital, organic unit which functions

The purpose of the gifts as manifestations of the Spirit is that the members of the church of God might be brought together.

well when all the members of the body work in harmony. Introducing the image, Paul spoke first about the one and the many (1 Cor 12:12). This led to the image of the body as a classic example of the one and the many (1 Cor 12:14).

Much of Paul's discourse is classic. For example, the personification of the members of the body, giving considerable verve to the metaphor, was used by Menenius. Paul's theological perspective provides uniqueness to his use of the image. To a large extent Paul's theological/ecclesiological perspective provides a framework for the metaphor without entering into the exposition of the image itself. Mention of Christ encompasses the metaphor (vv. 12, 27), but there is no mention of Christ within the exposition of the metaphor itself.

Basically what distinguished Paul's use of the body image from contemporary usage are (1) the idea that God has created the body, structuring it as he willed to do (vv. 18, 24), and (2) Paul's emphasis on the weaker and less honorable members of the body (vv. 22-24a). The two idiosyncratic ideas unite in Paul's peroration:

> God has so arranged the body, giving the greater honor to the inferior members, that there may be no dissension within the body, but the members may have the same care for one another. If one member suffers, all suffer together with it;[41] if one member is honored, all rejoice together with it. (1 Cor 12:24b-26)

On the basis of these remarks with their implied exhortation, Paul makes a profound ecclesiological assertion: "You are the body of Christ and individually members of it" (1 Cor 12:27). How can this be, one might ask. Paul had given the answer in his introduction: "In the one Spirit we were all baptized into one body—Jews or Greeks, slaves or free—and we were all made to drink of one Spirit" (1 Cor 12:13). Both incorporation into the one body and the activity of the members of the body result from the one Spirit.

The references to baptism and eucharist are patent, though the reference to the eucharist[42] is not as clear as is the reference to baptism where baptismal language is used. Previously Paul had spoken allusively about both baptism and the eucharist using the historical example of the Exodus:

> Our ancestors were all under the cloud, and all passed through the sea, and all were baptized into Moses in the cloud and in the sea, and all ate the same spiritual food, and all drank the same spiritual drink. For they drank from the spiritual rock that followed them, and the rock was Christ. (1 Cor 10:1-4)

Paul's use of baptismal language includes the words "Jews or Greek, slaves or free," a snippet from a baptismal formula that seems to have been used in the Pauline churches. A fuller version of the baptismal formula is cited in Gal 3:27-28.[43] Reflecting on the formula, Paul drew an important lesson pertaining to descent from Abraham[44]—an issue that had been a bone of contention among Galatian believers. Paul wrote:

> As many of you as were baptized into Christ have clothed yourselves with Christ. There is no longer Jew or Greek, there is no longer slave or

free, there is no longer male and female; for all of you are one in Christ Jesus.

It would be difficult to imagine a more forceful plea for unity in Christ that transcends the usual bases for distinctions among human beings, especially those based on ethnicity, class, or gender, the most fundamental social markers.[45]

The Gift of Prophecy

After his important rhetorical digression on the body of Christ, Paul returned to the topic at hand: the gifts of the Spirit (1 Cor 12:28-31). He first gave a list of gifts that begins with three enumerated gifts: "first apostles, second prophets, third teachers; then deeds of power, then gifts of healing, forms of assistance, forms of leadership, various kinds of tongues" (1 Cor 12:28). Paul's rhetoric led him to ask a series of rhetorical questions, each of which obviously calls for a negative response: "Are all apostles? Are all prophets? Are all teachers? Do all work miracles? Do all possess gifts of healing? Do all speak in tongues? Do all interpret?" (1 Cor 12:29-30).

These seven questions roughly correspond to the seven gifts cited in verse 28, but the two lists are not identical. Assistance and leadership appear in the list that is stated positively; the working of miracles and the interpretation of tongues appear in the series of rhetorical questions. When the two lists are combined, Paul has mentioned a total of nine different gifts. But only five of the gifts, healing, the working of miracles, prophecy, tongues, and the interpretation of tongues, appeared in Paul's first list of gifts (1 Cor 12:7-10). On the other hand, the first list included the utterance of wisdom, the utterance of knowledge, faith, and the discernment of spirits. All told, thirteen different gifts appear in the three lists combined; only three gifts appear on all three lists: healing, prophecy, and speaking in tongues.

The comparison of the gifts of prophecy and tongues is the burden of chapter 14. Paul himself possessed these gifts.[46] Forcefully, he wrote about the importance of the gift of prophecy in comparison with the gift of tongues, giving himself as an example: "I thank God that I speak in tongues more than all of you; nevertheless, in church I would rather speak five words with my mind, in order to instruct others also, than ten thousand words in a tongue" (1 Cor 14:18-19). Paul obviously preferred the use of the gift of prophecy to the exercise of the gift of tongues.

Comparing the two gifts, Paul gave several reasons why the gift of prophecy is to be preferred to the gift of tongues, why, in his own words, "one who prophesies is greater than one who speaks in tongues" (1 Cor 14:5). Among the reasons are that those who speak in tongues: (1) build themselves up (v. 4); (2) do not benefit people unless another charismatic person has the gift of interpretation (v. 6); (3) are not intelligible (v. 9); (4) do not use their minds (v. 14); (5) do not elicit an appropriate response from the assembly (v. 16); (6) are a sign only for unbelievers (v. 22); and (7) run the risk of leading outsiders to say that Christians have lost their minds (v. 23).

Paul clearly held the gift of prophecy in high esteem. It is one of just three gifts—and the only noncontroversial gift[47] among them—that appear in all three lists of gifts in chapter 12. The gift of prophecy later appeared in the list of gifts in Romans 12. In that chapter of his letter-essay, Paul wrote about the unity of the body and the different gifts of the Spirit in this way:

> As in one body we have many members, and not all the members have the same function, so we, who are many, are one body in Christ, and individually we are members one of another. We have gifts that differ according to the grace given to us: Prophecy, in proportion to faith; ministry, in ministering; the teacher, in teaching; the exhorter, in exhortation; the giver, in generosity; the leader, in diligence; the compassionate, in cheerfulness. (Rom 12:4-8)

Prophecy is a gift whose importance for the church was first emphasized by Paul in the concluding exhortation of 1 Thessalonians: "Do not quench the Spirit. Do not despise the words of prophets" (1 Thess 5:19-20). The importance of prophecy is further confirmed by the mention of this gift in the lists of gifts compiled by Paul's disciples (Eph 4:11; 1 Pet 4:10-11).

Prophecy is the only gift of the Spirit that appears in all six of the lists of charisms in the New Testament. Among the Spirit's gifts, prophecy would appear to be a sine qua non of any Christian church. In the absence of the gift of prophecy, the church of God cannot exist. The reason is easy to discern. The role of the prophet is to "speak the words of God" (1 Pet

4:11). Without God's word, in which the members of the church believe, the church cannot exist.

Jesus was a prophet (John 4:19); there must be a prophetic presence in the gathering of those who convene in his name (1 Cor 1:2). A prophet speaks not only by word; a prophet also speaks through actions. A prophet speaks of God in the spoken word and in the speaking word, the prophetic gesture. Like Jesus, the prophet speaks on behalf of God and on behalf of the people of God, for in the biblical tradition the God who reveals himself is the God of a people.

Coming Together to Pray and Prophesy

Paul emphasized that the purpose of the gifts was the building up of the church (1 Cor 14:5, 12). When the church came together the various gifts were much in evidence. Paul reminded the church at Corinth that he exercised his own prophetic gift in the midst of the assembly: "In church I would rather speak five words with my mind in order to instruct others also, than ten thousand words in a tongue" (1 Cor 14:19).

When the whole church came together,[48] almost inevitably there were problems. One problem seems to have been that they all wanted to use their gifts. The result was confusion in the assembly. For Paul this was scandalous: "If the whole church comes together and all speak in tongues, and outsiders or unbelievers enter, will they not say that you are out of your mind" (1 Cor 14:23)? According to the apostle to the Corinthians, order in the assembly was necessary:

> If anyone speaks in a tongue, let there be only two or at most three, and each in turn; and let one interpret. But if there is no one to interpret, let them be silent in church and speak to themselves and to God. Let two or three prophets speak, and let the others weigh what is said. If a revelation is made to someone else sitting nearby, let the first person be silent. For you can all prophesy one by one, so that all may learn and all be encouraged. (1 Cor 14:27-31)

It was not necessary for all to use their specific gifts when the community came together. It was not even necessary for all the prophets to speak, as Paul said: "Let two or three prophets speak." Others should contemplate the meaning of the prophet's words. When the assembly comes together, everything should be done in orderly fashion for the sake of the building up of the church, not in order that each one can demonstrate his or her prophetic gift: "When you come together, each one has a hymn, a lesson, a revelation, a tongue, or an interpretation. Let all things be done for building up" (*panta pros oikodomēn ginesthō*, 1 Cor 14:26).

Another issue that arose was the outward demeanor of those who gathered together in the assembly at prayer. Social commentators in Paul's day frequently addressed the issue of proper attire and the hairstyle to be worn when people appear in public. As he addressed the issue of the outward demeanor of men and women in the Christian assembly, Paul was doing as several of his contemporaries did. Paul wrote: "Any man who prays or prophesies with something on his head disgraces his head, but any woman who prays or prophecies with her head unveiled disgraces her head" (1 Cor 11:4-5).

> *Paul had previously given instructions on the demeanor of women who would pray and prophesy in the assembly (1 Cor 11:5). How could he now have said that women are to remain silent?*

The exhortation comes in the course of an enigmatic passage (1 Cor 11:3-16) that is quite difficult for people in our day to understand. Part of the difficulty arises from the fact that Paul does not otherwise speak of hair, and thus much of his vocabulary occurs only here;[49] another part of the interpretive problem arises from our lack of knowledge of Hellenistic social conventions; still another part arises from the fact that Paul makes use of a midrash. The result is that this section of Paul's letter constitutes a major problem for contemporary interpreters. The passage is a true crux,[50] but the bottom line of Paul's exhortation is clear: when men and women come together to pray and prophesy, they should be properly attired, looking like respectable men and women of the time.

Another problem regarding public worship stemmed from a reactionary backlash. Paul wrote:

> As in all the churches of the saints, women should be silent in the churches. For they are not permitted to speak, but should be subordinate, as the law also says. If there is anything they desire to know, let

them ask their husbands at home. For it is shameful for a woman to speak in church. Or did the word of God originate with you? Or are you the only ones it has reached? (1 Cor 14:33b-36)

This is another passage that has proven to be problematic for many among us.[51] It seems to be demeaning to women. Taken on face value, however, it does not ring true. Paul had previously given instructions on the demeanor of women who would pray and prophesy in the assembly (1 Cor 11:5). How could he now have said that women are to remain silent?

Though the words are Paul's, the thought is not; Paul's own thought is expressed only in the last verse of the passage. The double interrogative ("Did the word of God originate with you? Are you the only ones it has reached?") is Paul's rejoinder to those who wanted the church of God in Corinth to adopt the practice of Jewish assemblies,[52] in which women were not allowed to speak or pray publicly. If they wanted to know anything, they were to ask their husbands, presumably more learned in the Torah than they, what they wanted to know. Even today when Orthodox Jews and Muslims gather for prayer, the public gathering is reserved to men. Women are shunted off to someplace apart. Paul would have none of that. He challenged the claim of those who thought that they had a monopoly on the word of God.

Discussion and Study Questions

1. What does it mean for the church of God to be the Body of Christ? In the early church in Corinth? At the present time?

2. What are the different gifts given to and working among the members of your present church community?

3. What kind of unity does the Holy Spirit inspire within the church?

4. What does the charismatic nature of the church say about different forms of piety, parish, and church?

Chapter Four

"Saints in Christ Jesus . . . with the Bishops and Deacons"

Compared to the great epistles (Romans, 1–2 Corinthians, and Galatians), Paul's Letter to the Philippians is one of the shorter compositions in his legacy. It opens with words that call to mind the first words of the Letter to the Romans, "Paul and Timothy, servants of Christ Jesus, to all the saints in Christ Jesus who are in Philippi" (Phil 1:1; see Rom 1:1, 7).

Philippians is a letter that is difficult to situate. Scholars debate whether it was originally a single letter or whether the extant text is a composite document conflated from two or three earlier texts. They also debate among themselves as to whether Philippians was composed during an imprisonment of Paul at some time during the mid-fifties when Paul was in Ephesus or whether it was written during the period of Paul's Roman imprisonment in the early sixties.[1]

There is little doubt that Paul wrote the letter or that he had visited the Colonia Iulia Augusta Philippensis in Macedonia. Paul tells us that he had been shamefully treated in Philippi before traveling the Egnatian Way to Thessalonica a hundred miles away (see 1 Thess 2:2). Paul's brief remarks allude to the situation that Luke describes at length in Acts 16:11–17:1. Luke says that Philippi was the first "European"[2] city evangelized by Paul. In Philippi, Paul enjoyed the hospitality of a woman named Lydia, expelled a demon from a slave girl, was punished and imprisoned as a result of false accusations, miraculously escaped from prison, and then went on his way to Thessalonica. He was invited to do so by the Philippian authorities, apparently the duoviri themselves. Paul later passed through the region as he was on his way to Jerusalem at the end of the third missionary voyage (Acts 20:6).

According to the narrative in Acts 16, Paul's preaching took place in a location where a few women gathered for prayer outside the city. Among those who listened to Paul was a woman named Lydia, a Gentile merchant who was a Jewish sympathizer. Lydia's heart was opened by the Lord and she and her household (*ho oikos autēs*) were baptized. Later she invited Paul to stay in her home (*eis ton oikon mou*); Paul accepted the invitation. On the occasion of a later visit to the riverside place of prayer (*proseuchē*), Paul met a slave girl who suffered from demonic possession. The girl followed Paul and Silas for several days, causing troubles that would lead to Paul's imprisonment. After Paul was miraculously released from prison, the jailer was baptized along with his entire household (*hoi autou pantes*). The jailer opened his house to Paul (*eis ton oikon*),[3] laid on a spread of food, while the whole household[4] rejoiced because they believed in God.

The Lucan account of Paul's visit to Philippi indicates that the first household units in the community of believers in Philippi were those of Lydia and the jailer. Presumably both Lydia and the jailer were Gentiles. Lydia was led to believe because she had heard Paul's message; the jailer came to belief after having witnessed a wondrous event, a sign of God's power. Each of them was a head of a household and was joined in accepting the faith by the entire household. Both Lydia and the jailer offered hospitality to Paul. Thus, the household churches of Lydia and of the anonymous Philippian jailer became the foundation of the community of believers in Philippi.

Saints

Paul does not, however, address his letter to the church—or churches—at Philippi. Rather, he wrote "to all the saints in Christ Jesus who are in Philippi" (Phil 1:1b). Absent from the salutation is any specific reference to an assembly of Christians. Could this be because there was more than one house church in the city and the disharmony to which Paul refers in his exhortations to unity (Phil 1:27–2:18; 3:15–4:3) resulted from some sort of split among them? The reference to Euodia and Syntyche in Phil 4:2-3 would seem to suggest, however, that the differences in the community were differences of opinion among individuals rather than among groups.

It could be that the lack of reference to a church in the opening of Paul's letter simply reflects the existence of more than one house church in Philippi; Paul wanted to address all the believers in Philippi even if they did not normally come together in one place as did believers in Corinth (1 Cor 11:17-20). On the other hand, the time between Paul's visits to Philippi and his writing of the letter may have been so long ago that Paul had no recent experience of a gathering in Philippi. These reasons would have been similar to those which prompted Paul to address believers in Rome as "all God's beloved in Rome, who are called to be saints" (Rom 1:7).

Common to both of the salutations, Rom 1:7 and Phil 1:1, is the universal "all" (*pasin*), the phrase "who are in Rome/Philippi" (*tois ousin en Rōmē/Philippois*), and the descriptive epithet "saints" (*hagiois*). The latter is an honorific designation to be sure, reminding the respective communities of their dignity as God's own people. The characteristic epithet functions as a kind of *captatio benevolentiae,* an appeal to the good will of the listeners. At the same time, however, it is a subtle reminder of their vocation as God's holy people, a vocation whose implications Paul spells out as he continues the writing of his letter.[5]

Although Paul does not speak of a household gathering in Philippi, his letter to the Philippians suggests something about the domestic organization of the early church. Before closing the letter, Paul extends greetings to all the saints in Christ Jesus who are in Philippi (Phil 4:21) on behalf of "all the saints . . . especially those of the emperor's household" (*hoi ek tēs Kaisaros oikias,* Phil 4:22). Thus, the holiness motif encompasses the entire letter.[6]

Overseers

What distinguishes the salutation of Paul's Letter to the Philippians, not only from his letters to the four churches but also from the Letter to the Romans, is that the salutation makes specific reference to bishops and deacons. Paul writes: "To all the saints in Christ Jesus with the bishops and deacons" (*syn episkopois kai diakonois;* Phil 1:1).[7] The translation is anachronistic and somewhat misleading. "Bishops" and "deacons" are terms that today identify well-defined offices in the various Christian churches. The saints in Philippi at the time that Paul wrote to them were not as well organized as are our contemporary churches. Lest anachronisms be introduced into our reading of Paul's letters, it is better to speak of "overseers and helpers"[8] than to speak of "bishops and deacons" when the terms *episkopoi* and *diakonoi* appear in the New Testament.

Who were these overseers and helpers? What did they do? Paul does not speak about overseers in the extant letters except for this brief mention of them in Phil 1:1. Describing Paul's ministry, Luke mentions overseers only once, namely, in Paul's farewell discourse (Acts 20:28).[9] Clearly, Phil 1:1 is the oldest witness to the use of "overseer" in regard to church leadership in early Christian literature.

The Greek term *episkopos* ("overseer") appears in classical Greek literature. The term was applied to various people who exercised any number of different kinds of oversight. Homer, for example, used the term to describe the member of a ship's crew who had responsibility for watching over the cargo (*Odyssey* 8.163). Sophocles (*Antigone* 217) and Plato (*Laws* 8.849a) used the term to speak about people who served as guardians or supervisors. In the writings of Aristophanes, "overseer" is used of an intendant, the administrative official sent to a subject state (*Birds* 1022-1023). Plato uses the term in reference to women[10] who served as overseers for young married couples (*Laws* 6 [784a]), who functioned as overseers during athletic events, or who fed children (*Laws* 7 [795d]). An overseer, then, is a person who has supervisory responsibilities over things, events, or people. Paul does not tell us any more about the overseers among the holy people of God in Philippi. He has nothing to say about their responsibilities and areas of supervision and nothing to say about their qualifications, age, or gender.

The farewell discourse that Luke attributes to Paul in Acts 20:18-35 has, however, something to say about the responsibilities of overseers in a church. Among the characteristics of the literary genre[11] of the farewell discourse is that it is a posthumous composition. In the words of Joseph Fitzmyer, this particular farewell discourse is "the way that Luke wants Paul to be remembered."[12] Acts 20:18-35 is a reflection on Paul's work and ministry and speaks of those who will succeed him[13] after his departure. The discourse is, as it were, a kind of vicarious last will and testament composed by Luke on behalf of Paul.

According to Luke's report, Paul urged the elders who had come to meet him in Miletus to fulfill their responsibilities carefully: "Keep watch

over yourselves and over all the flock, of which the Holy Spirit has made
you overseers to shepherd the church of God" (Acts 20:28). Acts was written some twenty-five or thirty years after Paul's Letter to the Philippians.
That Luke spoke of overseers in his eulogistic reflection on Paul's life and
ministry in the church at Ephesus suggests that overseers were a common
feature in the churches that Paul left behind. Enhancing the idea that this
was indeed the case is the fact that Acts 20:28 represents the only occur-
rence of the term "overseers" in Luke-Acts.

Acts 20:28 contains the core of Luke's reflection on the ministry of
oversight. With his usual attention to the role of the Spirit in the life of the
church, Luke states that it is the Holy Spirit who "made" (*etheto*) the elders
of Ephesus overseers. The verb
etheto ("made") had a variety
of senses, many of which were
related to the technical jargon
of one or another kind of
activity. One of these meanings is "to put someone/some-
thing in a certain state or
condition," "make or establish
someone as" a wife, friend, and
so forth.[14] This is the meaning of the verb in Acts 20:28: The Holy Spirit
constituted the elders in their role as overseers of "the church of God."

*In Jewish society of the time,
elders were respected leaders
of the community, known not
for their age but for
their wisdom.*

The function of the overseers was to "shepherd the church of God"
(*poimainein tēn ekklēsian tou theou*; Acts 20:28).[15] Theirs was a pastoral
role. As good shepherds, they were to guard the flock against ravenous
wolves (Acts 20:29). The image of savage wolves as a metaphor for false
prophets and teachers was classic in the Jewish and Christian traditions of
the time.[16] The image of the shepherd as leader of the people has biblical
roots, perhaps coming from the time of David, the shepherd king (2 Sam
5:2). Ezekiel 34 contains a satirical condemnation of the leaders of Israel
who are like careless shepherds in their neglect of the people. The same
chapter contains the promise of a shepherd ruler who will care for the
people (Ezek 34:23).

A story about a lost sheep was preserved in the early church's Q tradition. In Matt 18:12-14, the saying is directed to church leaders (cf. Luke
15:1-7). The Fourth Evangelist used the image of the shepherd in one of
the "I am" (*egō eimi*) sayings: "I am the good shepherd" (John 10:11).[17] The

relationship between the shepherd and his flock is the dominant theme of John 10:1-16. This pastoral motif is reprised in an episode contained in the epilogue to the Fourth Gospel. John 21:15-17 describes the risen Jesus entrusting a pastoral mission to Simon Peter.

Luke's use of pastoral imagery to describe the function of leaders of the church is thus rooted in centuries-old tradition. The Dead Sea Scrolls also bear witness to the tradition. According to the scrolls, the leader of the community at Qumran was known as the *mĕbaqqēr*, the "overseer."[18] His functions included that of shepherding the flock:

> And this is the rule of the Overseer[19] of the camp. He shall instruct the Many in the deeds of God, and shall teach them his mighty marvels, and recount to them the eternal events with their explanations. He shall have pity on them like a father on his sons, and will heal all the afflicted among them like a shepherd his flock. He will undo all the chains which bind them, so that there will be neither harassed nor oppressed in his congregation. And everyone who joins his congregation, he should examine, concerning his actions, his intelligence, his strength, his courage and his wealth; and they shall inscribe him in his place according to his inheritance in the lot of light. (CD 13:7-12)

Luke's application of the imagery to those whom he had identified as "elders of the church" (*tous presbyterous tēs ekklēsias*, Acts 20:17) is striking.[20] In Jewish society of the time, elders were respected leaders of the community, known not for their age but for their wisdom. Philo explained:

> By senior (*presbyterous*) they [Jews] do not understand the aged and grey headed who are regarded as still mere children if they have only in late years come to love this rule of life but those who from their earliest years have grown to manhood and spent their prime in pursuing the contemplative branch of philosophy, which indeed is the noblest and most god-like part. (*Contemplative Life* 64, 67)

In Luke's presentation of Paul's farewell discourse, "elders" (*presbyterous*) and "overseers" (*episkopous*) are terms that describe the same group of church leaders.[21] The term "elders" draws attention to their qualities and characteristics; the term "overseers" to their function, explained by means of the traditional image of a shepherd taking care of the flock. These three ideas—elders, overseers, and shepherd—come together in another early church text that depends on Paul. The First Epistle of Peter addresses this exhortation to the leaders of the church:

> Now as an elder myself (*ho sympresbyteros*) . . . , I exhort the elders among you (*presbyterous en hymin*) to tend the flock of God (*poimanate to en hymin poimnion tou theou*) that is in your charge, exercising the oversight (*episkopountes*[22]), not under compulsion but willingly, as God would have you do it—not for sordid gain but eagerly. Do not lord it over those in your charge, but be examples to the flock. And when the chief shepherd appears, you will win the crown of glory that never fades away. (1 Pet 5:1-4)[23]

Although Paul writes about the overseer only once, the language of Phil 1:1 is traditional. The images associated with it are deeply rooted in Jewish tradition. The mosaic of the overseer that emerges from the Christian and Jewish literature of the era is that of the shepherd, a true elder, who cares for the sheep of his flock. The picture of a flock of sheep remains until now a striking image of the church.[24]

Helpers

Unlike "overseers," the term "helpers" (*diakonoi*) appears in several of Paul's letters, twelve times in all.[25] It is twice used of civil authorities (Rom 13:4 [2x]), twice of Christ (Rom 15:8; Gal 2:17), and six times of Paul and his coworkers (1 Cor 3:5; 2 Cor 3:6; 6:4; 11:15 [2x], 23). Another time the term is used of Phoebe (Rom 16:1). Paul commended Phoebe to the Christians of Rome: "I commend to you our sister Phoebe," Paul wrote, "a deacon[26] of the church at Cenchreae, so that you may welcome her in the Lord as is fitting for the saints, and help her in whatever she may require from you, for she has been a benefactor of many and of myself (Rom 16:1-2).

This commendation[27] helps to clarify what Paul means by "helpers" in Phil 1:1. Phoebe was a Christian of the church in Corinth's western port, on the Saronic Gulf. In the past she had helped Paul and many others. In the church of Cenchreae, she was a "deacon" (*diakonos*). Now the Romans are asked to welcome her and assist her in the unidentified task at hand.

In the Greco-Roman world the term *diakonos* was used to describe a waiter at table (Xenophon, *Memorabilia* 1.5.2), a servant (Herodotus, *Histories* 4.71, 72), a messenger (Aeschylus, *Prometheus* 942), and an attendant, one of the officials in a temple or religious guild.[28] An inscription found in the Lydian city of Metropolis uses a feminine form of the term to identify a woman who served as a religious official.[29] Paul used the masculine form of the word to describe Phoebe's role in the church at Cenchreae. A fourth-century Jerusalem inscription similarly describes a woman named Sophia as a deacon (*diakonos*, a masculine form), calling her a "second Phoebe."[30]

Phoebe

Paul does not further describe Phoebe's role in the church at Cenchreae. It is clear that she was a woman of means on whom Paul could rely with confidence. Given the analogous use of the term "deacon" in Greco-Roman epigraphs and its appearance in Phil 1:1, Phoebe must be seen to have had some official position in the church at Cenchreae, a religious guild of the era even if the church at Cenchreae was not officially recognized as such during Paul's life.

Phoebe's task was that of service. Discussing the church as the body of Christ in Rom 12:3-8, Paul gave a list of seven charisms. Prophecy was the first gift mentioned by Paul. The notation of this essential gift was followed by a listing of the gifts of service (*diakonia*),[31] teaching, exhortation, giving, leading, being compassionate.

Paul said that the gift of service should be used in serving (*diakonian en tē diakonia*, Rom 12:7). Fitzmyer comments: "Undoubtedly, he means that the person who serves should really put his or her heart into such service." It is not easy to determine exactly what Paul means by the gift of service. The service might have been some particular kind of service, for example waiting on tables (Acts 6:2) or taking a collection to Jerusalem (Rom 15:25, 31; 1 Cor 16:1-4; 2 Cor 8:4). Or "service" might have been something more general, as it was when Paul used the term to speak of himself and his coworkers actively engaged in building up the church, specifically through preaching.[32] Referring to Rom 12:7, Brendan Byrne says: "*diakonia* seems to refer to service performed within the community by certain persons set apart and commissioned by the church as a whole to see to various tasks and concerns."[33]

One might object that service, particularly when the word has the connotation of waiting on table or carrying a collection, is not a very "spiritual" activity. The point is well made, but in 1 Corinthians 12 Paul had argued that very point: the charisms are essentially gifts; they do not necessarily entail extraordinary manifestations. In 1 Cor 12:28, after the enumerated gifts of the apostolate, prophecy, and teaching, Paul cites the gifts of power, healing, and "forms of assistance, forms of leadership" (*antilēmpseis, kybernēseis*) before he closes the list with a mention of the gift of speaking in tongues. Forms of assistance and forms of leadership might not have been particularly striking gifts among those given to members of the Corinthian church.

Paul does not use either of the Greek terms "assistance" or "leadership" elsewhere in his writings, so it is difficult to determine exactly what he means by them. The two Greek words were commonly used in Greco-Roman times. The former, *antilēmpseis*, was used in a wide variety of meanings, including assistance. The latter, *kybernēseis*, was properly used as a nautical term to describe a helmsman or a pilot; metaphorically it was used to designate a guide or a governor. As gifts of the Spirit, "assistance" and "leadership" seem to be Paul's way of describing a helping hand and some form of leadership. These talents are not extraordinary, yet their exercise does contribute to the building up of the church. Something similar must be stated in regard to the gifts of giving (*ho metadidous*), leading (*ho proïstamenos*),[34] and being compassionate (*ho eleōn*). The participles designate ordinary kinds of activity. Prompted by the Spirit, those who use these gifts build up the church. Phoebe, then, was a charismatic[35] person who possessed the gift of service or administration.[36] She exercised her gift of service for the benefit of the church at Cenchreae.

Paul, Andronicus, and Junia

Writing to the Philippians, Paul identified himself and Timothy as servants, literally "slaves" of Christ Jesus (Phil 1:1). The title alludes to Paul's situation as a prisoner, considered from the theological perspective of Paul's relationship to the Lord. Writing to the Romans, Corinthians, and Galatians, however, Paul identified himself as an apostle. He used various descriptive phrases to underscore his apostolic authority (Rom 1:1; 1 Cor 1:1; 2 Cor 1:1; Gal 1:1). He was named apostle (Rom 1:1; 1 Cor 1:1); his authority derives from the will of God (2 Cor 1:1), not from his own will or that of any human authority (Gal 1:1).

Make no mistake about it: Paul was an apostle. He wanted the Corinthians to fully realize that he was an apostle when he called them to task for scandalizing some of the weaker members of the community by eating meat offered to idols: "Am I not an apostle? Have I not seen Jesus our Lord? Are you not my work in the Lord? If I am not an apostle to others, at least I am to you; for you are the seal of my apostleship in the Lord" (1 Cor 9:1-2). Paul, however, considered himself to be the least of the apostles because he had seen the risen Lord after just about everyone else in the first generation of Christian believers had seen the Lord (1 Cor 15:8-9).

In the peroration to his exposition on the gifts of the Holy Spirit in 1 Corinthians 12, Paul mentioned the apostolate. In 1 Cor 12:28, Paul enumerated the apostolate as the first of the charisms, but in Romans 12 Paul did not mention the apostolate among the charisms. His failure to do so may be because of the fact that Paul was not the apostle to the Romans in the sense that he was apostle to the Corinthians. Paul proclaimed the gospel to the Corinthians, thus establishing the church of God at Corinth. At the time that he wrote to the Romans, Paul had not visited the community, let alone evangelized them.

The apostle Paul had a unique and precise understanding of what it meant to be an apostle.[37] Brendan Byrne summarizes this understanding in this way: "For Paul, to be an apostle means to have seen the risen Lord, to have been commissioned and sent by him to found churches and to have demonstrated the genuineness of this commissioning through hard labors."[38]

The genuine apostle—as distinct from "false apostles" (2 Cor 11:13-15)[39]—has five essential qualities. (1) An apostle is one who has seen the risen Lord (1 Cor 15:7, 9). (2) The apostle has been commissioned (Rom 1:1; 1 Cor 1:1; 1 Thess 2:4).[40] (3) The apostle has been sent to preach the gospel through the power of the Spirit (1 Thess 1:5a); the etymology of the term (apostolos)[41] indicates a "sending," a mission. (4) In this way the apostle establishes a church of those who have received the gospel. (5) The true apostle is distinguished by the signs of the apostolate, not only miracles but also the witness of his or her life (2 Cor 12:12; cf. 1 Thess 1:5b).

Because the apostle establishes churches through the Spirit-empowered preaching of the gospel, the apostolate is the first charism. It is the foundational charism. Paul made a strong point of his being apostle to the

Corinthians in 1 Cor 9:1-2. In the same letter he graphically spoke about his foundational role, using the images of a mother (1 Cor 3:2), a planter (1 Cor 3:6), and one who lays a foundation (1 Cor 3:10).

Paul first mentioned an apostle in 1 Thess 2:7, where he spoke about himself, Silvanus, and Timothy as "apostles of Christ." In the extensive series of greetings at the end of the Letter to the Romans, he asked that greetings be extended to "Andronicus and Junia,[42] my relatives who were in prison with me; they are prominent among the apostles, and they were in Christ before I was" (Rom 16:7). The pair were Jewish Christians[43] who became believers before Paul did. In the words of James Dunn, they belonged to "the closed group of apostles appointed directly by the risen Christ in a limited period following his resurrection."[44] In praise of Junia, Chrysostom, the greatest of the Eastern patristic commentators, wrote: "How great the wisdom of this woman that she was even deemed worthy of the apostles' title."[45] Andronicus and Junia were prominent evangelists who had an important role in founding the church at Rome.

> *"Coworkers" (syn-ergōn) was almost a technical term in Paul's vocabulary, designating those who "work together" in the proclamation of the gospel.*

Euodia, Syntyche, Clement, and Epaphroditus

Phoebe was not the only woman with some sort of leadership task in the Pauline churches. Together with her husband, Aquila, Prisca preached the gospel with Paul and hosted a house church. In the Letter to the Romans, Paul commended women such as Mary, Tryphaena, and Tryphosa, who worked in the Lord (Rom 16:6, 12).[46] The merchant Lydia seems to have hosted a house church in Philippi (Acts 16:15, 40). Lydia is not mentioned in Paul's Letter to the Philippians, but two other women are. In the last chapter of the letter, Paul wrote: "I urge Euodia and I urge Syntyche to be of the same mind in the Lord. Yes, and I ask you also, my loyal companion, help these women, for they have struggled beside me in the work of the gospel, together with Clement and the rest of my coworkers, whose names are in the book of life" (Phil 4:2-3).

We do not know the identity of Paul's "loyal companion" (*gnēsie syzyge*)[47] nor do we know very much about Euodia and Syntyche, whose names are not otherwise mentioned in the New Testament. Obviously, there had been some difficulty between them that had negative repercussions on the unity of the community in Philippi. Paul appealed to his loyal companion to help reconcile the rift between the two women. This says something about Paul's vision of ministry. His understanding always was that people worked together in preaching the gospel and building up the church. He himself traveled with others and, more often than not, joined other missionaries with himself when he wrote letters to the churches. In Philippians, Paul identified Euodia, Syntyche, and Clement as individuals who had joined with him in furthering the cause of the gospel.

To emphasize the togetherness of Euodia, Syntyche, Clement, and Paul's anonymous companion in the service of the gospel, Paul used two compound words: they "struggled beside me" and are "my coworkers."[48] "Coworkers" (*syn-ergōn*) was almost a technical term in Paul's vocabulary, designating those who "work together" in the proclamation of the gospel.[49] In the New Testament, the verb "struggle beside [me]" (*syn-ēthlēsan [moi]*) appears only in the Letter to the Philippians (Phil 1:27; 4:3). The verb, an athletic metaphor,[50] is an expression of the agon motif that Paul often uses to express the struggle that he and others are engaged in on behalf of the gospel.[51] Such imagery had long been employed by Stoic moralists to speak about the struggle on behalf of the truth or the moral life. Paul used similar language to describe those who were struggling on behalf of the gospel.

Before bringing his letter to a close, Paul expresses his gratitude to the Philippians for the gifts that they had sent to Paul (Phil 4:15-20). A person named Epaphroditus had carried the Philippians' gifts to Paul; he returned to them bearing Paul's letter. In the meantime he had fallen gravely ill and had almost died (Phil 2:25-30). Paul described this faithful go-between in terms similar to those that he used in regard to Euodia, Syntyche, and Clement, calling him "my brother and coworker and fellow soldier, your messenger and minister to my need" (Phil 2:25).

No other person in the New Testament[52] earned such an array of descriptive epithets as Paul applied to Epaphroditus in Phil 2:25. Like Prisca and Aquila (Rom 16:4), Epaphroditus risked his life for Paul. Describing Epaphroditus as "my brother,"[53] Paul identified him as a man of faith. Calling Epaphroditus "my coworker," Paul recognized him as someone who worked together with Paul in the preaching of the gospel.

When Paul described Epaphroditus as my "fellow soldier," Paul was not saying that Epaphroditus was serving in the Roman army. Epaphroditus was no more a soldier than was Archippus (Phlm 2) or Paul himself. Like "struggle beside me," "fellow soldier" (*sy-stratiōtēn*)[54] is a metaphor belonging to a register of terms associated with the agon motif. The image speaks of a struggle on behalf of the gospel, with the additional nuance that the struggle involves some adversity, perhaps even strong opposition.[55]

Finally, Paul described Epaphroditus as "your messenger[56] and minister to my need" (*hymōn de apostolon kai leitourgon tēs chreias mou*). The two terms should probably be taken together, perhaps as a hendiadys with the meaning "your messenger sent to minister to my need."[57] Does this mean that Epaphroditus had been sent to serve as Paul's factotum? Or was there some specific service that he was to render to Paul? There is no answer to this question but Paul obviously used liturgical language to describe Epaphroditus' service.[58]

Should Paul's expression be taken as a hendiadys in which the two nouns ("messenger" and "minister") qualify one another, the designation of Epaphroditus as an *apostolos* would indicate nothing more than that Epaphroditus had been sent by the Philippians. In this context "apostle" would then mean nothing more than "messenger," as it does when Paul uses the word in 2 Cor 8:23.[59] It cannot, however, be altogether ruled out that Epaphroditus had worked with Paul in the foundation of the church at Philippi and thus would have been qualified to be called an apostle in the way that Paul normally understands this term.[60]

On the one hand, Paul's Letter to the Philippians contains relatively meager theological reflection on the nature of the church. On the other hand, the letter indicates that leadership within the church is a cooperative endeavor. Leadership within the church at Philippi was a matter of team ministry, involving different men and women in various ways. Among them were Paul, Timothy, Paul's loyal but unnamed companion, Euodia, Syntyche, Clement, and Epaphroditus. The name of Lydia should probably be added to this list of names. In the community, there were overseers and helpers. Paul used a number of descriptive phrases to describe the leadership team in Philippi. He called them brothers and sisters, coworkers, fellow soldiers, ministers, and apostles or messengers. The number of the saints at Philippi might not have been very large, but leadership among them entailed a cooperative effort.

Discussion and Study Questions

1. What does it mean to be a saint?

2. What is the role of the hierarchy in the church?

3. Do real apostles exist in the church today?

4. What do you think about the leadership role of women in the church?

Chapter Five

"The Head of the Body, the Church"

Writing to the Thessalonians, Paul recognized that a leadership cadre was already in place laboring on behalf of the church of the Thessalonians. Paul urged Thessalonian believers to recognize those leaders and to pay heed to the voice of the prophets among them. Although the church of the Thessalonians had been but recently established, there were already recognized leaders and prophets among them. As Paul preached the gospel and wrote to various churches, his reflection on community leadership continued. Paul recognized that leadership, the preaching of the gospel itself, was the work of the Holy Spirit.

As Paul wrote about people's varied responsibilities within the church, he developed precise language. Apparently Paul coined the term "charism" to speak about the responsibilities that came from the Spirit of God at work in the church. To illustrate how those within the church must work together to build up the church, Paul used the powerful image of the church as the body of Christ. In his longest letters, Paul employed this graphic and pregnant image of the body to designate the great churches of Corinth and Rome.

Colossians 1:15-20 is a magnificent piece of poetry that speaks about the role of Christ in creation and reconciliation.

After his death, Paul's language was continued in the churches that he left behind, but the meaning of that language changed as the community of believers grew in numbers and experienced the need to adapt to new circumstances. The Epistle to the Ephesians bears witness to the growing number of believers and the accommodation of those believers to the circumstances of the Greco-Roman Empire in the second half of the first century c.e. The text of the epistle is a virtual treatise on the church.[1]

In the judgment of many biblical scholars, the Epistle to the Ephesians is based on the Epistle to the Colossians. Thus, the Epistle to the Ephesians is a new and expanded edition of the earlier text. Much of the additional material found in Ephesians relates to the church. The finished product then becomes the extended essay on the church. Since Colossians itself was most likely not written by Paul but rather by one of his disciples, Colossians should be regarded as a deutero-Pauline work; Ephesians, as a trito-Pauline text.[2]

Colossians

The Epistle to the Ephesians uses the word "church" (*ekklēsia*) nine times, but Colossians uses the word only four times. Two of the appearances are to be found in the epistle's final greetings where the term has retained its traditional Pauline meaning, namely, a local assembly: "Give my greetings to the brothers and sisters in Laodicea and to Nympha and the church in her house.[3] And when this letter has been read among you, have it read also in the church of the Laodiceans" (Col 4:15-16a).

Colossians 1:15-20 is an expressive christological hymn; it is a magnificent piece of poetry that speaks about the role of Christ in creation (vv. 15-16) and reconciliation (vv. 18b-20). Verses 17-18a serve as a transition between the two strophes: "He himself is before all things, and in him all things hold together. He is the head of the body, the church."[4] The idea that Christ is the head and the church the body recurs a few verses later: "I am now rejoicing in my sufferings for your sake, and in my flesh I am completing what is lacking in Christ's afflictions for the sake of his body, that is, the church" (Col 1:24).

In these passages, Col 1:17-18a and 1:24, the word "church" is employed in a novel and different sense from the way that Paul had used the term and that the author himself would use it in Col 4:15-16. The way that the author of Colossians wrote about the church as the body of Christ represents a radical transformation of Paul's use of that powerful metaphor. For Paul the body of Christ was a local community of believers interacting with one another in a fashion similar to the way that members of a human body function together for the good of the entire body. The apostle made no distinction between one of the members and the body, nor did he distinguish the body (torso) from the head. Employing Paul's metaphor and using the insights of ancient physiology, the author of Colossians portrayed the dependency of the body on the head. He described people beguiled by false teaching and unsound practices as "not holding fast to the head, from whom the whole body, nourished and held together by its ligaments and sinews, grows with a growth that is from God" (Col 2:19). The verse subtly links the idea of God-given growth with the notion that the church is the body of Christ.

In his christological hymn (Col 1:15-20), an unknown author has made "the body of Christ, the church," a symbol of the reconciliation of all things through Christ. As the entire universe has been created and preserved through Christ, so too the church is centered on Christ "so that he might come to have first place in everything" (Col 1:18). The universe and the church, its symbol, are dependent on Christ in whom "all the fullness of God was pleased to dwell" (Col 1:19).

The use of the church as a cosmic symbol in Colossians means that "the church" no longer connotes a local assembly of believers but rather the entire "body" of believers. In the language of contemporary ecclesiology, the author of the Epistle to the Colossians used "church" (*ekklēsia*) to designate the universal church. Thus, "church" no longer represents a physical reality; rather, the term has become a metaphor denoting the ensemble of believers no matter where they are located.

Head and Body

The trito-Pauline author of Ephesians borrowed the head-and-body motif from Colossians, providing it with a shift in emphasis and much further development. Ephesians 1:15-23 is a deferred epistolary thanksgiving. It ends with a prayer of thanksgiving and praise of the cosmic Christ, and it includes a citation of Ps 8:7: "And 'he has put all things under his feet' and has made him the head over all things for the church, which is his body, the fullness of him who fills all in all" (Eph 1:22-23). The allusion is part of a scriptural apologetic in which the author used various verses of the Bible to reflect on the significance of Christ and the meaning of the Christian life.

What the author says about the church is striking. Reprising the cosmic motif from the christological hymn of Colossians, the author of Ephesians has described Christ's cosmic triumph as beneficial to the church. All of Christ's work seems directed to the church. This exaltation of the church was continued when the author described the church as "the fullness of him who fills all in all." In Colossians the fullness of the godhead was said to reside in Christ (Col 1:19); now that same fullness is said to reside in the church (see Eph 1:22-23; 3:19). The "fullness" of Christ has become an attribute of the church.

Prayer forms abound in the Epistle to the Ephesians. The doxology that concludes a prayer for the readers celebrates the exalted status of the church: "Now to him who by the power at work within us is able to accomplish abundantly far more than all we can ask or imagine, to him be glory in the church and in Christ Jesus to all generations, forever and ever. Amen" (Eph 3:20-21). This is the only doxology in the New Testament that mentions the church.[5] The exaltation ecclesiology that prompted the author to speak of the fullness of the godhead dwelling in the church led him similarly to present the church as linked in consort with Christ Jesus as the means through which glory is given to God.

Reconciliation in the Temple

Unity is a major theme of the Epistle to the Ephesians, whose author proclaims: "There is one body and one Spirit, just as you were called to the one hope of your calling, one Lord, one faith, one baptism, one God and Father of all, who is above all and through all, and in all" (Eph 4:4-6)—a memorable heptad! Key to the unity of the body is the reconciliation of Jews and Gentiles in Christ. Christ has overcome the traditional ethnic divide and has created in himself one new humanity in place of the previous two (see Eph 2:15). The author's images are graphic; his theology, profound:

He [Christ] is our peace; in his flesh he has made both groups into one and has broken down the dividing wall, that is, the hostility between us. He has abolished the law . . . that he might reconcile both groups to God in one body through the cross, thus putting to death that hostility through it. So he came and proclaimed peace to you who were far off and peace to those who were near; for through him both of us have access in one Spirit to the Father. (Eph 2:14-18)

Echoes of Colossians' christological hymn and its immediate context are to be found in Ephesians' proclamation of peace. Particularly striking is the link between reconciliation and the body of Christ (see Col 1:22). Yet there are striking differences between the way the author of Colossians and the author of Ephesians speak of reconciliation and the body. In Colossians, reconciliation is the reconciliation of evil men and women through the physical body of Christ who suffered and died. In Ephesians, reconciliation is reconciliation between Jew and Gentile, effected in the body of Christ, the church. For the author of this late text, the church, as the body of Christ, is the locus of ethnic reconciliation.

Juxtaposed with the image of the body is the image of the temple. The author of Ephesians did not state, as did the Synoptists (Matt 27:51; Mark 15:38; Luke 23:45), that the curtain of the temple was torn in two. The implication of Ephesians' use of the temple metaphor is that non-Jews are no longer confined to the court of the Gentiles:

So then you are no longer strangers and aliens, but you are citizens with the saints and also members of the household of God, built upon the foundation of the apostles and prophets, with Christ Jesus himself as the cornerstone. In him the whole structure is joined together and grows into a holy temple in the Lord; in whom you also are built together spiritually into a dwelling place for God. (Eph 2:19-22)

The pericope opens with political language[6] but soon switches to the construction language that recalls Paul's own language:[7] "aliens (*paroikoi*)[8] . . . members of the household of God (*oikeioi tou theou*) . . . built upon the foundation (*epoikodomēthentes epi tō themeliō*) . . . cornerstone (*akrogōniaiou*) . . . whole structure (*pasa oikodomē*) . . . built together into a dwelling place for God *synoikodomeisthe eis katoikētērion tou theou*)." Amid ponderous language rings the sound of construction, *oiko-*.[9]

Paul used construction imagery to good advantage in 1 Cor 3:9b-17. In that pericope, Paul previewed the idea that the house under construction is a temple. A similar movement is found in Eph 2:19-22, but the component metaphors have been radically altered and the construction image is employed in the pursuit of a different rhetorical argument. When Paul in 1 Corinthians used the metaphor, he used it to talk about the role of individual "contractors" working with different building materials to construct a single edifice. In Ephesians the construction metaphor is employed to portray the eschatological acceptance of the nations in the house of the Lord.[10] Instead of portraying the members of a community working together, as Paul did, with every person accountable for his or her own work, the metaphor used in Ephesians portrays an aspect of the eschatological hope of Israel.

Paul stated that he had laid the foundation, which is Jesus Christ (1 Cor 3:10-11). By preaching the gospel, Paul introduced Christ into the city of Corinth so that a community of believers was built on this foundation. In Ephesians the foundation consists of the apostles and the prophets.[11] The crucial role[12] of Christ in the construction is highlighted by the image of a cornerstone.[13] Typically an edifice is built outward and upward from the cornerstone. The cornerstone thus holds the entire construction together. In the construction described by the author, people rather than objects are the building material. Christ himself holds Jew and Gentile together[14] in the house of God.

The author's metaphor is mixed yet again as he switches from construction imagery (cf. Eph 2:14) to organic imagery (cf. Eph 4:16; Col 2:19). Through the life-giving power of the Spirit, the building "grows" into a holy temple, the dwelling place of God. The imagery is biblical. Biblical texts speak of both the temple in Jerusalem and in heaven as the dwelling place of God.[15] For the author of Ephesians the church is a temple[16] whose cornerstone is Christ. This holy temple provides for both Jew and Gentile access to God who dwells in the temple by the power of the Spirit.[17] In this way the biblical expectation[18] of an eschatological temple in which Jews and Gentiles together worship the one God of Israel is fulfilled.

The eschatological scenario suggested in Eph 2:19-22 continues in Eph 3:1-13 as the author reminisces about Paul's preaching of the gospel within the context of the eschatological mystery. The mystery was revealed not only to Paul (Eph 3:3) but also to the holy apostles and prophets. The mystery is that "the Gentiles have become fellow heirs, members of the same body, and sharers in the promise in Christ Jesus through the gospel" (Eph

3:6). The mystery is that Gentiles have become heirs to the promise made
to Israel because of the gospel that was preached to them. Being the recipients of the promise, the Gentiles are one with Israel.[19]

Paul's own role, the apostolate to the Gentiles, had as its purpose "to
make everyone see what is the plan[20] of the mystery hidden for ages in God
who created all things; so that through the church the wisdom of God in
its rich variety might now be made known to the rulers and authorities in
the heavenly places" (Eph 3:9-10). The mystery that had previously been
revealed to Paul, the apostles, and the prophets is to be made known to
hostile spiritual powers through the church. The very existence of the
church,[21] the breaking down of the barrier that had divided Jews and Gentiles, is a sign that the power of these hostile forces is about to be broken.
The church bears witness to the ultimate eschatological victory of the cosmic Christ.

Christ's Gifts

The seven-fold articulation of ecclesial unity in Eph 4:4-6 gives rise to
an image of the cosmic Christ whose portrayal is replete with language
drawn from 1 Corinthians 12. As was the case with the author's exploita-
tion of construction imagery in Eph 2:19-22, the metaphor has been radically altered; and, as was also the case with the earlier image, the metaphor
is employed to plead a point other than that exploited by Paul in 1 Corinthians 12–14.

Paul employed the image of a single body composed of various inter-
active members to show the importance of each and every charism of the
Spirit and to illustrate the way in which they might work together to the
advantage of the entire community. The author of Ephesians chose not to
use the Pauline neologism "charism" (*charisma*); rather he writes simply
about grace (*charis*).[22] He begins by affirming that a gift is given to each
one: "Each of us was given grace according to the measure of Christ's gift"
(*tēs dōreas tou Christou*, Eph 4:7). The affirmation recalls the language of
1 Cor 12:7, 11, but Ephesians attributes the gifts given to each one to Christ
who had ascended rather than to the Spirit, as did Paul.

Christ's gifts were that "some would be apostles, some prophets, some
evangelists, some pastors and teachers" (Eph 4:11). This list of just five gifts
is shorter than any of the three lists of charisms given by the apostle in

1 Corinthians 12. First Corinthians 12:28 and 29 lists apostles, prophets,[23] and teachers as the first three gifts of the Spirit to the church, the body of Christ. Two new gifts appear in the list given in Ephesians 4: evangelists and pastors (*tous de euaggelistas, tous de poimenas*). These gifts have no counterpart in Paul's own writings. The "evangelist" does, however, appear in Acts 21:8 and 2 Tim 4:5 to describe second-generation preachers of the gospel, Philip and Timothy. First Peter identifies Christ as a shepherd (*ton poimena*, 1 Pet 2:25) and as a chief shepherd (*tou archipoimenos*, 1 Pet 5:4). Apart from Eph 4:11 the New Testament never uses the term "shepherd" or "pastor" to describe a leader of the church.[24]

Apart from the shift by the author of Ephesians from the language of charism, the attribution of the gifts to the exalted Christ, and the introduction of gifts that Paul does not mention, the author's list of gifts is limited to gifts of didactic leadership. His list lacks the diversity of Paul's various lists of charisms. By so limiting the list of gifts, the reader is left to wonder what the author means when he writes that "each of us was given grace." The gifts that appear to be of exclusive interest to the author are the various gifts of proclamation and teaching.

This impression is confirmed in the inferential paraenesis that the author draws from his picture of Christ, the heavenly gift-giver. He dutifully notes that the gifts are given "to equip the saints for the work of ministry, for building up the body of Christ" (*ergon diakonias eis oikodomēn tou sōmatos tou Christou*, Eph 4:12). In the context of his discussion of the charisms, the author of Ephesians follows Paul, his mentor, in speaking about love. For him, however, love is not the greatest and most fundamental of gifts. Rather, he writes about love only in the terse phrase "in love" (*en agapē*), a phrase twice used to qualify the activity of the believer (vv. 15, 16).

In a single long sentence describing the gifts to be used in building up the body (vv. 11-16), the author writes about the unity of faith, knowledge of the Son of God, [frivolous] doctrine, and speaking the truth. His doctrinal emphasis is manifest. Paul used the image of the body to speak of the unity and interactivity of the local church; Ephesians uses the image of the body in reference to the universal church in order to speak of its growth:

> Speaking the truth in love, we must grow (*auxēsōmen*) up in every way into him who is the head, into Christ, from whom the whole body, joined and knit together by every ligament with which it is equipped,

as each part is working properly, promotes the body's growth (*auxēsin*) in building itself up in love. (Eph 4:15-16)

The point is well taken but it is a point other than that made by Paul in writing to the Corinthians and to the Romans. The author's physiological imagery is derived not from Paul but from the author of the Letter to the Colossians (Col 2:19).

The Body of Which He Is the Savior

Paul used the word "church" to identify a gathering of Christians in a particular locale. In two of his major letters, Romans and 1 Corinthians, Paul used the powerful image of the human body to describe the church. Both the terminology and the image recur repeatedly in the Epistle to the Ephesians with, however, manifest adaptation of application and implication. The use of the body image in Ephesians clearly depends at times on the prior usage of Colossians, which used the language of "church" to refer both to the church universal and to a local community of believers.

The author of the Epistle to the Ephesians explicitly links together the term "church" and the image of the body in only two passages of his text. These are Eph 1:22-23 and 5:22-33. The latter passage is rich in ecclesiological insights but they are sometimes difficult to comprehend because the author has incorporated them into the framework of a household code taken over from the Epistle to the Colossians (Col 3:18–4:1;[25] Eph 5:21–6:9). The result is a passage in which the language of late first-century marital relationships informs the description of Christ and the church. At the same time, elements of the author's ecclesiology inform his description of the marital relationship.

Earlier in the epistle, the author had used the metaphors of the human body, politics, construction, and organic growth to speak about the church. Now he uses the image of the husband and wife to portray the relationship between Christ and the church. This use of the metaphor was preceded in the biblical tradition by imagery in which the marital relationship between husband and wife was used to describe the relationship between Yahweh and his people, Israel (Jer 3:1; Isa 54:6-7; Ezek 16:10-14). The Book of Hosea used the infidelity of Gomer, whom God commanded the prophet to marry, as a symbol of Israel's infidelity to Yahweh. Indeed, Israel's infidelity was often described as "adulterous."[26] The biblical metaphor was readily grasped because the same term, *berith*, "covenant," was used to describe the relationship between Yahweh and Israel and the relationship between a husband and wife.

Appropriation of this biblical imagery to speak of the relationship between Christ and the church appears to be a characteristic phenomenon in late-first-century Christianity,[27] but the author of Ephesians has exploited the imagery in a most explicit fashion. Before recapitulating his paraenetic advice to husbands and wives, he says: "This is a great mystery, and I am applying it to Christ and the church" (Eph 5:32). More literally translated, the sentence would read: "This is a great mystery; I am speaking about Christ and the church."[28]

Exploiting the marital imagery allows the author to reprise the motif of Christ as the head of the church, which is his body (Eph 1:22-23; 4:15). The presence of the motif in this literary context makes it clear that the headship of Christ over the church connotes Christ's authority over a church that is subject to him. The idea had previously been expressed in Col 1:18.

The notion that Christ is the "savior" (*sōtēr*) of his body,[29] the church, offers much food for thought on the nature of the church. To the naive reader of Ephesians, the title "savior" evokes the theological idea of redemption. This notion cannot be ruled out from the meaning of this title in Eph 5:23,[30] but there is more to the meaning of the title than that. Within the framework of marital imagery, the title, on the one hand, suggests the salvation of a woman from the fate of loneliness and the social stigma that accompanied childlessness,[31] not to mention the lack of fulfillment of a woman's own maternal instinct. On the other hand, a "savior" was generally one who offered favors and benefactions to those who were saved. As a savior, a husband offered gifts to his wife. Thus, the image of Christ, the savior of his body, the church, suggests that Christ gives gifts to the church (see Eph 4:7-13).

The marital imagery allows the author of Ephesians to speak of Christ's love for the church (Eph 5:25), an idea that receives its unique expression in this context. Christ's love for the church is twice presented as the exemplar for a Christian's love for his wife (Eph 5:25, 29).[32] As the epistle speaks of Christ's love for the church, emphasis is placed on Christ's active role with regard to the church. The primary expression of Christ's love for the church is his self-sacrifice on behalf of the church: "Christ loved the church and gave himself up for her" (Eph 5:25). The latter phrase, "gave himself up for her" (*heauton paredōken hyper autēs*) uses the technical language with which the early church described Christ's passion.[33] Christ's total self-oblation on behalf of the church was the essential manifestation of his love for the church.

The result of Christ's passion grounded in his love for the church is that the church is "made holy by cleansing . . . with the washing of water by the word" (Eph 5:26). Because of Christ's passion, the church is sanctified; it belongs to God. What belongs to God must be purified, as the biblical tradition so often attests.[34] Philo says that a man is forbidden to enter the temples "save after bathing and cleansing his body" (*Unchangeableness of God* 8). The purification and sanctification of the church "is carried out by means of and in the form of a bath with water."[35] "By the word" (*en rhēmati*), the author's qualification of this bath makes it clear that he is writing about a ritual lustration. Christian readers recognize in the phrase an allusion to the ritual of baptism.[36] Because of Christ's loving action, the church is holy and unblemished.[37]

Further reflection on this bath in the light of the marital imagery of Eph 5:22-32 yields additional nuances. Ephesians 5:26-27 evokes notions of a bride's preparation for marriage.[38] The bridal bath (*loutron*[39] *nymphi-kon*[40]) was an important feature of the Hellenistic marital ritual. Hellenistic society considered procreation to be the principal purpose of marriage. Since water was a source of fertility, the bridal bath was important not merely because it consisted of physical washing but also because the bridal bath was a significant fertility rite. The symbolic bath was intended to assure progeny for a woman and the husband she was about to marry.

If Christ's love for the church was principally manifest in the self-oblation by which Christ acquired the church as his very own, his love was not limited to this initial act. The church belongs to Christ as his very body. Common sense dictates that a person take care of his or her own body: "No one ever hates his own body, but he nourishes and tenderly cares for it, just as Christ does for the church, because we are members of his body" (Eph 5:29-30).

This sentence is offered as an explanation[41] of the reason why husbands should love their wives. As an element in the author's paraenesis, it provides two reasons why husbands should love their wives: the common-sense dictum that a person takes care of his own body and the example of Christ's love for the church. Read from the perspective of the author's ecclesiology,[42] the sentence offers two important ideas that had not previously been expressed.

First, the sentence speaks of Christ's on-going love for the church. His love for the church was not confined to his once-only self-oblation on behalf of the church; rather it is continued in the nourishment and tender care that Christ provides for the church. The idea that a husband should provide food for his wife and that he should cherish her was part of the marriage contract in antiquity.[43] He promised to "care for and nurture and clothe her."[44] Another text says that he is to "love, care for, and attend to her."[45] Similarly Christ nurtures[46] the church and expresses his love in tender affection[47] for his church.

Because of Christ's passion,
the church is sanctified;
it belongs to God.

Second, Eph 5:30 notes: "we are members of his body" (*melē esmen tou sōmatos autou*). The author of Ephesians had written about being members "of one another" (Eph 4:25). The language of 5:30 comes from 1 Cor 12:12-26 and had not previously appeared[48] in this epistle. That it does is an indication of the lingering memory of Paul's idiom. The pseudepigrapher borrowed Paul's metaphor, configuring it to the new and rich, albeit different, nuances of his own ecclesiology.

Discussion and Study Questions

1. Does the church's self-understanding, its ecclesiology, continue to develop? Why or why not?

2. How can the church of today function as an agent of reconciliation, especially among peoples of different cultures and religious backgrounds?

3. How does the relationship between husband and wife help us better understand the nature of the church? How does our understanding of the church help us to better understand the nature of Christian marriage?

4. Do you see or experience any tension between a universal ecclesiology and a local ecclesiology in the church today?

Chapter Six

"The House of God"

The Epistle to the Colossians and the Epistle to the Ephesians represent one trajectory in the development of Pauline ecclesiology. These two epistles borrowed Paul's ecclesial metaphors, particularly those of the building and the body, developing them from the perspectives of a cosmic Christology and a universal church. The Pastoral Epistles, composed towards the end of the first century C.E., develop Paul's ecclesiology along another, more practical and less theoretical, trajectory. They exploit the Pauline image of the household.[1] The image was particularly appropriate. The Greco-Roman household served as the organizational model for the author's practical directives for the church.

Two of the three so-called Pastoral Epistles are ostensibly directed to Timothy, the other to Titus. Timothy and Titus were among Paul's closest coworkers. They served as Paul's personal emissaries when Paul was unable to go somewhere in order to accomplish some specific apostolic endeavor. Given the time frame within which the Pastoral Epistles were composed, it is highly likely that Timothy and Titus, as well as Paul, were already dead by the time the epistles were written. It is appropriate, therefore, to speak of a phenomenon of double pseudonymity with regard to the Pastoral Epistles. The stated recipients, as well as the stated author, belong to the domain of literary fiction.

The three epistles are customarily called the Pastoral Epistles, but it is useful to distinguish among them since they do not share the same literary genre. The contents of 1 Timothy and Titus are similar to those of later documents on church order, such as the early second-century *Didache*, the third-century *Didascalia Apostolorum*, the turn-of-the-century *Apostolic*

Church Order, the fourth-century *Apostolic Constitutions*, and the fifth-century *Testamentum Domini*. First Timothy and Titus are the oldest extant examples of the genre, a quasi-juridical text on church order.[2] The material contained in 2 Timothy is of a different sort. Its contents, language, and style type it as a testamentary text[3] in the form of a letter.

With regard, then, to the ecclesiological insights proffered by the Pastoral Epistles, it is primarily to the First Epistle to Timothy and the Epistle to Titus that the reader must turn. It is all but impossible to make a definitive judgment as to which of the two texts was composed first. Strong arguments can be, and have been, advanced in favor of the literary priority of one or the other.

Overseers

One who reads these epistles in their canonical sequence first meets 1 Timothy, the longer of the two texts pertaining to church order. One of the noteworthy features of 1 Timothy is the attention devoted to the "overseers and helpers," who first appeared in the New Testament in Phil 1:1. A long passage containing one pericope on the qualifications of overseers and another on the qualifications of helpers or servers can be read in 1 Tim 3:1-13. The qualifications of the overseer are given in a list of sixteen virtues, only one of which is specifically Christian.

The way in which the author sets out these qualities allows his list to be typed as a catalogue of virtues, a typical pattern of speech in Hellenistic rhetoric.[4] The Pastor states that the overseer is to be above reproach, married only once, temperate, sensible, respectable, hospitable, an apt teacher, not a drunkard, not violent, gentle, not quarrelsome, not a lover of money, a good household manager, a successful father,[5] and a person who enjoys a good reputation (1 Tim 3:2-7). In addition, the Pastor notes that the would-be overseer should not be a recent convert (see 1 Tim 3:2-7).[6] Except for the last, these desirable qualities are among those that people would expect to find in a reputable person, then and now.

A striking feature of the Pastor's[7] list of the overseer's virtues is a parenthetical remark inserted in verse 5: "If someone does not know how to manage his own household, how can he take care of God's church?" The rhetorical question clearly suggests that there is an analogy between the management of one's own household and the care of the church of God. If a person cannot take care of his own household, there is little chance that he can take care of a larger group that gathers in a believer's house, perhaps in his very own house.

In Titus 1:7-9, there is a list of an overseer's qualifications similar to the list found in 1 Tim 3:2-7. According to Titus, the overseer must be blameless, hospitable, prudent, upright, devout, self-controlled, one who loves goodness, and not arrogant, addicted to wine, violent, or greedy. To this series of eleven social virtues, the Pastor adds one specifically Christian quality, namely, that the overseer must have a firm grasp of the word that is trustworthy. For the most part, the qualities are similar to the qualities listed in 1 Tim 3:2-7, but the way that the Pastor presents them helps to clarify the role and responsibility of the overseer.

The Pastor added an important qualifying phrase in apposition to "the overseer": "a bishop, as God's steward," must be blameless. . . . In Greco-Roman society, the steward (*oikonomos*) was a well-placed, powerful, and highly respected functionary. Normally a slave, the steward was the household manager[8] in charge of other household slaves. His responsibilities were analogous to a modern chief-of-staff. The Pastor's

> "If someone does not know how to manage his own household, how can he take care of God's church?"
> (1 Tim 3:5)

appositional phrase thus describes the role of the overseer as one of oversight over those who belong to the household of God, effectively the church that gathered in someone's home. From this perspective, the rhetorical question of 1 Tim 3:5 makes full sense. The overseer must possess household management skills so that he can take care of God's church, the household of God. The overseer described in both 1 Timothy and Titus is a person who has management responsibilities in the household of God.

A Theological Interlude

Although 1 Timothy and Titus are for the most part practical documents, they are occasionally punctuated by short passages rich in theological content. One such passage is a brief remark that follows the exposition of the qualities of the overseer and servers in 1 Timothy 3:

> I hope to come to you soon, but I am writing these instructions to you so that, if I am delayed, you may know how one ought to behave in the household of God, which is the church of the living God, the pillar and bulwark of the truth. (1 Tim 3:14-15)

Ostensibly the passage offers a reason why the so-called letter was written. It offers behavioral guidelines to be followed during Paul's absence. This motif is part of the pseudepigraphic character of the letter. Paul is absent; he is not to return. Hence, the instructions are to be followed *ad diem,* indefinitely.

The descriptive triad contained in these verses is one of the richest ecclesiological statements in the entire New Testament. It identifies the church as "the household of God," "the house of God" (*oikō theou*).[9] The description serves to explain why the overseer is a steward (Titus 1:7) and why household management skills are so important for the proper exercise of ecclesiastical oversight. The imagery derives from Paul's construction metaphor (1 Cor 3:9b-17) but reflects the situation of a local church meeting in someone's home. The local church is God's household. God, however, is neither an absentee landlord nor absent from the household. God dwells within his own house, among his own people (see 1 Cor 3:16-17; Eph 2:22). A house is a dwelling place; the house of which the Pastor speaks is God's dwelling place.

The second member of the Pastor's descriptive triad is given in a relative clause, "which is the church of the living God." This additional element in the author's titular ecclesiology serves two purposes. First of all, it clarifies that the house about which the Pastor is writing is not the house of one or another deity. Authors as different as the historian Herodotus (*Histories* 8.143) and the dramatists Euripides (*Phoenician Maidens* 1373) and Aristophanes (*Clouds* 600) had used the word *oikos* to designate a temple.[10] The Pastor's "house of God" is the house of the "living God." The living God is the God of Abraham, Isaac, and Jacob, designated by his primal trait, "living."[11] God is active and dynamic; God communicates life.

Second, the relative clause identifies the temple of the living God not as a building made of stones but as a temple composed of people.[12] It is an assembly, a "church." Construction imagery recurs, nonetheless, in the third member of the Pastor's ecclesiological triad. The house, the assembly, is "the pillar and bulwark of the truth." These two pieces of construction evoke the idea of a solid instruction. Taken together as a hendiadys, "pillar" and "bulwark" suggest a solid foundation.

The assembly itself is the firm foundation for the "truth." This "truth" is the truth(s) of faith, the full knowledge of which is characteristic of the community's existence.[13] The Pastor's imaginative description of the church as the pillar and bulwark of the truth is similar to the description in the Dead Sea Scrolls of the community at Qumran: "a foundation of truth for Israel, for the Community of the eternal covenant" (1QS 5:5-6).[14] With his description, the Pastor identified an important function of his church: it is to preserve and support the truth. This delineation of the function of the church arises from the beleaguered situation of the church in the Greco-Roman world during the late first century c.e. Repeatedly the Pastoral Epistles warn their recipients against teachers of falsehood and their false teaching.[15] Confronted by opponents from without and eschatological apostasy from within (1 Tim 4:1-3), the church must remain the pillar and the bulwark of the truth.

This function of the church is the reason why the Epistle to Titus identified the only specifically Christian responsibility of the overseer as it did: "He must have a firm grasp of the word that is trustworthy in accordance with the teaching, so that he may be able both to preach with sound doctrine and to refute those who contradict it" (Titus 1:9). Describing this double-task function of the overseer, the Pastor employed some of his church's characteristic jargon. "The trustworthy word" alludes to pithy confessions of faith, such as those scattered throughout the Pastorals.[16] These sayings are believable and are to be believed. "Sound doctrine" is an expression borrowed from philosophic discourse which used hygienic idioms to describe teaching that leads to healthy behavior and sound relationships.[17]

With regard to the truth, the overseer had a double responsibility: he was to preach the truth; he was to defend against error. This responsibility, so clearly stated in Titus 1:9, is the reason why the overseer's being an "apt teacher" (*didaktikon*) appeared among the list of qualifications in 1 Tim 3:2. This characteristic was also cited among the qualities that Timothy, successor to Paul as the Lord's servant, must possess (2 Tim 2:24).

Elders

Each of the two lists of qualifications for the overseer found in the Pastorals mentions being "hospitable" (*philoxenon*, 1 Tim 3:2; Titus 1:8). This social grace was particularly important for a person who had household managerial responsibilities, as did the overseer of God's household. Hospitality is a desirable quality for any householder; it was especially important for the manager of the household of God. The house served the early church as a locus for evangelization and catechesis. There, traveling missionaries might find lodging, perhaps having the occasion to read a letter written by Paul. Had the leaders of the house churches been lacking in hospitality, the mission of the church would have been severely compromised.

In listing the qualifications of the overseer (Titus 1:7-9), the Epistle to Titus did not cite the kinds of familial responsibilities that appear in 1 Tim 3:2, 4, fidelity to one's wife and the successful rearing of children. These very qualities are, however, listed among the traits of the elders whom "Titus" is to appoint in every town. The elder must be someone who is "married only once, whose children are believers, not accused of debauchery and not rebellious" (Titus 1:6). These characteristics reveal that elders to be appointed are good husbands and fathers, people who have demonstrated that they have managed their own households well. Their experience shows that they have what it takes to manage the household of God (see 1 Tim 3:4-5).

Combining a short list of an elder's qualifications with a longer list of the overseer's qualifications as he does (Titus 1:6-9), the Pastor implied that the elder and the overseer are one and the same person.[18] "Elder" evokes the person's stature and qualities; "overseer," his function.[19] Jewish elders were presumed to be prudent and to be versed in the Torah and traditions of the people.[20] Similarly, elders in the household of God were expected to have full knowledge of the truth. Only in this way would they be capable of exercising their double responsibility with regard to the truth.

Elders, said the author of Titus, were to be appointed in every town (Titus 1:5), that is, the various towns in which the gospel had been preached. These appointments were for the sake of order in the community. The Pastor's reflection indicates that the church of the late first century was concerned with its organization, order, evangelical responsibility, and succession in ministry. The Second Epistle to Timothy addressed at length the issue of succession in the form of an epistolary farewell from Paul to Timothy.[21]

The Epistle to Titus was also concerned with succession in ministry. Having presented Paul's apostolate within a temporal framework of eternity (Titus 1:1-3)[22] and having noted that Paul considered Titus to be his faithful son, the epistle instructed Titus to appoint elders. The chain of succession was thus: from Paul to Titus; from Titus to the elder–overseer.

First Timothy does not link the elder and the overseer as did Titus. First Timothy, nonetheless, proposed a bill of rights for elders, with two provisions:

> Let the elders who rule well[23] be considered worthy of double honor, especially those who labor in preaching and teaching; for the scripture says, "You shall not muzzle an ox while it is treading out the grain," and "The laborer deserves to be paid." Never accept any accusation against an elder except on the evidence of two or three witnesses. (1 Tim 5:17-19)

The first provision relates to the support of the elder;[24] the second to his reputation within the community.

The Pastor argues for the provision of support by citing a passage from scripture and a saying. The scriptural citation is a provision of agricultural law found in Deut 25:4, which is similarly used by Paul in 1 Cor 9:9. The second citation, identified as "scripture," is similar to a Q saying reprised in Matt 10:10 and Luke 10:7. The Pastor's arguments from authority are clear enough. What he meant has been a subject for discussion among exegetes.[25]

These are the two questions: (1) Did the Pastor require that elders receive double pay? and (2) Did the Pastor suggest that some elders are engaged in a ministry of the word while others are not? The issues are moot; I would argue that the Pastor urged that elders, particularly those who were esteemed for their preaching and teaching, be held in high regard and have their material needs taken care of by the church.[26]

Provision for the elder's right to justice likewise echoed the Jewish scriptures. Deuteronomy 19:15 states: "Only on the evidence of two or three witnesses shall a charge be sustained."[27] The story of Daniel and Susanna illustrates the importance of at least two concurring witnesses (Daniel 13). Accordingly 1 Timothy—the epistle is actually directed to a community[28]—does not accept as credible any accusation made against an elder unless there be at least one corroborating witness.

Helpers

"Helpers" (*diakonoi*) are not mentioned in the Epistle to Titus, but the author of 1 Timothy arranges the third chapter of the epistle[29] so that a list of helpers' qualifications (1 Tim 3:8-9) is given immediately after his exposition of the qualities of overseers (1 Tim 3:1-8). As was the pattern of the Pastorals, only one specifically Christian quality appears in the list of the helper's virtues. Helpers were to be serious, not double-tongued, not addicted to wine, and not greedy for money. In addition, they were to hold fast to the mystery of the faith with a clear conscience. After a brief interlude (vv. 10-11), the Pastor continued his list of qualities with reference to the helper's responsibilities as a family man: "Let [helpers] be married only once, and let them manage their children and their households well" (1 Tim 3:12).

The qualities demanded of the helper are similar to the traits that should characterize the overseer. The separation of personal qualities from relational qualities recalls a similar separation in Titus 1:6-9. The verses that separate the two parts of the Pastor's list demand particular attention since the Pastor makes reference to a process of scrutiny for the "candidate to the diaconate": "let men first be tested; then, if they prove themselves blameless, let them serve as deacons" (1 Tim 3:10).[30]

Unfortunately the Pastorals made no further reference to this scrutiny. That the process was rather formal is indicated by the author's use of the verb "be tested" (*dokimazesthōsan*). The verb was a technical term used in the political sphere to designate a process of scrutiny for office, akin to the process of legislative hearings held before a person is appointed to public office in contemporary government. The passive voice of the verb leaves open the question as to who conducts the scrutiny. It may be that the entire church was involved in the process. One thing is certain: scrutiny must precede diaconal service.[31]

The Pastorals make no provision for the emolument of those engaged in the role of helper. Instead, 1 Timothy speaks of their standing in the community and in the eyes of God: "Those who serve well as deacons gain a good standing for themselves and great boldness in the faith that is in Christ Jesus" (1 Tim 3:13). Their standing[32] does not mean that their good service qualifies them for promotion to a higher responsibility in the church. The idea of promotion to higher office is foreign to the Pastorals. The "standing" of the helpers was a reference to the regard in which they were held by God and God's people.

Likewise, Women

Another interrupting verse in the Pastor's list of the helper's virtues mentions women: "Women likewise must be serious, not slanderers, but temperate, faithful in all things" (1 Tim 3:11). Who were these women? Why did the Pastor provide a separate list of their traits?

Some interpreters have suggested that the Pastor was referring to helpers' wives,[33] as did Polycarp in *Phil.* 4:2. This suggestion labors under a number of serious exegetical difficulties. First of all, in 1 Tim 3:11 the Pastor had not yet mentioned that helpers were expected to be married (v. 12). Second, were the Pastor to be making reference to helpers' wives, he should have used a personal pronoun—*their* women, meaning "their wives"—as did Polycarp in the aforereferenced passage. Finally, the Pastor introduced the verse with "likewise" (*hōsautēs*), just as he had previously introduced the list of the helpers' traits by writing "helpers likewise" (*diakonous hōsautēs*, v. 8). He has developed three lists of virtues, those for overseers, those for helpers, and those for "women."

These women are woman helpers, female *diakonoi*.[34] The Pastor gave a short list of qualifications for female helpers. These *diakonoi* were to be serious, not slanderous, and temperate. To these three virtues, the Pastor added a specifically Christian quality, just as one specifically Christian trait was added to the lists of qualifications for overseers and helpers. The woman helper is to be "faithful in all things," full of faith in every regard.

Why did the Pastor give a separate list of qualifications for a woman? A superficial answer might be that she was obviously not the "husband of one wife,"[35] and in the social circumstances of the Greco-Roman world, she would not have been primarily responsible for the rearing of her children unless her husband had died. In fact, Hellenistic moralists from the time of Aristotle were well aware that some characteristics were more appropriate to women and their social roles than they were to men and their roles in society and vice versa. Philosophers also observed that some virtues common to both men and women were expressed differently in the lives of virtuous men and women. With similar awareness of the differences between men and women, the Pastor appears to have thought it appropriate to give a list of desirable traits that ought to characterize women who served the church as helpers.

The Pastoral Epistles do not speak about helpers beyond the list that is given in 1 Tim 3:8-13. What they did to help the community is left unstated. One can only surmise that the communities for which the epistles were written knew what it was that helpers might do to help them build up their assembly as a true household of God.

Liturgy

Paul's First Letter to the Corinthians indicated that believers prayed and prophesied when they came together as church. When the whole church came together, they celebrated their *eranos*, with its commemoration of the institution of the eucharist. The members of the community gathered on the first day of the week. On that occasion the collection was made for God's holy people in Jerusalem.

When the assembly came together for prayer, some order was necessary lest there be complete cacophony. To avoid the confusion, Paul set down some simple rules, appealing to God who is not a God of disorder but a God of peace (1 Cor 14:33a):

> When you come together, each one has a hymn, a lesson, a revelation, a tongue, or an interpretation. Let all things be done for building up. If anyone speaks in a tongue, let there be only two or at most three, and each in turn; and let one interpret. But if there is no one to interpret, let them be silent in church and speak to themselves and to God. Let two or three prophets speak, and let the others weigh what is said. If a revelation is made to someone else sitting nearby, let the first person be silent. For you can all prophesy one by one, so that all may learn and all be encouraged. (1 Cor 14:26b-31)

The teaching activity of the early church was based on the scriptures.

Paul's plea for order in the liturgical assembly was continued by the Pastor, who set down regulations for the community at prayer (1 Tim 2:1-

7). The Pastor first directed that the community's prayer include a variety of prayer forms: supplications, prayers, intercessions, and thanksgivings (1 Tim 2:1). The community was to (1) call on the name of God, (2) thank God for favors received, and (3) ask God to satisfy the community's needs. The Pastor specifically directed that prayers and thanksgivings be offered on behalf of everyone, even kings and those who exercised civil authority (1 Tim 2:1-2). The inclusivity of the believers' prayer was to countermand any exclusivity or elitism in prayer. The Pastor gave a reason why members of the community should pray for rulers and civic authorities: they were to pray for those in authority so that the community might live a tranquil and peaceful life in society.[36]

Paul directed that men and woman have appropriate hairstyles when the community came together for prayer (1 Cor 11:4-15). Similarly, the Pastor gave directives on posture, dress, and demeanor (1 Tim 2:8-12). Men were expected first to wash or "purify" their hands. Men were to pray with their arms outstretched, the traditional gesture of petition and peace. Rancor and controversy should be banished from their hearts when they pray. As for women, they were to shun ostentation in attire, coiffure, and jewelry. Their religious attitude was to be manifest in their good works.[37]

Women, moreover, were not to teach; rather they were to learn in silence (1 Tim 2:12). To contemporary Western readers,[38] this last injunction represents a step backward from Paul's directives indicating that both men and women were to have their hair properly arranged when they prayed and prophesied in the assembly.[39] The directive must be understood within the context of one of the Pastorals' primary concerns, namely, that the church and its members should actively strive to conform to existing social customs so as to win acceptance in the society in which they lived.

First Timothy 4:13 suggests that the scriptures were read and that a "homily" was given when the church came together. In 1 Tim 4:13, "Timothy" was directed to pay heed to the public reading of scripture,[40] exhortation, and teaching. His hortatory and didactic activity was apparently based on the reading. "All scripture," that is, the Jewish scriptures, says 2 Tim 3:16-17, ". . . is useful for teaching, for reproof, for correction, and for training in righteousness, so that everyone who belongs to God may be proficient, equipped for every good work." The teaching activity of the early church, which Paul described as being a gift of the Spirit (1 Cor 12:28), was based on the scriptures. Teaching was essentially a reflection on the meaning of the Christ event in the light of the Jewish scriptures;[41] it was also a reflection on the life of the Christian believer in the light of those same scriptures.

Ritual

As a leader of the church, "Timothy" is told not to neglect the gift (*charismas*) that is in him, given "with the laying on of hands by the council of the elders" (*meta epitheseōs tōn cheirōn tou presbyteriou*, 1 Tim 4:14). Similar descriptive phraseology is found in 2 Tim 1:6: "I remind you to rekindle the gift of God that is within you through the laying on of my hands" (*dia epitheseōs tōn cheirōn mou*). The exclusive focus on Paul in the latter passage is most likely due to the testamentary nature of 2 Timothy; one of its principal themes is the idea that Timothy was the successor to Paul in the exercise of his ministry.

It is anachronistic to speak of this imposition of hands[42] as an ordination ritual, but the use of the gesture to symbolize transference of power and appointment to office is similar to a practice in late first-century and early second-century Judaism, the *semikhah*. The Jerusalem Talmud says that Rabbi Johannan ben Zakkai, a leading first-century c.e. rabbi who died shortly before the Pastoral Epistles were written, ordained his disciples, the rabbis Eliezer ben Hyrcanus and Joshua ben Hananiah, with a ritual imposition of hands.[43] This same passage notes that in earlier times each rabbi ordained his own pupils.

A third reference to an imposition of hands occurs in 1 Tim 5:22, where the Pastor directs that hands not be imposed hastily on anyone.[44] The text may, on the one hand, refer to an "ordination ritual," similar to that by which Timothy received his charismatic gift. First Timothy 5:22 would then enjoin the leader of the community not to coopt anyone into ministry with undue haste lest the leader participate in the sins of those who have not been sufficiently scrutinized. On the other hand, some patristic authors[45] argue that this verse, which comes immediately after a passage on sinners, relates to a ritual of reconciliation of sinners.

In one of its important "epiphany" passage,[46] the Epistle to Titus speaks about salvation with obvious reference to the baptismal ritual:

> But when the goodness and loving kindness of God our Savior
> appeared, he saved us, not because of any works of righteousness that

we had done, but according to his mercy, through the water of rebirth and renewal by the Holy Spirit. This Spirit he poured out on us richly through Jesus Christ our Savior, so that, having been justified by his grace, we might become heirs according to the hope of eternal life. (Titus 3:4-7)

Echoes of Paul's letters are heard when the author speaks of works, righteousness, grace, and heirs.[47] The pericope offers a variety of profound soteriological insights, including the idea that believers are saved through the waters of baptism. Baptismal imagery is reflected in the Pastor's writing about water and plentiful pouring. The abundance of water symbolizes the profusion of the Spirit's power effective in baptism. The Spirit effects a rebirth[48] and renewal so that believers become heirs. Paul would have written "joint heirs with Christ" (Rom 8:17).

Social Welfare

With an intrusive digression inserted into a household code (1 Tim 5:1–6:2), the Pastor wrote at length about widows in the church (1 Tim 5:3-16). He distinguished three groups of widows: (1) real widows; (2) widows with surviving children or grandchildren; and (3) young widows. He urged the young widows to seek fulfillment in a second marriage (vv. 11-14). He reminded children and grandchildren that they have a responsibility to care for widowed mothers and grandmothers (vv. 4, 8).[49] Most of his attention was, however, directed to elderly women who are "real widows."

These real widows were women who had no one to care for them. In the eyes of society they were all alone (v. 5). As the biblical widows before them, they were among "the poor," the *anawim*, who having led righteous lives could now rely only on God. These real widows were the object of the Pastor's concern.[50] He directed that their names be put on a list (v. 9) and that the members of the assembly take care of them, providing for their sustenance and other needs. It is the church's responsibility to care for these widows, but the Pastor notes that if any of these widows had living relatives who were believers, responsibility for caring for these widows falls primarily on the shoulders of these relatives (v. 16).[51]

Discussion and Study Questions

1. Are the forms of prayer that you experience in the public prayer of the church today as universal as was the prayer of the Pastor's community?

2. What qualities are most needed in the leaders of the church today?

3. What are the most important forms of social welfare to which your local church should be devoted?

4. What kind of organizational structure would best enable the church of today to fulfill its mission?

Chapter Seven

"Apostles to Be with Him and to Be Sent Out"

Within the decade after Paul's death, Mark[1] decided to put into narrative form some of the oral traditions about Jesus that had been circulating in Christian circles. The narrative took the form of a short story about Jesus. Subsequent generations know this story as the Gospel according to Mark. The story was written at about the time that Jerusalem was razed, its Temple destroyed. By that time those who knew Jesus personally were almost all dead. The church wanted to preserve their memory. The inspired Mark wanted to preserve the memory of how they preached and talked about Jesus after his death. The result was the first written short story about Jesus, the oldest of the Christian Gospels.

Entering the House

Many commentators have observed that whereas the Gospel according to Matthew focuses on the teaching of Jesus and the Gospel according to Luke highlights the great journey of Jesus to Jerusalem, the Gospel according to Mark keys in on the miracles of Jesus.[2] Narrative accounts of miracles constitute a substantial part of the Markan story.

The first miracle story narrated in Mark's Gospel is the shortest. It is the tale of the cure of Peter's mother-in-law. The story has a domestic setting; all in all, it is a domestic story: "they entered the house of Simon and Andrew. . . . Simon's mother-in-law was in bed . . . and she began to serve them" (Mark 1:29-31).[3]

Those who read the Markan story surely observe that much of his narrative takes place in and around a house. The account of the cure of Simon's mother-in-law is a family story.[4] It is the story of a pair of brothers (Mark 1:16) who followed an enigmatically phrased invitation from Jesus to follow him and fish for people. Peter seems to have been the older of the two brothers. Jesus went with the brothers to the house where they lived. Peter, Andrew, and Jesus were accompanied by another pair of fishermen brothers who had similarly responded to the call to discipleship. Entering the house, they learned that Peter's mother-in-law was ill with a fever. They informed Jesus about the situation. Immediately Jesus cured the mother-in-law. As proof of the miracle,[5] Mark said that the mother-in-law immediately rose; she then served a meal to her son-in-law and his guests. The discerning reader is aware that the first disciples of Jesus witnessed a demonstration of Jesus' power at home.

> *The Gentile woman would not take no for an answer, even arguing with Jesus when he was hesitant to do what she asked.*

Form critics have suggested that the *Sitz-im-Leben*, the social situation in which the stories of Jesus' miracles had been rehearsed, was a gathering of Christians who talked about the manifestations of Jesus' wonderful power.[6] These gatherings took place in the homes of Christian believers. Mark's narrative reflects this same setting in three other stories that tell about the manifestation of Jesus' power.

The story of Jesus' cure of the paralyzed man is well known for its setting in a house (Mark 2:1-12).[7] Few Christians forget the difficulty encountered by the four stretcher-bearers who wanted to bring the paralytic to Jesus. The dramatic effort made by the stretcher-bearers in order to make a hole in the roof so that the paralytic could be let down into the presence of Jesus is unforgettable. Few readers of this story are aware that Jesus was "at home"[8] and that crowds had gathered in front of the door of the house. The at-home scene is one in which Mark portrayed crowds gathered around the door of a disciple's house, eager to see what was happening inside.

The story of the paralytic is just one example of the many cures and exorcisms done by Jesus at home while crowds gathered in front of the door (Mark 1:32-34).

Another dramatic tale of an event that occurred at home is the Markan story of the raising of Jairus's daughter from the dead (Mark 5:22-23, 35-43).[9] Attention must be paid to its domestic setting. Mark told the story in such a way that the entire scene was controlled by Jesus. Although great crowds followed Jesus to see what would happen and although the mourners laughed at Jesus, only the girl's parents and a select triumvirate of Jesus' disciples entered the house. Only this chosen group—the parents, Peter, James, and John—was allowed to see Jesus' imparting life to the child. Only they saw Jesus' power at work.[10] Only they could speak about it, although Jesus told them not to do so—at least not then.[11]

A fourth Markan story with a domestic setting is the account of the exorcism of the daughter of the Syrophoenician woman (Mark 7:24-30).[12] The story is set in two different houses. Jesus is said to have entered a home in the region so that he could escape from the crowds, but he was unable to do so. An aggressive and importunate Gentile woman of mixed ancestry heard about Jesus and managed to enter the house. She begged him to cure her daughter of demonic possession. She would not take no for an answer, even arguing with Jesus when he was hesitant to do what she asked. She relented only when Jesus told her that the demon had left her daughter. When he told her to go, she went home. Arriving at her own home (*eis ton oikon autēs*), she found that the demon had left her daughter, who was now peacefully lying on her bed (*epi tēn klinēn*). This exorcism is an example of the demonstration of Jesus' power from afar. From a house located some distance away, Jesus was able to manifest his power "at home."

The House of Simon

Strategically placed in the Markan passion narrative,[13] just prior to the first steps in Judas's betrayal and the preparation for the Passover meal, is a story about Jesus set in the house of Simon the leper (Mark 14:3-9). Jesus was sitting at table when an unnamed woman anointed his head. The anointing provoked controversy on the part of some who were present. Jesus' pointed response focused on the care of the poor, the interpretation of a gesture related to his own death, and the proclamation of the gospel.

The next narrative account of a meal at home is the story of the Passover meal and the institution of the eucharist (Mark 14:17-25), when the distribution of bread and wine was accompanied by the interpretive words referring to Jesus' death. Years later, Christians recalled that liturgical gesture when they came together in one another's homes to celebrate their love feasts.[14]

The story of the call of Levi shows that discipleship leads to the celebration of meals at home (*en tē oikia*) with tax collectors and sinners, no matter how scandalous that might be (Mark 2:13-17). After Jesus' appointment of the Twelve, he went home (*eis oikon*), apparently intending to eat a meal with the appointees, but the crowd prevented them from doing so (Mark 3:20).

The Markan story spoke about the proclamation of the gospel. "Truly I tell you," Jesus said, "wherever the good news is proclaimed (*kērychthē to euangelion*) in the whole world, what she [the woman who anointed Jesus] has done will be told in remembrance of her" (Mark 14:9). Jesus' words employed the technical vocabulary used to designate early Christian preaching, "kerygma" and "gospel."

The good news was proclaimed when people told one another about what Jesus had done, when they spoke about the wonderful power of God that was at work in him. The Gerasene demoniac, from whom Jesus expelled a legion of unclean spirits, wanted to remain with Jesus. Instead, Jesus told him: "'Go home (*eis ton oikon*) to your friends, and tell them (*apangelion*) how much the Lord has done for you, and what mercy he has shown you.' And he went away and began to proclaim (*kēryssein*) in the Decapolis how much Jesus had done for him" (Mark 5:19-20a). The paralytic who came to Jesus through the roof and the blind man whom Jesus cured at Bethsaida were also "sent home" (*eis oikon autou*) by Jesus (Mark 2:11; 8:26). Presumably these two likewise spoke about the mercy that the Lord had shown them.

Mark's narrative reminds contemporary readers that stories about the wonderful power of God at work in Jesus and the meaning of Jesus' activities were told at home. Mark similarly tells his readers that discussions about the meaning of Jesus' teaching also took place at home. It was in the house (*eis oikon*, Mark 7:17), away from the crowd, that the disciples asked Jesus about the meaning of Jesus' enigmatic teaching on defilement, the "parable" of Mark 7:14-15. There in the house Jesus explained to his disciples what true evil was.

It was in the house (*eis oikon*, Mark 9:28) that these same disciples asked Jesus about exorcisms. Jesus explained that some demons cannot be expelled except by the power of prayer (Mark 9:29). It was in the house (*eis tēn oikian*, Mark 10:10) that the disciples queried Jesus about the meaning of the prophetic proclamation that human beings are not to rend asunder what God had joined together. Responding to their request, Jesus taught them about divorce and remarriage (Mark 10:11-12).

An ironic twist in the Markan motif of the disciples' asking Jesus questions is the one that Jesus posed to his disciples when he was in the house (*en tē oikia*, Mark 9:33). The question was simple enough. Jesus simply wanted to know what they were arguing about while they were en route. It turned out that they had been arguing about who was the greatest among them. On discovering that this was the source of their disagreement, Jesus gave the Twelve a lecture on leadership and authority (Mark 9:35-37). To emphasize the importance of the lecture, Mark portrayed Jesus as having sat down. Then he called the Twelve over and gave his lecture. Sitting was the traditional posture of rabbis while they were engaged in teaching.[15]

House Church

Other echoes of the house church are found here and there throughout the oldest Gospel's narratives. The early church's use of kinship language to designate believers is reflected in the story about Jesus' true kindred (Mark 3:31-35)[16] and the teaching that those who abandon their natural families for the sake of the gospel[17] will receive a new family a hundred times over (Mark 10:29-31). This teaching also speaks of leaving one's home and acquiring new homes. Believers enjoy a kinship, a relationship between siblings, that is not based on blood and genes.

The twice-told Markan story of the feeding of the multitude (Mark 6:32-44; 8:1-10) has much to say about the early church. It is the only miracle story that appears in all four canonical Gospels (see also Matt 14:13-21; 15:32-39; Luke 9:10b-17; John 6:1-5). This is probably the result of the story being frequently told when believers gathered to celebrate the Lord's Supper, an echo of which appears in the eucharistic "ritual" of Mark 6:41: "take . . . look up . . . blessed . . . broke . . . gave . . . and they ate" (see Matt 14:19-20; Luke 9:16).[18] Noteworthy is the fact that the twice-told narrative in Mark and Matthew reflects the telling of the story and celebration of the eucharist in both Jewish and Gentile contexts. The coloring and setting of the narrative in Mark 6 is decidedly Jewish, that of Mark 8 clearly Hellenistic.[19] The latter narrative notes that the people were not in their own homes when they ate the meal that Jesus offered (v. 3).

Mark's version of Jesus' missionary charge to the Twelve (Mark 6:6b-13), considerably expanded in Matthew 10, shows the importance of the house and of hospitality. Sent out without any provisions, the evangelists had need of hospitality if they were to complete their mission. Jesus' brief discourse, however, warns the missionaries not to gad about from house to house,[20] perhaps to seek better lodgings or a finer meal.

Finally, two significant parables in Mark's Gospel employ the image of a house in speaking about the followers of Jesus. One of these parables is the parable of the house divided against itself (Mark 3:23-27). The other is a well-known parable calling Jesus' disciples to an attitude of eschatological watchfulness (Mark 13:32-37). The little tale tells the story of the master of a house who goes on a journey and returns at an unexpected hour. The lesson to be learned is that the master's servants should not be asleep when the master arrives. Christians who heard this story could not fail to recognize the Lord as the master evoked by the parable, themselves as the servants, and the church as the house of which the Lord is master (*kyrios tēs oikias*, v. 35).

Disciples and the Twelve

The way in which an author constructs his or her characters is an essential element of any story. This is as true of Mark's short story about Jesus as it is for any contemporary novel worth reading. Commentators frequently observe that the Gospel according to Mark is really a story about Jesus and the disciples. The disciples stand out from the crowd as followers of Jesus. The crowds are interested observers in Mark's story; the disciples follow after Jesus.[21]

Two short episodes at the beginning of the Markan tale narrate the call of two pairs of brothers, Simon and Andrew, and James and John (Mark 1:16-18, 19-20). All four were fishermen. Mark 2:14 gives the story of the call of a tax collector named Levi. These three "call stories" follow the same narrative scheme: (1) Jesus sees someone, whose name is cited by the evangelist; (2) he calls that person; (3) the individual abandons what he was doing;[22] and (4) follows Jesus.[23] The scheme evokes the authority of Jesus as well as the immediate and complete response. Mark's "immediately" (*euthus*, Mark 1:18, 20) is a narrative trait adding a little eschatological urgency to a story that comes just after Mark's summary notation of Jesus' proclamation of the (eschatological) Kingdom of God. With regard to the call to discipleship, those who read Mark's Gospel from an ecclesiological perspective should also note that each of the four fisherman, as well as the tax collector, enjoyed a meal with Jesus and the other disciples after his call (Mark 1:31; 2:15-17).

An enigmatic promise, "I will make you fish for people" (*poiēsō hymas genesthai alieis anthrōpōn*,[24] Mark 1:17), follows the command[25] that Jesus directed to Peter and Andrew. Apart from the following call of James and John, the Markan story makes no further reference to fishing. The reader is left to wonder about the meaning of the parabolic promise.

In Mark's story of Jesus, it is clear that Simon quickly became the leader of the disciples.[26] Jesus visited the house of Simon and Andrew; he cured Simon's mother-in-law (Mark 1:29-31). The following morning "Simon and his companions" (*Simon kai met'autou*, Mark 1:36) went to look for Jesus, who had gone out to pray. The emergence of Peter as a leader among Jesus' disciples continues until the end of Mark's narrative. After Jesus had died and been raised, a young man dressed in white told the women who came to the tomb to anoint Jesus' body: "Go, tell his disciples *and Peter* that he is going ahead of you to Galilee; there you will see him, just as he told you" (Mark 16:7).

Simon is not alone in being distinguished among Jesus' followers in the Markan story. Mark 3:13-19 describes a scene whose significance is symbolized by its location on a mountain, where Jesus selects a small group of disciples and summons them into his presence: "He called to him those whom he wanted and they came to him" (Mark 3:13). There on the mountain, Jesus constituted his group of twelve.[27] He made[28] them "the Twelve."

As the narrative tradition about Jesus developed, it was clear that twelve was a symbolic number. "The Twelve" has an identity somewhat independent of the individual identities of those who make up the Twelve. Thus, Paul wrote about an appearance of the Risen Jesus to the Twelve (1 Cor 15:5), but it is rather unlikely that Judas the betrayer was with them when the appearance took place (Mark 14:10, 43; Matt 26:14, 47; Luke 22:47; John 6:71). Luke's Acts tells the story of Peter taking a leadership role in filling up the complement of the Twelve after Judas's death (Acts 1:15-26). Matthias was chosen. According to Luke, Matthias received the "position of overseer" (*episkopēn*).[29]

The number twelve symbolizes the twelve tribes of Israel, whom the Twelve are to judge. The symbolism has an eschatological nuance that must not be overlooked.[30] The group of the Twelve is to be associated with Jesus' proclamation of the Kingdom of God. When the enigmatic Son of Man appears on his throne for the renewal of all things, the Twelve are to sit "on twelve thrones, judging the twelve tribes of Israel" (Matt 19:28; Luke 22:30).[31] The language of this saying bespeaks a leadership role rather than a merely judgmental one.

The symbolism and eschatological nuance of "the Twelve" comes to the fore in the Book of Revelation's vision of the New Jerusalem: "It has a great high wall with twelve gates . . . and on the gate are inscribed the names of the twelve tribes of Israel. . . . And the wall of the city has twelve foundations, and on them are the twelve names of the twelve apostles of the Lamb" (Rev 21:12-14). Within the eschatological people of God the Twelve have a foundational and leadership role.

Mark says that Jesus named the Twelve "apostles" (*hous kai apostolous ōnomasen*, Mark 3:14),[32] giving them a three-fold charge. They were (1) to be with him;[33] (2) to be sent out to proclaim the message; and (3) to have authority to cast out demons. Another pericope, Mark 6:7-13, explains the name "apostle" and sums up the role of the apostles: "He called the Twelve and began to send them out two by two. . . . So they went out and proclaimed that all should repent. They cast out many demons. . . ."[34] Their role as Jesus' companions is the stuff of which Mark's narrative is made (Mark 4:10; 11:11; 14:17).

Simon, to Whom He Gave the Name Peter

Giving the list of the names of the Twelve, Mark highlighted three names by appending the nicknames that Jesus gave to each of them. Mark also drew attention to the treachery of one of the Twelve: "He appointed the Twelve:[35] Simon (to whom he gave the name Peter); James, son of

Zebedee, and John, the brother of James (to whom he gave the name Boanerges, that is, Sons of Thunder); and Andrew, and Philip, and Bartholomew, and Matthew, and Thomas, and James son of Alphaeus, and Thaddaeus, and Simon the Cananaean, and Judas Iscariot, who betrayed him" (Mark 3:16-19). This list does not include the name of Levi, who had been called to discipleship but did not receive the apostle's mission.

Similar lists of the names of the Twelve appear in Matt 10:2-4; Luke 6:14-16; and Acts 1:13. The Gospels of Matthew and Luke begin the list of twelve names with the names of the two pairs of brothers. In Acts, Luke begins the list with the group of three highlighted by Mark. Luke omits the name of Thaddaeus from both of his lists. Instead of the name of Thaddaeus, Luke cites the name of Simon who was called the Zealot. The freedom shown by the evangelists in giving names and the order in which they list the names demonstrate the importance of "the Twelve." The symbolic importance of "the Twelve" is more important than their individual names and the order in which they appear.[36]

On all four New Testament lists of the names of the Twelve, the name of Simon[37] appears first. Both Mark and Luke emphasized the name Peter: "to whom he gave the name Peter" (Mark 3:16); "whom he named Peter" (Luke 6:14). Matthew has a less striking "also known as Peter" (*ho legomenos Petros;* Matt 10:2) literally, "the one called Peter."[38] Having noted that Jesus gave Simon a nickname (Mark 3:16), Mark called Simon by the nickname throughout the Gospel account. He did not use the name Simon again in his story except for the wake-up call in Mark 14:37, a call in which Jesus addressed Peter as "Simon," but Mark noted that Jesus' words were addressed to Peter.

The way that the four passages consistently give the name of Simon before the names of the eleven others indicates that Simon had a special role among Jesus' disciples. As the Markan narrative unfolds, Peter's role is that of the spokesperson who speaks on behalf of the disciples. Thus, Peter appears at Caesarea Philippi, confessing Jesus to be the Messiah (Mark 8:29). He is the one among the disciples who spoke of their having left everything in order to follow Jesus (Mark 10:28). Although the disciples were with Jesus as they passed by the accursed fig tree, it is Peter who points out that it had withered (Mark 11:21). The disciples chimed in with Peter when he later said that he would not deny Jesus (Mark 14:31). Peter's outspokenness occasionally leads to his being reprimanded by Jesus (Mark

8:32-33; 14:28-31[39]). Despite his unthinking bravado,[40] Peter remained the disciples' spokesperson.

Among the disciples, those to whom Jesus gave a nickname—Simon, James, and John—appear to be an elite group of three. Apart from the parents, these three were the only people to witness Jesus' raising the daughter of Jairus from the dead (Mark 5:35-43). Only they witnessed the transfigured Jesus (Mark 9:2-8). They had a private conversation with Jesus about the coming eschaton (Mark 13:3-8 [31]).[41] They were with Jesus when he distanced himself from the other disciples in Gethsemane (Mark 14:32-42).

Among the three, Peter stood out. He served as their spokesperson, as he did when making the importune offer of three tents on the mountain where the Transfiguration occurred (Mark 9:5-6). When the trio fell asleep in Gethsemane, it was Peter to whom Jesus spoke about not being able to stay awake for even an hour (Mark 14:37).

The End of the Story

Given the role of Peter as the disciples' spokesperson and the role that he had among the elite three, it is hardly surprising that the women who discovered the empty tomb were told by the young man dressed in white that they were to go to the disciples and to Peter and tell them that the Lord would see them in Galilee (Mark 16:7).

This is the final mention of Peter in the oldest narrative about Jesus. He is a person who receives a message from a trio of women, Mary Magdalene, Mary the mother of James, and Salome, who had gone to Jesus' tomb bringing spices and intending to anoint his body. Instead, they discovered the empty tomb and were the first recipients of the Paschal proclamation. They were the first to hear the good news, "He has been raised; he is not here" (Mark 16:6). After the resurrection these three women were the first to receive a heavenly commission, as modest as it might have been. They were told to tell the disciples and Peter to get on the move and go where they will be able to see Jesus.

The women's fear, with which the Markan story ends, proved unsettling for later generations of Christians.[42] Unknown scribes added a postscript to the story (Mark 16:9-20). This epilogue echoes scenes from the other canonical Gospels and contains a number of features that attest to the ecclesiology that developed during the first few centuries of the church's existence.

The postscript portrays Mary Magdalene as the woman who announced to Jesus' companions, presumably the Twelve,[43] that Jesus was alive.[44] This epilogue attests to an appearance to "the eleven themselves" (*autois tois endeka*) while they were at table (v. 14). It speaks of the commission to the eleven "go into all the world and proclaim the good news to the whole of creation" (Mark 16:14), a commission that they carried out (v. 20). This mission and the worldwide proclamation of the gospel contrast with the limited mission of the twelve described in Mark 6:7-13. Those who believe the gospel message and are baptized will be saved (v. 16); they will experience some of the same powers that the Twelve themselves had experienced (vv. 17-18; see Mark 6:13).

> *Despite his unthinking bravado, Peter remained the disciples' spokesperson.*

Epilogue

The Gospel according to Mark is lacking in explicit ecclesiological insights. The attention that Mark draws to the importance of the house in the mission of Jesus is particularly significant nonetheless. The transformation of kinship language from its use describing those bound by blood to those bound by discipleship is likewise significant. Mark's narrative also shows the importance of "the Twelve," hearkening back to the church's link with Judaism and anticipating the fulfillment of the eschatological promise. Along the way, Mark shows that Jesus' disciples were not an undifferentiated group. Leadership roles began to emerge as soon as there were disciples. Among them, twelve were named apostles and Peter was the spokesperson. The mandate given to the Twelve is a paradigm for the church's mission of proclaiming the gospel, in word and in deed.

Discussion and Study Questions

1. What is the significance of the fact that Jesus chose *twelve* of his disciples to be apostles?

2. What was the role of Simon Peter among the Twelve?

3. Does the church really happen "at home"?

4. What is different between the ending of Mark's Gospel and the ending of Matthew's Gospel?

Chapter Eight

"On This Rock I Will Build My Church"

For centuries, going back to the time of Augustine and beyond, the Gospel according to Matthew was thought to be the oldest canonical Gospel. Since the beginning of the third century, this single story about Jesus served the church as its primary source for Sunday readings.[1] Matthew's is the only canonical Gospel to use the word "church" (*ekklēsia*; Matt 16:18; 18:17 [2x]). Words taken from Matt 16:18 are emblazoned in large letters on the interior of the dome of St. Peter's Basilica in Rome. Thus, the Gospel according to Matthew was widely regarded as the church's Gospel throughout the course of many centuries.

Since the emergence of the historical-critical approach to the church's scriptures, however, scholars have come to the conclusion that Matthew's story about Jesus is, in fact, a new revised edition of the story that Mark had written. The revision was made by a Jewish-Christian author who experienced the need for Jewish Christians to have a story about Jesus that was tailor-made for their idiom and tradition.

It was very important for Matthew's community to have such a story about Jesus. The Gospel was written in the eighties, barely ten years after the destruction of Jerusalem and the razing of its Temple. Bereft of control over their land and of the use of their beloved Temple, Jews of various stripes sought to understand the meaning of the scriptures for their times. Inspired by the great rabbis of the early first century C.E., Hillel and Shammai, leaders of the two dominant groups of Pharisaic Jews known to history as the schools of Hillel and Shammai, intensified their efforts to define the Jewish ethos with their interpretation of the scriptures.

One small group of Jews, acknowledging the crucified Jesus as the Messiah, sought to interpret his story and their own existence in the light of the Jewish scriptures. The Gospel according to Matthew is the literary legacy of this effort, a story about Jesus written for Jewish Christians in the light of the Jewish scriptures on the basis of the story about Jesus written by Mark.[2]

The First Disciples

To a large extent the Matthean Gospel recasts the Markan story so that it has become a story about the formation of "the church."[3] At times Matthew's redactional interest is subtly expressed; at other times it is quite explicit. To discern Matthew's editorial hand at work, a reader can begin with the account of the call of the first disciples (Matt 4:18-22). When this episode is compared with its parallel in Mark (Mark 1:16-20), the evangelist's editorial hand can be seen at work. Matthew highlights the idea that Jesus called two pairs of brothers, noting from the very outset that Simon is the one called Peter (*ton legomenon Petron*), even though the conferral of this nickname does not occur until Matt 16:18.[4] Jesus' enigmatic promise about fishing for humans is addressed to the first pair of brothers, Simon and Andrew, as it is in Mark.

After summarizing Jesus' Galilean ministry, preaching, teaching, and healing (Matt 4:23),[5] Matthew offers his memorable portrait of Jesus the Teacher, the Sermon on the Mount (Matt 5:1-8:1).[6] Matthew's setting of the scene is the first part of a ring construction (see Matt 7:28–8:1). On a mountain reminiscent of Sinai, Jesus assumes the authoritative position of a teaching rabbi; he sits. In the fashion of students approaching their masters, Jesus' disciples (*hoi mathētai autou*) come to him. The evangelist highlights what it is that Jesus says with the repetitive "he began to speak, and taught (*edidasken*) them, saying."[7] In a series of catechetical-like instructions, Jesus teaches his disciples as he gives the beatitudes, offers a midrash on selected passages of the scriptures, and comments on the traditional practices of piety, almsgiving, prayer, and fasting. The instruction continues with a variety of teachings that Matthew has culled from the Q-source.

The peroration of the Sermon on the Mount brings the discourse to a close by speaking about hearers and doers, contrasting the image of a house built on a rock, which stands solid in the middle of a terrible storm, with the image of a house built on sand, which fell mightily to the ground when the storm arrived (Matt 7:24-27). The contrasting metaphors have been taken from Matthew's Q-source.[8] His editorial hand is evident in the apocalyptic quality that he imparts to the storm (Matt 7:25, 27) and in the attention that he draws to the foundation of each of the houses: "Everyone then who hears these words of mine and acts on them will be like a wise man who built his house on rock" (Matt 7:24). The house built on rock (ōkodomēsen autou tēn oikian epi tēn petran) holds firm despite the ravages of the storm; the house built on rock weathers the storm. The evangelist's use of the double metaphor is a good example of literary foreshadowing with paraenetic intent. A discerning reader of the Matthean story cannot help but think ahead to Matthew's story of the keys and of the church "built on a rock" (epi tautē tē petra oikodomēsē, Matt 16:18).

Following the mountaintop formation session, the reader of Matthew's Gospel comes to two chapters dealing with Jesus' miracles (Matthew 8–9). Mark, Matthew's principal source at this point, narrated an exorcism in the synagogue of Capernaum, followed by Jesus' visit to the house of Simon and Andrew, where he cured Simon's mother-in-law. Matthew, however, begins his account of Jesus' working miracles with the story of a cleansing of a leper (Matt 8:1-4), which is followed by a story of

On a mountain reminiscent of Sinai, Jesus assumes the authoritative position of a teaching rabbi; he sits.

healing from afar. Only then does the evangelist speak about Jesus' visit to the house where the sick mother-in-law was lying ill with a fever (Matt 8:14-17).

Matthew's account of this visit is shorter than its parallel in Mark. Matthew's focus is on Jesus, Peter, and the sick woman. Peter is identified by his nickname, Peter, rather than by his given name, Simon. Matthew then continues to call him Peter until the end of his Gospel narrative.[9] The only exceptions are Matt 10:2 and 16:16, where the double name "Simon

Peter" occurs, and Matt 16:17 and 17:25, where Jesus calls him by his given name, Simon. In Matthew's story of the cure of Peter's mother-in-law, Matthew's focus on Peter is sharpened by the omission of any reference to other disciples. Even Andrew has been dispossessed of his home, as it were. The house is no longer the house of Simon and Andrew (Mark 1:29); rather, the house is now "Peter's house" (*tēn oikian Petrou*, Matt 8:14). There in Peter's house Jesus manifested his power, curing one of his kin.

The Twelve Disciples

Matthew used the literary device of a ring construction to create the Sermon on the Mount as the instruction of Jesus' disciples (Matt 5:1–8:1) He made use of the same literary device to create the second major discourse in his story, the so-called missionary discourse (Matt 10:1–11:1). "Jesus" and "his twelve disciples" (*tous dōdeka mathētas autou*) provide the encompassing vocabulary.

Jesus' "twelve disciples"[10] are a group. The Twelve are no longer a select group from among a larger group of disciples (Mark 3:13-15); they are his twelve disciples. They are *the* disciples and there are only twelve of them![11] In Mark, the appointed Twelve were given a three-point charge: (1) to be with Jesus; (2) to be sent out and proclaim the message; and (3) to cast out demons (Mark 3:14-15). Having omitted the first part of the charge, Matthew has separated the second and third parts from each other; he reversed their sequence and inserted the names of the Twelve between the two elements of the charge. The compositional effort serves Matthew's theological interests. Designated "apostles," the twelve are not so much called to be with Jesus as they are "to be sent out."[12] This part of the mission statement serves almost as an explanation of the name "apostles," which the Twelve now have.

Before describing their mission, the evangelist spoke of the authority, the power (*exousian*) that Jesus gave them.[13] As in Mark, that power is the power to cast out demons, but Matthew added an explanation: "to[14] cast them out and to cure every disease and every sickness" (Matt 10:1). The Matthean Jesus gave the twelve disciples the power that he himself had exercised in casting out demons and in curing, as just illustrated in Matthew 8–9. The language that the evangelist used to explain the authority given to the twelve disciples echoes the language of his summary account of the ministry of Jesus (Matt 9:35).

In similar fashion, Matthew has explained the charge to preach. Mark's version read simply, "to be sent out to proclaim the message" (*hina apostelle autous kēryssein*, Mark 3:14). According to Matthew, Jesus sent (*apesteilen*) the Twelve out with these instructions:

> Go nowhere among the Gentiles, and enter no town of the Samaritans, but go rather to the lost sheep of the house of Israel. As you go, proclaim the good news (*kēryssete*), "The kingdom of heaven has come near." Cure the sick, raise the dead, cleanse the lepers, cast out demons. . . . (Matt 10:5-8)

The restriction of the mission of the twelve apostles to the house of Israel is striking. The twelve apostles are not to go among Gentiles nor are they to go among the Samaritans; rather they are to go only to the lost sheep of the house of Israel. No such restriction is found in Mark's version of the charge. Matthew's restrictive phrase implies that the Twelve are to continue Jesus' historical mission. Of that mission the Matthean Jesus himself declared: "I was sent only to the lost sheep of the house of Israel" (*ouk apestalēn ei mē eis ta probata ta apolōlota oikou Israēl*, Matt 15:24).[15] In like fashion, the twelve apostles are to go "to the lost sheep of the house of Israel" (*pros ta probata ta apolōlota oikou Israēl*). Jesus' prophetic vision of the crowds "like sheep without a shepherd" (*hōsei probata mē echonta poimena*,[16] Matt 9:36) provided the occasion and the need for Jesus to give the Twelve their mission. They were sent out to be the shepherds of Israel.

And what are these twelve to say when they go to the lost sheep of the house of Israel as they have been told to do? They are to preach, saying: "The kingdom of heaven has come near" (*hoti ēngiken hē basileia tōn ouranōn*, Matt 10:7). This is the message of Jesus himself (Matt 4:17). This is the message of John the Baptist as well (Matt 3:2). The detail is important in Matthew's scheme of things; it demonstrates the continuity between the preaching of John the Baptist, Jesus, and the twelve apostles. It is a single, continuous mission carried out by three "generations" of preachers. Matthew thus affirms the continuity of what Christians might call the preaching of the Old Testament prophets, the preaching of Jesus, and the preaching of the church.

For Matthew, the fact that there are twelve disciples/apostles and no more than twelve is extremely important. These twelve play the role of the patriarchs of old in the renewal of Israel: "Truly I tell you, at the renewal of all things, when the Son of Man is seated on the throne of his glory, you who have followed me will also sit on twelve thrones, judging the twelve tribes of Israel" (Matt 19:28; Luke 22:30).[17] Given the importance that he attaches to the symbolic mission of the twelve disciples/apostles, Matthew's list of their names is singularly important:

> These are the names of the twelve apostles: first, Simon, also known as Peter, and his brother Andrew; James son of Zebedee, and his brother John; Philip and Bartholomew; Thomas and Matthew the tax collector; James son of Alphaeus, and Thaddaeus; Simon the Cananaean, and Judas Iscariot, the one who betrayed him. (Matt 10:2-4)

Significant elements of Matthew's ecclesiology emerge when his list of the twelve apostles is compared with the lists of the twelve names in Mark 3:16-19 and Luke 6:14-16.[18] In Matthew the members of the group are called the twelve apostles (*tōn dōdeka apostolōn*). Simon is enumerated as "first" (*prōtos*), the only one of the Twelve to whom a numeral is assigned. Among the Twelve the nickname of Simon alone is given. He is the one "also known as Peter" (*ho legomenos Petros*, Matt 10:2; see Matt 4:18). Rather than stating explicitly that the Twelve were sent out "two by two" (Mark 6:7; cf. Luke 10:1), Matthew presents a list of names consisting of six pairs.[19]

The evangelist has slightly changed the order of the names found in his Markan source. Rather than relegate Andrew to fourth place on the list, Matthew pairs him with his brother at the head of the list. On the revised list, the evangelist places the name of Thomas ahead of the name of Matthew. Then comes a significant addition. The evangelist identifies Matthew as "the tax collector" (Matt 10:3). He is the only one of the twelve on the list whose profession is identified.[20]

The detail is important, reflecting the singular prominence of the Twelve from the evangelist's unique perspective. Mark 2:14-17 narrates the call[21] of a man named Levi, the son of Alphaeus, who was sitting at a tax collector's table when he was summoned by Jesus. Without identifying him as the son of Alphaeus, Luke similarly describes the call of a tax collector named Levi (Luke 5:27-32). The same story appears in Matt 9:9-13 except for the fact that the tax collector is now called Matthew, not Levi. Rudolf Pesch offers a plausible explanation of the name switch.[22] The call story in Mark (Mark 2:13-14) shows that the tax collector was called to be a disciple of Jesus; like the fishermen, he abandoned his livelihood to go and follow Jesus. In his narrative Matthew equated the Twelve, the disciples, and the apostles. According to Pesch's theory, twelve was the full complement; there could be no more than twelve apostles or twelve disciples. The name of the tax collector did not appear on Mark's list of the Twelve, but he was a disciple. For Matthew, that meant that his name should have appeared on the list of the Twelve. A name switch solved his problem. He made the tax collector fit into the list of the Twelve by changing his name from Levi to Matthew in Matt 9:9-13 and identifying him as Matthew, the tax collector, in the list of the names of the Twelve.[23] The job specification calls the reader to think back to the earlier narrative, where the name of Matthew first occurs.

Mark's list of the names of the Twelve included the names of James and John, to whom Jesus gave the nickname Boanerges, which means "sons of thunder" (Mark 3:17). An episode late in Mark's narrative describes their importunate request: "Grant us to sit, one at your right hand and one at your left, in your glory" (Mark 10:37). The unseemly request led to Jesus giving a lecture on the nature of authority from the perspective of the Kingdom of God (Mark 10:35-45). The lecture ended with Jesus' prophetic utterance, "The Son of Man came not to be served but to serve, and to give his life as a ransom for many" (Mark 10:45). The episode, which makes note of the tension between the two brothers and the other ten apostles (Mark 10:41), was appropriated by Matthew. This evangelist, however, placed the inappropriate request on the lips of the mother of the sons who are identified but remain nameless throughout the narrative (Matt 20:20-28).[24] The way in which Matthew describes the dramatic scene represents yet another of his redactional improvements of the image of the disciples; the mother was out of order; James and John were not.

Another improvement of the image of the Twelve in Matthew is the evangelist's characterization of the disciples as "men of little faith" (*oligopistoi*).[25] The descriptive epithet is always found on the lips of Jesus. The evangelist first uses the term in the Sermon on the Mount when Jesus addresses his immediate audience, the disciples, as "you of little faith"

(Matt 6:30). The vocabulary comes from the sayings source Q,[26] used by Matthew in the composition of his narrative.

The idiom apparently suited Matthew's image of the disciples. After the stilling of the storm, Jesus upbraided the disciples as "you of little faith" (Matt 8:26). This would have been a harsh remark were it not for the fact that the original Markan version of the story described them as men of no faith (Mark 4:40). Matthew's Jesus again called the disciples men of little faith[27] when they showed that they did not really comprehend what it was that Jesus did when he fed the crowds (Matt 16:8). Later, when the disciples asked Jesus why they were unable to expel the demon from the boy who was possessed, Jesus replied: "Because of your little faith" (Matt 17:20). Daniel J. Harrington says that this story "really concerns the disciple's little faith (*oligopistia*)."[28] According to Matthew, the disciples are men of little faith, *oligopistoi*. The epithet is two-sided: the disciples have room, much room, to grow in their faith, but they do have faith and that is a big improvement over having no faith at all, the way that Mark describes them in Mark 4:35-41 and 9:14-29.

Simon Peter

Matthew singles out one disciple/apostle among the Twelve as a man of little faith, *oligopistos*. That individual is Peter (see Matt 14:28-33). Peter was terrified when a powerful wind arose as he was walking on the water. Unnerved by fear, he began to sink under the waters. Jesus responded to Peter's frightened plea for help with a helping hand but chided: "You of little faith, why did you doubt?" (Matt 14:31). Matthew appended his account of this episode to an earlier narrative of Jesus' walking on water (Matt 14:22-27; Mark 6:45-52).[29] Prior to introducing the episode, Matthew had spoken about Peter only when he followed the Markan outline, that is, in the call of the first disciples (4:18-20), the cure of the mother-in-law (8:14-17), and the listing of the Twelve (10:1-4). In each instance the evangelist clearly but subtly enhanced the image of Peter. With the episode of Peter walking on the water, the evangelist's narrative focus on Peter achieves greater intensity. Now Peter appears in the Matthean narrative when he had not been mentioned in the evangelist's narrative source, the Gospel according to Mark.

Jesus' walking on water is a theophany. The scenario is reminiscent of biblical and Jewish motifs. The first chapter of the Book of Jonah and Ps

107:23-32 contain similarly graphic descriptions of storms at sea. Jonah 2 and Ps 69:1, 15 describe the shouts for help that come from the mouths of those who are drowning. The Qumran *Hodayot* (Thanksgiving Hymns) and the *Testament of Naphtali* employ the metaphor of rescue from drowning to speak of people being saved from the ravages of persecution (1QH 3:6, 12-18; 6:22-25; 7:4-5; *T. Naph.* 6:1-10).

This Petrine insert[30] illustrates the way that the evangelist Matthew builds upon Peter's role as spokesperson for the disciples,[31] Peter's role in Mark. In the episode Peter responds to Jesus' self-revelation and his urging the disciples to "fear not."[32] With some hesitation Peter recognizes Jesus as Lord. Peter wants to be with Jesus; he wants to do as Jesus had done.[33] Invited to do so, Peter was able to walk on the water at Jesus' command. When Peter began to fear, he started to sink. He was a man of little faith, who had to cry out to be rescued.[34] Thus, the evangelist portrays Peter as an example, showing that the disciples are men of little faith.[35]

Thereafter, the role of Peter as representative of the Twelve and spokesperson is developed more vividly in Matthew's story than it had been in Mark's.[36] This is particularly apparent in Matt 15:15 (a request for an explanation of a parable); 18:21 (a question about forgiving); and 19:27 (a question about discipleship).

With the request "explain this parable to us," Matthew's Peter on behalf of the twelve disciples asks Jesus to explain his puzzling statement about things that defile a person (Matt 15:15). According to Matthew's Markan source, "when he [Jesus] had left the crowd and entered the house, his disciples asked him about the parable." In Matt 18:21, the evangelist introduces a Q logion on forgiveness with a remark from Peter: "Then Peter came and said to him, 'Lord, if another member of the church[37] sins against me, how often should I forgive? As many as seven times?'" In Luke the logion appears in a catena of sayings that treat of scandal, repentance, and forgiveness (Luke 17:1-4).

In addition to the story of Peter walking on the water and then sinking, the narrative of the temple tax (Matt 17:24-27) is another episode featuring Jesus and Peter that appears in Matthew but not in Mark or Luke. Linguistic and stylistic analysis of the text reveals the patently Matthean character of the narrative. Strategically placed after the second announcement of the passion (Matt 17:22-23)[38] and located before the discourse to church leaders (Matt 18:1–19:1), the episode shows the collectors of the tax implicitly acknowledging Peter's leadership role among the disciples.[39]

These leaders asked Peter: "Does your teacher[40] not pay the temple tax?" (Matt 17:24).

The origins of this tradition are somewhat obscure.[41] The episode centers on the payment of the temple tax[42] required by Jewish law (Exod 30:11-16; Neh 10:32). At the time of the composition of the Gospel, more than a decade after the destruction of the Temple, Roman authorities collected the double drachma as a *fiscus judaicus* for the maintenance of the Roman shrine of Jupiter Capitolinus. The question posed by the tax collectors is similar to the one that Pharisees and Herodians asked of Jesus (Matt 22:17; Mark 12:14; Luke 20:22). The narrative is characterized by a relatively high Christology and expresses the conviction that Jesus' disciples are children of God. Given these circumstances, were free[43] adult Christian males required to pay a tax for the Temple, now diverted to the temple of Jupiter Capitolinus?[44]

At the time when Matthew composed his Gospel, the issue was ultimately one of the Jewish identity of the Jewish-Christian community. Were the "temple tax" to be paid, the members of the community would appear to be Jews in the eyes of the authorities and would expect to enjoy the relative religious freedom generally accorded to Jews. The episode portrays a Solomonic judgment. As children of God, Christians were not obliged to pay the temple tax; in principle, they were exempt. It would have been, however, a prudent thing for them to do so. In passing, the narrative shows that God, through Jesus, provides for the church in its actual social condition and material (financial) need.

Matthew 16:18 is the first time that the word "church" (ekklēsia) appears in the tradition of the written Gospels.

Jesus' Church

In many ways, and certainly in terms of the subsequent historical development of the church, the most important Petrine text in the Gospel according to Matthew is Peter's confession of faith. In Matthew's narrative the promise of the keys of the Kingdom (Matt 16:17-20)[45] follows Peter's confession (Matt 16:13-16). The confession itself belongs to the triple tradition,[46] but the hand of Matthew the redactor is to be seen in the designation of Peter as "Simon Peter"[47] and the expansion of the confession by the addition of "the Son of the living God." These editorial emendations anticipate the beatitude and promise that follow.

The beatitude, an affirmation of good fortune, pronounces Simon as blessed because he has been the recipient of divine revelation. This is manifest in Simon Peter's ability to proclaim Jesus as "the Son of the living God" (Matt 16:16).[48] Using a rhetorical contrast, the evangelist underscored the idea that divine revelation is the source of Simon's happiness. It is not some human source that has communicated to Simon the content of his proclamation; it is rather God himself who has done so: "Flesh and blood has not revealed this to you, but my Father in heaven" (Matt 16:17). The reader recognizes in the description of God as "my Father in heaven" the language of Matthew the redactor.[49] The import of this description is such that a comparison is made between Jesus, the son of the Father in heaven, and Simon, the son of Jonah.[50] Simon's sonship is merely human; Jesus's sonship is of another kind. Only God could reveal that. Peter is blessed because he has received a divine revelation.

Jesus' words, "And I tell you" (*kagō de soi legō*), solemnly introduce the promise, imparting to it some formality: "You are Peter, and on this rock I will build my church, and the gates of Hades[51] will not prevail against it" (Matt 16:18). This is the first time[52] that the word "church" (*ekklēsia*) appears in Matthew's narrative, the first time that the term appears in the tradition of the written Gospels.

What is implied by Simon's new name[53] and the promise given to him? The Greek text of Matthew gives the name as "Peter" (*Petros*); older New Testament texts give the name as "Cephas" (*Kēphas*),[54] a Greek transliteration of an Aramaic word used to designate a rock, a crag. Apparently the nickname had not previously been used in either Aramaic or Greek. The name suggests solidness. Anything built on "Peter," a rock, is built on a solid foundation. The church built on this foundation stands firm against the power of death,[55] just as a house built on rock stands firm against rains, floods, and winds (see Matt 7:24). The church built by Jesus is built to last.

According to the biblical tradition, a new name implies a change of function. The evangelist has explained Peter's new role in the second promise made by Jesus: "I will give you the keys of the kingdom of heaven, and whatever you bind on earth will be bound in heaven, and whatever you loose on earth will be loosed in heaven" (Matt 16:19). With this promise the evangelist has mixed his metaphors.[56] Peter is no longer portrayed as a solid foundation for a construction; rather he is presented as the doorkeeper or manager of the edifice.[57] The metaphor derives from traditional Jewish usage, as does much of the material particular to Matthew.[58] For example, the Mishnah identifies the followers of the great first-century c.e. rabbis Hillel and Shammai as the house of Hillel (*beth Hillel*) and the house of Shammai (*beth Shammai*).[59] Now the followers of Jesus are implicitly described as a "house," language that fits in well with the venue of early Christian gatherings as well as with the language of such early Christian texts as 1 Tim 3:15.

In Jewish tradition the key of David[60] refers to the authority of the teachers of the Law. In rabbinic usage,[61] "binding and loosing" evoked the idea of making authoritative decisions with regard to the Law, declaring that something was forbidden or permitted. Occasionally the metaphor was used in reference to expelling someone from or reconciling them to the community. Within a Jewish community such as Matthew's Jewish-Christian community, the metaphor suggested teaching and disciplinary authority.

Jesus' utterance on the keys of the Kingdom (Matt 16:19) is readily understood when it is compared with a Q saying that appears in slightly different forms in Matt 23:13 and Luke 11:52.[62] In Luke the saying is: "Woe to you lawyers! For you have taken away the key of knowledge; you did not enter yourselves, and you hindered those who were entering." The Matthean counterpart is: "Woe to you, scribes and Pharisees, hypocrites! For you lock people out of the Kingdom of Heaven."

Thus, in Matt 16:19 Peter is effectively portrayed as having been assigned the role of chief rabbi of the Jewish-Christian community.[63] For that community Peter is the authentic interpreter of the Law as understood and taught by Jesus. He continues the mission of Jesus to the house of Israel (Matt 15:24). Among Matthew's contemporaries, various other teachers were recognized as authentic interpreters of the Law, carrying on the tradition of the legendary rabbis Hillel and Shammai. Among the disciples of Jesus, Peter is the foundation of the church,[64] the authentic interpreter of the Law, carrying on the tradition of Jesus.

Listen to the Church

The fourth major discourse in Matthew's narrative is the Instruction for Church Leaders (Matt 18:1–19:1). The idea of binding and loosing is used again in this speech. In Matt 16:19, the imagery is found in a logion addressed to Peter alone; in Matt 18:18, a similar logion is addressed to the disciples.[65] In the instruction the logion follows a series of graduated directives for dealing with sinners:

> If another member of the church sins against you, go and point out the fault when the two of you are alone. If the member listens to you, you have regained that one. But if you are not listened to, take one or two others along with you, so that every word may be confirmed by the evidence of two or three witnesses. If the member refuses to listen to them, tell it to the church; and if the offender refuses to listen even to the church, let such a one be to you as a Gentile and a tax collector. Truly I tell you, whatever you bind on earth will be bound in heaven, and whatever you loose on earth will be loosed in heaven. (Matt 18:15-18)

The purpose of these instructions is the reconciliation of the sinner to the community. The Jewish setting is obvious, particularly in regard to the two or three witnesses[66] and the reference to the Gentile and tax collector. The first instruction (v. 15) deals with the correction of a "sibling"; twice the Greek text employs the word *adelphos*, "brother."[67] A member of the community against whom an offense has been committed has a responsibility to take the initiative in correcting his or her sibling[68] and thus try to heal the strain on the family relationship. Only if the one-on-one attempt fails should the help of others be sought.

If the second attempt to encourage conversion and reconciliation fails, the issue should be brought before the entire assembly, the church (*ekklēsia*).[69] If the efforts of the assembly prove to be futile, the recalcitrant sinner is to be ostracized and excommunicated. He is to be no more considered a member of this Jewish-Christian community than a Gentile would be considered as a member of an ethnic Jewish community.

The three-step procedure outlined in Matt 18:15-17 is similar to one followed by the community at Qumran, which also had to deal with the issue of sinners within its midst:

One should reproach one another in truth, in meekness and in compassionate love for one's fellow-man. No one should speak to his brother in anger or muttering, or with a hard [neck or with passionate] spirit of wickedness, and he should not detest him [in the fore]sk[in] of his heart, but instead reproach him that day so as not to incur a sin because of him.[70] And in addition, no one should raise a matter against his fellow in front of the Many unless it is with reproof in the presence of witnesses. (1QS 5:24–6:1; cf. CD 9:2-3)

Matthew underscored his Jewish-Christian community's authority to excommunicate[71] the obstinate sinner by reprising the logion of Matt 16:19, which he has introduced by the solemn and authoritative lemma,

"Remember, I am with you always, to the end of the age" (Matt 28:20b).

"truly I tell you" (*amēn legō hymin*): "Truly I tell you, whatever you bind on earth will be bound in heaven, and whatever you loose on earth will be loosed in heaven" (Matt 18:18). Within the context of the discourse to the church, the idiom refers to the expulsion of a person from the community.[72] The authority for such excommunication is that of the one who says "truly I tell you."

This introductory formula appears again in Matt 18:19. The lemma introduces the rationale for the procedure that the community is to follow: "Again, truly I tell you, if two or three of you agree on earth about anything you ask, it will be done for you by my Father in heaven. For where two or three are gathered in my name (*duo ē treis synēgmenoi eis to emon onoma*, I am there among them" (Matt 18:19-20). What the church does is ratified by God.

Jesus' explanatory utterance offers a description of the church. The church is a gathering of two or more people in the name of Jesus. Matthew 18:20 is the christological center of the entire discourse to the church: when the church gathers, Jesus is present. This idea is thoroughly Jewish, albeit phrased in Christian terms.[73] The Mishnah similarly stated: "If two sit together and words of the Law [are spoken] between them, the Divine Presence rests between them" (*m. ʾAbot* 3:2). The logion found in Matt 18:20 makes a profound ecclesiological statement in terms that are thoroughly Jewish.

The Great Commission

The idea of Jesus' presence with his disciples appears again in the finale of the Gospel according to Matthew. This finale is rather different from the conclusion to Mark's story of Jesus. Mark's narrative comes to an abrupt end, seemingly interrupted. Matthew's narrative apparently comes to a conclusion in Matt 28:15, when it takes a new turn with an episode without parallel in the other canonical Gospels (Matt 28:16-20).[74]

The scenario is that of the group of the Twelve, without the traitor Judas who had killed himself (Matt 27:5), assembled on a Galilean mountain. This was a place to which Jesus himself had directed them to go (Matt 28:10). Prior to his death, the disciples had regularly approached Jesus with solemnity; now, after his death, Jesus approaches the disciples, speaking to them about the authority that is his.[75] With plenipotentiary authority, Jesus gives the eleven disciples a triple commission before making a solemn promise.

The words of this great commission[76] are well known: "Go therefore and make disciples of all nations, baptizing them in the name of the Father and of the Son and of the Holy Spirit, and teaching them to obey everything that I have commanded you" (Matt 28:19-20a). With the commission's first clause, Matthew links the mission to the Gentiles to a command of the exalted Jesus and the formation of the twelve disciples. Having been formed as disciples, they are to form other disciples in turn. In the second clause, the eleven disciples are told to baptize in the name of the Father and of the Son and of the Holy Spirit. The baptismal formula, without parallel in the New Testament,[77] reflects the practice of early Christian liturgy. In the commission's final clause, the evangelist indicates that the formation of disciples consists of teaching them to learn and observe what Jesus had taught.[78]

The ecclesial implications of the great commission are obvious. The commission is a command to extend Jesus' mission to the house of Israel beyond Israel to the Gentiles. In fulfilling their mandate, the disciples are not alone. Jesus' words, "Remember, I am with you always, to the end of the age" (Matt 28:20b),[79] express the promise with which Matthew concludes his story. This promise brings his entire narrative to a close in a ring construction that harkens back to Matthew's initial disclosure of Jesus' identity, Emmanuel, "God with us" (Matt 1:23). The apocalyptic horizon of the promise recalls the apocalyptic scheme of the opening genealogy in the Matthean story. This final promise of the exalted Lord to be with his disciples recalls the words of the formative instruction: "Where two or three are gathered in my name, I am there among them" (Matt 18:20), a veritable definition of the church.

Discussion and Study Questions

1. In what ways is the church of Matthew's Gospel a Jewish church?

2. What do Jesus' words to Peter, "You are Peter and on this rock I will build my church," mean for the contemporary church?

3. Are the members of the church today like Peter and the eleven other apostles, men and women "of little faith"?

4. Matthew's Jewish-Christian church was characterized by its Jewish heritage and culture. Is the church of today still characterized by its heritage and particular culture?

Chapter Nine

An Ideal Community

Matthew's revision of the Gospel according to Mark portrayed the twelve disciples as the core group from which the renewed Israel would emerge. These twelve learned from Jesus, the master teacher, and were sent out to continue his mission to Israel. Prior to his death, Jesus announced that Peter was to be the chief rabbi in the new community, the Jewish-Christian "church." After his death, the risen Jesus commissioned the Twelve to bring to the Gentiles the teaching that they had received from Jesus.

A few years after the composition of Matthew's Gospel, the evangelist known as Luke made his own revision of the Markan text. Unlike the Matthean revision that had been tailored to a Jewish-Christian community, Luke's revision was an adaptation of Mark's narrative for the benefit of Gentile Christians (Luke 1:3; Acts 1:1).

Luke's intention is implied by his telling of the story of the commissioning of the seventy-two[1] (Luke 10:1-12) and in his rendition of the Parable of the Great Supper (Luke 14:15-24; Matt 22:1-14). In his version of the parable, the third invitation is extended to those who live outside the city: "Go out into the roads and lanes, and compel people to come in, so that my house may be filled" (*hina gemisthēmou ho oikos*)" (Luke 14:23). The story of the commissioning of the seventy-two is, in fact, a parallel to the story of the mission of the Twelve (Luke 9:1-6).

Luke's aim is clearly manifest in the second part of his two-part work, the Acts of the Apostles.[2] Luke's thesis is expressed in the words of Jesus to the Eleven: "You will be my witnesses in Jerusalem, in all Judea and Samaria, and to the end of the earth"[3] (Acts 1:8). The story of the church

is a continuation of the story of Jesus. Spirit-endowed preachers bore witness to Jesus. Chief among them are Peter, who witnessed in Jerusalem;
Philip, who evangelized in Samaria; and Paul, who is the witness to the end
of the earth. These three are the heroes of the Lucan narrative.

Luke frequently used the word "church" (*ekklēsia*) to describe the
results of their testimony. He often mentioned the *ekklēsia* in Jerusalem,
though he more often implied the location of the church in the Holy City
than he explicitly stated its specific geographic venue (Acts 5:11; 8:3; 12:1,
5; 15:4, 22; 18:22; cf. 8:1; 11:22). Luke also wrote about the church in Antioch (Acts 13:1; cf. 11:26; 14:27; 15:3) and mentioned the churches in Judea,
Galilee, and Samaria (Acts 9:31). With regard to the Pauline mission, he
wrote about "the church of God" in Ephesus (Acts 20:28; cf. v. 17). He
noted that Paul and Barnabas appointed elders in each church, commend-
ing them to the Lord (Acts 14:23), and that after Paul's split from Barnabas
and Mark, Paul and Silas showed pastoral care for the churches of Syria
and Cilicia (Acts 15:41; cf. 16:5).[4]

The Gospel According to Luke

In contrast with Matthew and his own usage in Acts, Luke did not
employ the word "church" in writing his story of Jesus. The ecclesial elements of his story about Jesus center on the idea of a mission, that is, both
the mission of the Twelve and the mission of the seventy-two, and the formation of a leadership cadre for the church in Jerusalem.

Following Mark, Luke portrayed the selection and commissioning of
the Twelve (Luke 6:12-16; 9:1-6). He also describes, however, a further mission of seventy or seventy-two disciples. It is difficult to discern any specific referential factor in the symbolic number but Luke's intention is
clearly to describe a mission beyond that of the Twelve, who were sent to
the house of Israel. The numerical figure, seventy or seventy-two, suggests
the "universal" mission of the church. Jesus' sending of these disciples fore-
shadows the mission to the Gentiles narrated in Acts. The missionary
charge given to this larger group (Luke 10:1-12) is patterned after the missionary charge given to the Twelve (see Luke 9:1-6), but they, unlike the
Twelve, are not called "apostles."

Although Luke offers a summary of the Twelve's accomplishment of
their mission (Luke 9:6), he does not provide a narrative summary of the

activity of the seventy-two. In its stead Luke reports that the disciples returned with joy and that Jesus experienced an apocalyptic vision. In the vision Jesus saw the fall of Satan. Because of the vision, Jesus was able to encourage the disciples by announcing that their names were written in heaven (Luke 10:18-20). Luke's use of this apocalyptic imagery represents a departure from his normal practice of avoiding and even removing apocalyptic motifs from the story, but it provides a futuristic quality to the mission of the seventy-two.

Simon Whom He Named Peter

In addition to retelling the story of Jesus in such a way that the mission to the Gentiles is anticipated,[5] Luke has recast the entire Gospel narrative so that it speaks of the formation of those who will assume leadership positions in the church, those who will bear witness to Jesus in the church of Jerusalem after the resurrection. In his story about Jesus, Luke noted that after a night of prayer on the mountain, Jesus called his disciples and chose twelve of them "whom he also named apostles" (*hous kai apostolous ōnomasen*, Luke 6:13). The first name on the list is that of Simon,

Luke's intention is to describe a mission beyond that of the Twelve who were sent to the house of Israel.

"whom he named Peter" (*hon kai ōnomasen Petron*, Luke 6:14). Thereafter, Luke calls this chosen apostle by his nickname. The choice of the Twelve, named apostles, with Peter as their leader and spokesperson, provides the link between Luke's story of Jesus and his story of the early church.

Luke's retelling of the story of Jesus in such a way as to focus on the leadership of the church in Jerusalem is apparent in the attention that he pays to the figure of Peter. This Petrine interest is reflected in both subtle and explicit ways.[6] Thus, in Luke's retelling of the story of the woman who had been suffering from hemorrhages for twelve years (Luke 8:42-48; Mark 5:24-34), Peter's role as spokesperson appears quite clearly: "Jesus asked, 'Who touched me?' When all denied it, Peter said, 'Master, the crowds surround you and press in on you'" (Luke 8:45). In Luke's Markan source, a similar response to Jesus' question is found on the lips of "the disciples" (Mark 5:31).

The evangelist's interest in Peter is also evident in the way that Luke works with the sayings of Jesus, the material of the "double tradition."[7] For example, Luke has inserted a short dialogue between Peter and the Lord into a group of sayings[8] on vigilance and faithfulness (Luke 12:35-48; cf. Matt 24:42-51): "Peter said. . . . And the Lord said" (Luke 12:41-42a). The introductory lemmas focus on a conversation between Peter and the Lord.

What Peter uttered was really a question: "Lord, are you telling the parable for us and for everyone?" The parable in question is the Parable of the Lord and the Watchful Slaves. Jesus answered Peter's question with a question, "Who then is the faithful and prudent manager (oikonomos) whom his master (ho kyrios) will put in charge of his slaves (epi tēs therapeias), to give them their allowance of food at the proper time?" (Luke 12:42). In the parable the "lord" (kyrios) was identified as a householder (oikodespotēs, Luke 12:39). Jesus' rhetorical question to Peter suggests that the parable of the lord who went on a trip is really directed to the leaders of the community. In the household of God,[9] these leaders have a role to play analogous to that of the manager of a great household. Among their responsibilities is that of providing food for the lord's servants.

More striking than the traces of Lucan redaction in Luke 8:45 and 12:41 is Luke's story of the miraculous catch of fish (Luke 5:1-11). The story is without parallel in the other Synoptic Gospels but is similar to a tale found in the epilogue to the Fourth Gospel (John 21:4-11). According to Luke, Jesus was walking along the Lake of Gennesaret when he saw two empty fishing boats. He asked Simon, whose mother-in-law he had previously cured and who was the owner of one of the boats, to take him out a bit so that he could speak more effectively to the crowds who had gathered to hear God's word. Thus, Simon's boat served as the makeshift pulpit for Jesus' preaching the word of God to the crowds.

According to the story, after Jesus spoke to the crowds, he instructed Simon to let down the nets for a catch. The fisherman protested that such an effort would be useless; he and his companions had toiled the night through and had caught nothing.[10] Nevertheless, Simon relented. Having once dropped the nets, Simon caught such a large haul of fish that his partners had to come and help with the catch. Thereupon, Simon Peter fell to his knees, confessing, "Go away from me, Lord, for I am a sinful man!" (v. 8). Luke concluded the story by observing that the fishermen became

Jesus' disciples: "When they had brought their boats to shore, they left everything and followed him" (Luke 5:11).

In composing his narrative, Luke described Simon as acknowledging that Jesus is Lord and, on the occasion, the evangelist used the nickname "Peter" for the first time. To appreciate the import of this story, the reader must be aware that this is the first of the call narratives in the Gospel according to Luke. In the story James and John are identified as Simon's partners (*koinōnoi*), yet they are so identified only after Peter's confession of faith (v. 10; cf. v. 7). There was at least one other person in the boat with Simon—note the verbs in the plural in verses 6-7a—but that person is not identified.[11] It is, therefore, rather striking that Jesus' promise is addressed only to Simon: "Jesus said to Simon, 'Do not be afraid;[12] from now on you will be catching people'" (Luke 5:10). The verbs of the saying are in the singular. Simon is to catch people; James and John are his partners in this endeavor.

Jesus' last celebration of Passover provided another occasion for Luke to spotlight Peter. Luke told his readers that Jesus sent Peter and John to "go and prepare the Passover meal" (Luke 22:8). Neither Mark nor Matthew indicates that it was Jesus who took the initiative in arranging for the celebration of the Passover. In Mark and Matthew, the disciples ask Jesus about the celebration (Mark 14:12-13; Matt 26:17-18). In Mark two anonymous disciples are sent to make the preparations; in Matthew the task falls to "the disciples." In the Gospel of Luke, Peter and John, Peter's companion in the Acts of Apostles,[13] perform the task.

Luke subsequently interrupted Mark's narrative account of the meal in order to provide the readers with Jesus' farewell discourse (Luke 22:24-38). The evangelist pieced the discourse together in mosaic-like fashion, borrowing material coming from his various sources.[14] The nature of the genre of the farewell discourse is such that the discourse speaks about the situation of those who are left behind. The typical farewell discourse includes words of encouragement to those who remain, urging them to strive for unity among themselves and providing for some form of leadership among them.

The scenario of the Lucan farewell discourse depicts the apostles (Luke 22:14) arguing among themselves about who was the greatest (Luke 22:24). Jesus' response contrasts the greatness of the apostles with the greatness of kings and other civic authorities (Luke 22:25-26).[15] Jesus then asks a pair of pointed rhetorical questions: "For who is greater, the one

who is at the table or the one who serves? Is it not the one at the table?"
(Luke 22:27). This enables Jesus to speak about the nature of the disciples'
faithfulness. The first part of the discourse goes back and forth between
leadership and discipleship. Jesus offered himself as the example of a servant– leader;[16] his eschatological kingship was to provide parameters for
the apostles' leadership.[17]

The second part of the farewell discourse (22:31-32) is properly Lucan
material:[18] "Simon, Simon, listen! Satan has demanded to sift all of you like
wheat, but I have prayed for you[19] that your own faith may not fail; and
you, when once you have turned back, strengthen your brothers." Jesus'
words are directed to Simon alone. Four words in the second person singular are found in Jesus' address to Simon: I have prayed for you (*sou*) . . .
your (*sou*) faith . . . you have turned back (*epistrepsas*) . . . your (*sou*) brothers" (Luke 22:32).[20]

The double vocative, "Simon, Simon," recalls the biblical use of the
double vocative in narratives that recount the call of such figures as Abraham and Paul (cf. Acts 9:4; 22:7; 26:14; Gen 22:11). Jesus' mention of Satan
suggests that although Satan has tried to put the disciples through a sieve
and separate some from others, Simon will ultimately withstand the chal-
lenge. Jesus has prayed for him, that his faith not fail. After his conversion,
his turning back (*epistrepsas*), Simon was to strengthen his brothers
(*stērison tous adelphous sou*). As a man of unfailing faith, Simon was to
support, encourage, and strengthen his brother apostles, leaders who act as
servants at table. Thus, Jesus, who was about to die, is portrayed as having
given personal responsibility to Simon to be a support for his brother
apostles. In this way he was to assume some of the functions of Jesus, who
was about to leave this life.

The third unit of the Lucan farewell discourse (Luke 22:35-38) recalls
the missionary discourse of Luke 10. Luke 22:35-36 clearly refers back to
Luke 10:4; those who had been told to take with them neither purse nor
bag are now to do so. The reference in this discourse to the sword anticipates the passion narrative, in which "one of them[21] struck the slave of the
high priest and cut off his ear" (22:49-51, v. 50).

Luke's interest in Simon Peter appears again in the final chapter of the
Gospel. His account of the women at the tomb is followed by a short
episode featuring Peter: "But Peter got up and ran to the tomb; stooping
and looking in, he saw the linen cloths by themselves; then he went home,

amazed at what had happened" (Luke 24:12).[22] In a later episode, the two disciples who met the risen Jesus on the road to Emmaus returned to Jerusalem. They gave this report: "The Lord has risen indeed, and has appeared to Simon" (Luke 24:34). With these two verses (Luke 24:12, 34), the evangelist has portrayed Peter as the first apostolic witness to the resurrection. The tradition is reflected in an early credal formula that was cited by Paul in 1 Cor 15:3-5: "He [Christ] appeared to Cephas."[23] Luke has portrayed Peter as an authoritative witness to both the empty tomb and a resurrection appearance. These are the two narrative forms in which the church's early belief in the resurrection of Jesus has been handed down.

The Acts of the Apostles

Peter's name is absent from the concluding pericopes of Luke's long narrative (24:36-48). The first of the two (Luke 24:36-43) recounts the story of an appearance of the risen Jesus to the eleven. Luke's account of the episode focuses on Jesus' identity and includes a meal. The second pericope (Luke 24:44-49) describes the commissioning of the eleven and recalls a divine promise: "You are witnesses of these things. And see, I am sending upon you what my Father promised; so stay here in the city until you have been clothed with power from on high" (Luke 24:48-49). All this happened before Jesus' ascension to heaven. Part two of Luke's two-part work tells the story of how the divine promise was realized and how the apostles fulfilled their mandate.

Acts is a story of the early church, the only history of the early years of the Christian movement. It is history in the way that people of that era wrote history. They aimed not for the kind of objectivity that would become an ideal, albeit often not attained, for historians of the eighteenth and later centuries. Hellenistic historians wrote for a manifest purpose. They did not hide their bias. Secular historians generally wrote to praise the emperor or other civil authorities. Luke wrote to demonstrate the spread of the good news from Jerusalem to the Hellenistic world.

The theme of Acts is spoken by the risen Jesus, who said to the apostles chosen during his life among them: "You will receive power when the Holy Spirit has come upon you; and you will be my witnesses in Jerusalem, in all Judea and Samaria, and to the end of the earth" (Acts 1:8).

The Foundation of the Church

The high points of Luke's history of the early church are undoubtedly his etiological narrative of the origin of the Gentile mission, his description of the church of Jerusalem as an ideal model of the church, and his account of the unity between Paul's Hellenistic churches and the mother church at Jerusalem. The etiological narrative begins with the apostles coming together in the presence of Jesus (Acts 1:6); it ends with a summary description of the first three thousand[24] converts (Acts 2:41-42). Between the beginning and the end of the interpretive narrative come (1) Jesus' promise of the gift of the Spirit (Acts 1:6-11); (2) the filling of the complement of the Twelve (Acts 1:15-26); (3) the gift of the Spirit (Acts 2:1-13); (4) an inaugural address (Acts 2:14-36); and (5) the first converts (Acts 2:37-42).

Each of these episodes merits careful reflection; each of them has much to say about Luke's understanding of what would come to be known as "the church."[25] The related incidents of the promise and gift of the Spirit (Acts 1:6-11; 2:1-13) portray the apostles as continuing the mission of Jesus. The apostles had been chosen by Jesus (Acts 1:2). The risen Jesus gave them a mission (Acts 1:8). Their mandate is to bear witness to Jesus (Acts 1:8). Jesus instructed them through the power of the Holy Spirit (Acts 1:2), which had previously descended upon him in physical form (Luke 3:21-22). The same Holy Spirit came upon the apostles in physical form (Acts 2:1-13); they preached the gospel by the power of the same Spirit (Acts 2:14-36).

The gift of the Spirit enabled this small group of Galileans to speak in the power of the Spirit in such a way that Jews from the Diaspora, together with some proselytes, were able to understand their discourse about the wonderful deeds of God's power. Those who listened were Parthians, Medes, Elamites, Mesopotamians, Judeans, and Cappadocians, along with some people from Pontus, Asia, Phrygia, Pamphylia, Egypt, Libya, and Rome—people with a wide diversity of native languages. The preaching of the gospel in the Diaspora was thus effectively foreshadowed in the celebration of the first Christian Pentecost.

Between Jesus' promise of the Spirit and the conferral of the Pentecostal gift, Luke narrates a scene in which Peter, the apostles' spokesperson, takes the initiative in assuring that the Twelve are brought to their full numerical complement. Peter's speech on the occasion tells about the influence of the Holy Spirit in the process of bringing the group to their full number. In addition, Peter cites a biblical text (Ps 109:8)[26] as a warrant for the filling of the numerical complement before the mission begins. Of the two candidates for the vacant position, Matthias was chosen to assume "the place in this ministry and apostleship" (*ton topon tēs diakonias tautēs kai apostolēs*, Acts 1:25). With the choice of Matthias, "the Twelve" were again twelve in number.[27]

Luke's narrative mentions two essential traits of apostleship, at least from his point of view. First, the apostle is one who has been with Jesus and the disciples from the time of Jesus' baptism until the time of his ascension. Second, the apostle is one who bears witness to the resurrection of Jesus.[28] To these can be added a third characteristic of the apostle; the apostle is one who has received the enabling gift of the Spirit (Acts 2:1-13).

Another element in Luke's etiological narrative of the church is his account of the inspired Pentecost discourse given by Peter.[29] In this paradigmatic address, Peter served as the spokesperson for the Twelve (Acts 2:14). Peter spoke only briefly about the ministry of Jesus; he concentrated on the death and resurrection of Jesus. This is the heart of the early Christian kerygma (cf. 1 Thess 4:14; 1 Cor 15:3-5). Luke presents Peter as

> *Those who listened to the apostles were Parthians, Medes, Elamites, Mesopotamians, Judeans, and Cappadocians, along with some people from Pontus, Asia, Phrygia, Pamphylia, Egypt, Libya, and Rome—people with a wide diversity of native languages. The preaching of the gospel in the Diaspora was foreshadowed in the celebration of the first Christian Pentecost.*

having interpreted both the resurrection of Jesus and the descent of the Holy Spirit on the Twelve in the light of the Jewish scriptures, particularly Pss 16:8-11; 110:1; and Joel 2:28-31.[30] It was the common faith of the early church that Jesus "was raised on the third day in accordance with the scriptures" (1 Cor 15:4).

The Pentecostal discourse concluded with an appeal for conversion (Acts 2:40). Those who accepted Peter's message (*ton logon*, Acts 2:41) were baptized. The reception of the kerygma by the three thousand was evidenced by their conversion and their baptism. Acceptance of the gospel message and reception of baptism led to the participation of thse neophytes in the life and fellowship of the church in Jerusalem: "They devoted themselves to the apostles' teaching and fellowship, to the breaking of bread and the prayers" (Acts 2:42).

A Model Church

Luke has portrayed the church in Jerusalem as a "model church."[31] This occurs especially in three cameo passages found in the first segment of the Acts of the Apostles, Acts 2:42-47; 4:32-35; and 5:12-16. Each of these summaries provides significant insights into Luke's notion of the community in Jerusalem as an ideal church. In the words of Joseph Fitzmyer, the first of these Lucan compositions is "an idyllic description of the life of the primitive Christian community in Jerusalem, its spontaneity, harmony, and unity, its devotion to prayer and Temple worship."[32]

In this first summary, the church at Jerusalem is presented as a group of people who have responded to the kerygma with acceptance of the message and with baptism, who then become members of the community, joining with those who preceded them in faith. Following the pattern of Luke's model, it can be said that the church has four essential characteristics: its adherence to the teaching of the apostles, fellowship, the breaking of the bread, and prayer (2:42).

The "teaching of the apostles" (*tē didachē tōn apostolōn*)[33] differs from the proclamation of the kerygma. Teaching followed the neophytes' acceptance of the gospel message. Teaching included the apostolic witness to the deeds of power, wonders, and signs that God did through Jesus (2:22). It was also a matter of interpreting the words and works (see Acts 1:1) of Jesus in the light of the scriptures. "Fellowship" (*koinōnia*)[34] suggests that the community shared some elements of life in common. Fellowship entails a sharing of meals (Acts 2:46) and some sharing of material possessions (Acts 2:44; 4:32-35). The community's sharing of food and possessions was such that the church at Jerusalem may well have called itself a *koinōnia*, a community.[35]

A characteristic activity of the church in Jerusalem was the breaking of bread (*tē klasei tou artou*). "Breaking of bread" is the way that Luke describes the early Christian celebration of the eucharist (see Luke 24:30, 35; Acts 2:42, 46; 20:7, 11; 27:35; cf. 1 Cor 10:16). The breaking of bread by the gathered assembly bore witness to Jesus and was a celebration of the community's common life. The fourth trait highlighted in Luke's first portrayal of the model church in Jerusalem was its life of prayer. The plural noun *tais proseuchais* used by the evangelist suggests that the community employed different forms of prayer,[36] including praise of God (2:47). For the Jewish-Christian community in Jerusalem, prayer would have included participation in Temple worship (2:46), as was evidenced by Peter and John's visit to the Temple for afternoon prayer (Acts 3:1).

Luke's first summary description of the Jerusalem church emphasized the link between the community and the preaching and teaching of the apostles, the eucharist that was celebrated "at home" (*kat' oikon*, 2:46), and the impression made on outsiders by the life of the community. The witness of their life together was such that other people continued to join the community (2:47).

Luke's second cameo (Acts 4:32-35) highlights the *koinōnia* that consists in the sharing of possessions and focuses on the unity of the community: "the whole group of those who believed were of one heart and soul" (4:32). This sharing of possessions[37] so that there was no needy person among those who gathered was both a sign and a means of their unity. The language used by the evangelist suggests that a Deuteronomic ideal of community[38] was at work in his ideation of the community of believers. In similar fashion, the Dead Sea Scrolls attest to the Qumranites' self-understanding as a *yahad*, a community.[39] The ideal portrayed by Luke in Acts 4:32-35 was not altogether unusual in first-century c.e. Jewish reform movements.

A common Hellenistic proverb in the topos on friendship affirmed that "friends hold all things in common."[40] This notion was so widespread that Luke Timothy Johnson can say: "there can be no doubt Luke is appropriating that tradition."[41] The ideal of the church as a unified community would have appealed to both the Jewish and the Gentile elements within the community for whom Luke was writing. Luke does not, however, say how the church in Jerusalem lived up to this ideal in real life. Was the sharing of possessions mandatory or voluntary? Was it a matter of common ownership of all possessions or selling possessions so that everyone might benefit? Neither Luke's second summary nor 2:44-45 provides definitive answers to these questions.[42]

As in the first summary, the terse description of the church in Jerusalem in Acts 4:32-35 describes the members of the assembly as "those who believed" (*pisteuontes*, 2:44; 4:32).[43] The apostles are described as those who proclaimed the kerygma, who gave "testimony to the resurrection of the Lord Jesus" (*to martyrion tēs anastaseōs tou kyriou Iēsou*, 4:33). It is the apostles who had the responsibility to supervise the sharing of possessions (Acts 4:35; 5:2).[44]

Luke's third summary description of the church in Jerusalem appears in Acts 5:12-16. The summary portrays the apostles as continuing Jesus' prophetic mission, working signs and wonders (5:12; see Luke 24:19; Acts 2:22; 4:30). What God did through them was an answer to the community's prayer (4:29-30). Luke's description points to the singular power of God working through the apostles (5:13). Along with the preaching of the kerygma and the example of the community's life, the signs and wonders worked through the apostles were means by which God moved people to believe and join the community (Acts 2:41, 47; 5:14). All three summaries point to the role of the apostles in the life and faith of the church in Jerusalem (2:42; 4:33, 35; 5:12). Only the third summary highlights the unique role of Peter[45] among the apostles (5:15).

Mission to the Gentiles

The mission that the risen Jesus gave to the Twelve was that they be "witnesses in Jerusalem, in all Judea and Samaria, and to the end of the earth" (1:8). All three Lucan summaries in Acts highlight the importance of the apostolic witness in Jerusalem, but as Luke develops the narrative plot of Acts, it becomes readily apparent that the apostles were not the ones who bore witness to Jesus in Samaria. Neither were the apostles the ones who carried the gospel message to the end of the earth. Those roles fell to Philip and Paul respectively.

Both the Samaritan mission and the mission to the Gentiles were, however, warranted and confirmed by the apostles, particularly by Peter. In response to a complaint by the community's Hellenistic members that Hellenistic widows were being neglected in the distribution of the daily ration,[46] the Twelve called the entire community together. They chose seven men of good standing. This symbolic number, seven, signified completeness or totality.[47] The apostles prayed for the seven and laid hands on them (Acts 6:1-6). Among the seven was Philip, whose role was to proclaim the Messiah to the Samaritans (8:5-7, 12-13). Once the apostles heard about the success of Philip's preaching, they sent Peter and John. This pair of apostles confirmed the mission to the Samaritans by prayer; the two imposed hands on the Samaritans that they might receive the Holy Spirit. Peter and John then preached the gospel message to the Samaritans as they made their way back to the church in Jerusalem (8:14-25).

The mission of Paul was similarly warranted and confirmed by the apostles. Luke subtly introduced the young Saul into his narrative in the account of the stoning of Stephen, that is, prior to the evangelization of Samaria (8:1). Even after Saul had come to believe in Jesus the Messiah,[48] believers in Jerusalem continued to be afraid of him. Their fear was overcome when Barnabas took Paul to the apostles, testifying that the Lord had appeared to Paul and that he had spoken boldly in the name of Jesus (9:27). Paul was then able to enjoy the fellowship of the apostles. He joined with them in speaking about the Lord in Jerusalem (9:28).[49] When later some Hellenists attempted to kill Paul, the disciples sent Paul back to his native Tarsus (9:29-30).

Paul remained in Tarsus until Barnabas came to get him and brought him to Antioch (11:25-26). The two of them evangelized the city for a year. When the believers of Antioch heard about a famine, they organized a collection for believers in Judea and commissioned Paul and Barnabas to take the collection to Jerusalem on their behalf (11:29-30). After their mission to Jerusalem was fulfilled, Paul and Barnabas returned to Antioch, where the Holy Spirit launched their mission to the Gentiles. They were commissioned for the task by the laying on of hands (13:2-4).

Before describing this mission, Luke noted that the church in Judea, Galilee, and Samaria had been built up (9:31; see 1:8) and that Peter had experienced a heavenly vision (Acts 10:9-16). He then preached the gospel to Cornelius (Acts 10:34-43) and ordered that the Gentile Cornelius should be baptized together with his companions. Peter took the initiative in affirming that these Gentiles had received the Spirit (Acts 10:47). He confronted Jewish Christians who were astounded by the idea that the Holy Spirit had been given to Gentiles and that they had accepted the word of God (10:45-48; 11:1-18). Calling these dubious Christians up short, Peter said: "If then God gave them the same gift that he gave us when we believed in the Lord Jesus Christ, who was I that I could hinder God?"

(11:17). From the perspective of Luke's narrative plot, Peter's vision, the announcement of the kerygma to the Gentile centurion, and Cornelius's baptism provide a precedent for Paul's mission to the Gentiles.

By itself this precedent did not completely resolve the issue of uncircumcised Gentiles being accepted as believers by Jewish Christians. After Paul and Barnabas returned to Antioch at the end of the first missionary journey, some Jewish Christians came to Antioch, disturbing the peace of the community. Dissension arose because the intruders took issue with the practice of accepting Gentiles as members of the community of believers without requiring observance of the Mosaic Law and circumcision (Acts 15:1). Paul and Barnabas and some of the others were appointed to go to Jerusalem to discuss the question "with the apostles and elders" (15:2).

The scene that follows gives an account of the decision of the Jerusalem church (Acts 15:4-35). This is the turning point in Luke's story of the early church.[50] According to Fitzmyer, "The apostolic and presbyteral college of Jerusalem officially recognizes the evangelization of Gentiles, which had been initiated by Peter and carried out on a wide scale by Barnabas and Paul."[51] Luke's account of the "Council of Jerusalem" is a conflation of earlier traditions[52] which he has put together in order to advance his theological agenda, his claim that Jewish and Gentile Christians can and must co-exist in the community of believers.

Luke's account of the Council of Jerusalem is a dramatic presentation of and plea for unity between the Jerusalem church and Gentile churches.

Luke began his account of the meeting in Jerusalem on an irenic note. He observed that when Paul and Barnabas came to Jerusalem, they were welcomed by the church and the apostles and the elders (*paredechthēsan apo tēs ekklēsias kai tōn apostolōn kai tōn presbyterōn*). The repeated appearance of the elders in Luke's narrative (Acts 15:2, 4, 6, 22, 23; 16:4) indicates that a group of elders was associated with the apostles in the leadership of the Jewish-Christian church in Jerusalem.[53] The leadership team, apostles and elders, endorsed the mission of Paul and Barnabas to the Gentiles. They did not require that Gentile Christians be circumcised, and they approved table fellowship between Jewish and Gentile Christians, provided that the latter meet some minimal conditions of hospitality.[54] Peter and James, the leader of the Jerusalem church,[55] took the lead in the Spirit-inspired decisions. The decisions were then formalized in a letter[56] sent to the Gentile churches of Antioch, Cilicia, and Tarsus.[57] This letter was to have been delivered not only by Paul and Barnabas but also by representatives of the church in Jerusalem who were chosen by the apostles and elders, with the entire assembly participating in the decision.

Luke's account of the Council of Jerusalem is a dramatic presentation of and plea for unity between the Jerusalem church and Gentile churches. The mission to the Gentiles was confirmed by the power of the Spirit, who inspired the decision. The apostles to the Gentiles[58] consulted with the apostles and elders in Jerusalem; in turn, the Jerusalem church sent its representatives to the Gentile churches. The apostles and elders, led by Peter and James, endorsed a Gentile mode of being Christian that did not require circumcision and approved table fellowship between Jewish and Gentile Christians.

Luke's account of the relationship between the Gentile mission and the church in Jerusalem did not end with his narration of the gathering in Jerusalem. When Luke told the story of Paul's third missionary journey (Acts 18:23–20:38), he spoke of Paul's resolve to return to Jerusalem (19:21; 20:16). Paul was determined to go to Jerusalem (21:15) despite the Syrian disciples' fear for his safety (21:4). When he arrived in Jerusalem, Paul was welcomed by the Christians of the city (21:17). He then met with James and "all the elders" (*pantes hoi presbyteroi*, 21:18) and told them about the success of his mission to the Gentiles (21:19).

In the Acts of the Apostles the Lucan thesis of fellowship between Jewish and Gentile elements within the community of believers is told in narrative form. With the account of the Council of Jerusalem in Acts 15 and the story of Paul's journey to Jerusalem, difficulties not withstanding (Acts 21:1–22:21), Luke highlighted the apostle Paul's desire to maintain the unity between the Gentile mission and the church in Jerusalem.

This same desire is evidenced in Paul's letters. He was an apostle by the will of God, but he spoke about his visits to Jerusalem, where he met the pillars of the church (Gal 1:18–2:1). In his letters he described his active promotion of a collection for the saints in Jerusalem.[59] Paul's letters and Luke's Acts have literary forms that are quite different each other. Despite their literary and rhetorical differences, Paul's letters and the Acts of the Apostles are one in affirming that the ethnic divide between Jew and Gentile is transcended in the community of believers.

Discussion and Study Questions

1. What should the Lucan farewell discourse (Luke 22:24-38) say to the leaders of the contemporary church?

2. What is the significance of the gift of the Holy Spirit to Jesus' disciples?

3. Does your own church give evidence of traits similar to those Luke describes as being present in the church of Jerusalem (Acts 2:42)?

4. Does your church measure up to the ideal of the model church in Jerusalem? If so, in what ways? If not, why not?

Chapter Ten

We Who Believe

The understanding of the church gleaned from a reading the Fourth Gospel and the Johannine Epistles is quite different from the ecclesiologies of the Pauline corpus. It is different still again from the ecclesiologies of Mark and of the Synoptic authors, who developed their own insights into the church on the basis of Mark's story about Jesus.

Raymond Brown's classic little study describes the Johannine church as "The Community of the Beloved Disciple."[1] Paul Minear writes about the "Logos Ecclesiology" of the Fourth Gospel.[2] In a study of Johannine ecclesiology, Johan Ferreira speaks of the Gospel's "christological ecclesiology." This last description points to the origin, character, and purpose of the Johannine community:

1. A *christological ecclesiology* had as its basis or origin the revelation given by the Johannine Christ, that is, the Word; the community has been brought into being by the Word;
2. a *christological ecclesiology* emphasizes the intimate and exclusive inner life of the community as joy in the word, unity, and love for one another; and
3. a *christological ecclesiology* emphasizes the purpose of the community which is to continue the sending of the Son into the world.[3]

This threefold description points to the singularity of Johannine ecclesiology within the wide array of ecclesiologies reflected in the New Testament corpus.

Simon Peter and the Twelve

The Fourth Gospel speaks of the Twelve,[4] but it does not list their names nor does it identify them as apostles.[5] The traitorous Judas (John

6:71) and the doubting Thomas (20:24) are persons who are specifically identified as "one of the Twelve." Andrew, Philip, and the sons of Zebedee make an appearance in the Fourth Gospel,[6] but the author provides not a clue that they are to be included among the Twelve.

The Twelve appear in a short passage (John 6:67-71) circumscribed by a ring construction featuring the Twelve. The pericope is sandwiched between an account of the defection of some of Jesus' disciples (John 6:60-66) and an account that illustrates the unbelief of Jesus' relatives (John 7:1-9). The intervening passage speaks about faith and defection, giving Simon Peter and Judas, son of Simon Iscariot, as examples. Peter assumes the role of spokesperson for the Twelve, responding as he does to Jesus' question, "Do you also wish to go away?"

Peter's response is phrased in the first person plural: "Lord, to whom can we go? You have the words of eternal life. We have come to believe and know that you are the Holy One of God" (John 6:68-69). Peter speaks on behalf of the Twelve. His confession articulates their belief—eventually the faith of the entire Johannine community—that Jesus alone is the revealer. Peter's confession of faith anticipates Jesus' own self-revelation as the one whom the Father has sanctified (John 10:36).

As is the case in the Synoptic tradition, Jesus responds to this confession of faith by speaking about the hard reality of his passion and death.[7] The focus of the Johannine Jesus' response is on the Twelve: "Did I not choose you, the Twelve? Yet one of you is a devil" (John 6:70). Then, in a parenthetical remark so characteristic of the Fourth Gospel,[8] the evangelist then identifies "the devil" for the benefit of his readers: "He was speaking of Judas, the son of Simon Iscariot, for he, though one of the Twelve, was going to betray him" (John 6:71). The betrayer is none other than "one of the Twelve" (*heis ek tōn dōdeka*).

One of the Twelve has been singled out as the betrayer; another epitomizes the doubts of the Twelve after Jesus had been raised from the dead (John 20:24).[9] Simon Peter is never specifically identified as "one of the Twelve." In the second part of the Fourth Gospel (John 13–20), he pales in comparison with the Beloved Disciple.[10] Peter appears again with the Beloved Disciple in John 21, an epilogue to the Fourth Gospel. The narrative features the rehabilitation of Peter after his threefold denial of Jesus and Peter's commissioning as shepherd (John 21:15-17).[11] The commissioning echoes the self-revelatory image of Jesus as shepherd, suggesting

Peter's function in the early church[12] after the departure of Jesus.[13] The shepherd image[14] contrasts Peter's ecclesial role with his livelihood as a fisherman.

Reference to Peter as a fisherman appears in the Fourth Gospel only in the epilogue (John 21:1-14). The narrative focuses on a miraculous catch of fish[15] and the role of the Beloved Disciple as the one who recognizes the risen Lord. The setting of the narrative identifies a group of seven people who were together at the time of the incident: Simon Peter, Thomas called the Twin, Nathanael of Cana in Galilee, the sons of Zebedee, and two other disciples (John 21:2).

"We have come to believe and know that you are the Holy One of God" (John 6:69).

The group are identified as "disciples" (*mathētai*, John 21:1, 2) but not as "apostles," a term that the Fourth Evangelist resolutely avoids.[16] The Fourth Gospel does not speak of this select group of disciples as being at the origin of either the Samaritan mission (see John 4:28-30, 39-42) or the Gentile mission (John 10:16).

The epilogue to the Fourth Gospel contrasts the figure of the Beloved Disciple with that of Peter (John 21:7-8, 20-23), as does the body of the Gospel. The community from which the Gospel emerged—the "we" of the community sayings (John 1:14, 16; etc.)—appears to have been dependent on a tradition that derives from the witness given by that disciple (John 21:24). The Beloved Disciple is the hero of the community; hence, Brown's characterization of it as the "Community of the Beloved Disciple."

In postresurrection times this Johannine community was certainly distinct from and independent of Christians associated with memories of the Twelve and of their spokesperson Peter. The uniquely Johannine story of the call of the first disciples (John 1:35-51)[17] can be construed as a narrative account of the community's distant origins.[18] Leadership of the community is attributed to the Paraclete, and the Holy Spirit is given as a legacy of the departing Jesus (John 14:16, 26; 15:26-27; 16:7-15).

The community's claim to have benefitted from the witness of the Beloved Disciple permitted the development of both a Christology and an ecclesiology different from the Christology and the ecclesiology of postresurrection Christians who principally benefited from the memory of Peter and the Twelve. Brown designated these groups of Christians as "apostolic churches" notwithstanding the evangelist's own reluctance to use the word "apostle."

The Farewell Discourse(s)

Almost one quarter of the Fourth Gospel, John 13–17, has the literary form of a farewell discourse.[19] The nature of the genre is such that literary compositions in this form speak about those who have been left behind by a departing hero. The farewell addresses attributed to Jesus and to Paul by Luke (Luke 22:24-38; Acts 20:18-35)[20] have much to say about Luke's ecclesiology, especially with regard to his view of leadership in the church. The Second Epistle of Paul to Timothy reflects on the ministry of Paul and the task of Timothy in much the same way. Thus, it is to be expected that the farewell discourse chapters in the Fourth Gospel will also have much to say about the community that the departing Jesus has left behind.

Among the important ecclesiological notions expressed in the discourse are the idea of leadership as service, the coming of the Advocate, the bond of mutual love, and the unity of the community. The setting of this Gospel's farewell discourse is a meal[21] that took place prior to Passover, just before Jesus' departure for the Kidron Valley garden, where his betrayal and arrest would occur (John 18:1). During the course of the supper, as the story is told, Jesus doffed his outer garment and proceeded to wash his disciples' feet. The ever-blustery Peter would have none of it. Jesus overrode his objections, but Peter continued to misunderstand what was happening (John 13:9).[22]

The farewell discourse(s) begin(s) in earnest after this narrative introduction. Jesus speaks to his fellow diners about the meaning of his gesture: "You also ought to wash one another's feet. For I have set you an example, that you also should do as I have done to you. Very truly, I tell you, servants (*doulos*) are not greater than their master (*tou kyriou*), nor are messengers (*apostolos*[23]) greater than the one who sent them (*tou pempsantos*)" (John 13:14b-16). The proverbial saying[24] appears again, in even clearer reference to Jesus' impending death, in the second part of the farewell discourse

(John 15:20). This exhortation on leadership as self-sacrificing service recalls a similar exhortation in the farewell discourse of Luke 22:24-38, especially verse 27.

Jesus' promise of the Spirit (John 14:16-17, 26; 15:26-27; 16:7-15)[25] is another important element in Johannine ecclesiology. Farewell discourses generally speak about who is to be in charge once the departing hero has left. In Christian parlance, such discourses can be said to address the issue of succession in ministry. In the Fourth Gospel, Jesus is succeeded by the Spirit. Like Jesus, the Spirit is a revealer sent by the Father; the Spirit is the teacher par excellence (John 14:26; 16:13). The Spirit is, in the words of the Johannine Jesus, "another advocate": "I will ask the Father, and he will give you another Advocate (*allon paraklēton*) to be with you forever" (John 14:16). There is a tandem relationship between Jesus and the other "Advocate,"[26] a name given to the Spirit insofar as the Spirit is the one who continues the ministry of Jesus.

As Jesus is "the truth"[27] (John 14:6), the Advocate is "the Spirit of truth" (John 14:17). The Spirit is to guide the disciples into all truth (John 16:13): "The Advocate, the Holy Spirit whom the Father will send in my name, will teach you everything, and remind you of all that I have said to you" (John 14:26). After Jesus' departure, the Advocate is the source of teaching and anamnesis. The Advocate gives witness on behalf of Jesus; the disciples are to do likewise (John 15:26-27). The Advocate glorifies Jesus and communicates what is of Jesus to the disciples (John 16:14-15).

Like Jesus, the Advocate is neither known to the world[28] nor accepted by the world (John 14:17; cf. 1:9-10). There is opposition between the world and the Advocate, just as there was between Jesus and the world. The Advocate, petitioned by Jesus and sent by the Father, is given to the disciples of Jesus for the dual task of bearing witness to Jesus and of confronting the "world" in which they are to live (John 15:18-19). "When he comes," the departing Jesus announces, "he will prove the world wrong about sin and righteousness and judgment" (John 16:8).[29]

One element of Jesus' legacy to the disciples is his gift of peace (John 14:27). Another is his gift of the new commandment: "I give you a new commandment that you love one another. Just as I have loved you, you also should love one another" (John 13:34; cf. John 15:12).[30] The mutual love of the disciples is their characteristic feature. Their mutual love is a mark of recognition, the mark of the Johannine community. Mutual love is the mark of the Johannine "church": "By this everyone will know that you are my disciples, if you have love for one another" (John 13:35).

Considered from the standpoint of the literary genre of its context, the new commandment of the departing Jesus is an exhortation to unity.[31] It is a hortatory utterance urging the disciples to stay together after Jesus returns to the Father. The unity and togetherness demanded by the command is a characteristic of the farewell discourse genre, which frequently pleads for unity among those who are left behind. What distinguishes Jesus' command from parallel literary exhortations and from its biblical antecedent (Lev 19:18)[32] is what makes it new. The commandment is new because the disciples of Jesus are to love one another as Jesus himself had loved them.

The love command's comparative phrase, "just as I have loved you," implies a great deal more than mere example. Jesus loved the disciples as the Father loved him (John 15:9). The Father's love for Jesus is the source of everything that he has and the source of his mission (John 3:35; 5:20). Jesus abides in the Father's love (John 15:10); the disciples are to abide in Jesus' love (John 15:9). A twofold chain of relationships is involved. There is a chain of commandment and a chain of indwelling. The two chains are interrelated. The disciples of Jesus are to love one another as Jesus, who loved them as the Father had loved him, loved them.[33] From the other perspective, the disciples who love one another abide in Jesus just as Jesus abides in the Father.

The mutual love that the disciples have for one another is the visible mark of their unity. It is also the means by which they abide in Jesus and in the Father. This indwelling is the ultimate reality of the community, the Johannine church. It is the object of Jesus' prayer: "I ask (erōtō) not only on behalf of these, but also on behalf of those who will believe in me through their word, that they may all be one. As you, Father, are in me and I am in you, may they also be in us, so that the world may believe that you have sent me" (John 17:20-21; see John 17:11).[34]

Jesus' prayer continues with a petition for this mutual indwelling: ". . . that they may be one, as we are one, I in them and you in me, that they may become completely one, so that the world may know that you have sent me and have loved them even as you have loved me" (John 17:22b-23). The Greek phrase translated "that they may be completely one" (hōsin teteleiōmenoi eis hen) implies that the Father (God) is the agent who brings about the complete unity of the disciples.

Jesus' prayer for the unity of the community means that the unity of the disciples effected by the Father transcends the apparent individualism of the disciples' relationship with Jesus. Called individually (John 1:29-51; cf. 20:16), the disciples have a profound unity that only the Father can give. Their unity is of another order than even the unity of the sectarian community at Qumran, which considered itself a community, a unity (*yahad*). The term may well have been the Qumran community's self-designation:[35] "The Community shall set apart a holy house for Aaron, in order to form a most holy community" (1QS 9:5). They are to "constitute a Community in law[36] and possessions" (1QS 5:2). The unity of the Johannine community is of another sort; it is the work of the Father, who responds to Jesus' prayer.

Christological Ecclesiology

Johan Ferreira considers that John 17:20-26, with its prayer for unity, functions as a programmatic statement concerning the existence of the community.[37] He identifies as central to John 17 the notion of glory, with its various implications for Johannine Christology. The glorification of Jesus is effected by the Father in Jesus' death; the glorification continues to happen in the history of the Johannine community.[38] Jesus' glorification is realized in his authority and power over all creation (*exousian pasēs sarkos*) to give eternal life to all whom the Father has given him. Eternal life is given to those chosen[39] by the Father and by Jesus, his agent, in their unity with one another.[40] In this way, the unity of the disciples for which the departing Jesus prayed is linked to his glorification on the cross.[41]

Those chosen by Jesus have not been taken out of the world, nor will they be. They do not belong to the world; they belong to Jesus and to the Father (John 17:6, 11, 24). Those chosen by Jesus are God's own people, God's holy ones, the saints. Jesus prays for their sanctification: "Sanctify them (*hagiason autous*) in the truth.... As you have sent me into the world, so I have sent them into the world" (John 17:17-18). This singularly Johannine notion of holiness links sanctification to the mission of Jesus. The mission of Jesus is continued in the mission of the chosen and sanctified people for whom Jesus prays. Ferreira concludes: "from the requests in vv. 20 to 23 it appears that the community's *raison de être*[42] is to continue the sending of the Son."

The community of the Beloved Disciple has been graced with its reception of the Word of God. The idea is beautifully stated in the prologue to the Fourth Gospel: "And the Word became flesh and lived among us, and we have seen his glory, the glory as of a father's only son, full of grace and truth" (John 1:14). Jesus revealed to his disciples both the name of the Father (John 17:6, 26) and the words that he himself had received from the Father (John 17:8, 14). "For John," Ernst Käsemann writes, "the Church is basically and exclusively the fellowship of people who hear Jesus' word and believe in him; in short, it is the community under the Word."[43]

The Johannine author offered an evocative figure to express the life-giving and fruit-producing unity between Jesus and his disciples: the image of the true vine (John 15:1-11). The image evokes the biblical use of this figure to speak of Israel (Isa 27:2-6; Ezek 19:10-11; Ps 80:8-19; Qoh 24:27; *2 Bar.* 39:7).[44] In the farewell address Jesus explained his use of the image as it applied to him and his disciples: those who abide in Jesus are those in whom his word abides (John 15:7). Those

> *The disciple is one who has come to Jesus through the witness of someone else, who has an encounter with Jesus, and then bears witness to Jesus to yet another person. The pattern of discipleship is a chain of witness.*

who abide in his love are those who keep his commandments, of which there is apparently only one, the commandment to love one another as he had loved them (John 15:10, 12).

The Fourth Gospel's manner of presenting the death and resurrection of Jesus results in a uniquely Johannine configuration of the domestic motifs of the early church.[45] Thus, the anointing of Jesus in the house at Bethany with three family members present (John 12:1-8) is a proleptic image of the post-Easter experience of the household of God.[46] In the scene of the mother of Jesus and the Beloved Disciple at the foot of the cross (John 19:25-27), kinship relationships are radically transformed. The Beloved Disciple is effectively described as Jesus' sibling. With the glorification of Jesus in his death and resurrection, the disciples become Jesus' brothers and sisters (John 20:17).[47]

Mission and Ritual

The basic insights of Johannine ecclesiology are essentially expressed in the farewell discourse, in which the departing Jesus presents a vision of the disciples whom he is to leave behind as he returns to the Father. On the whole this vision is innocent of the practical consequences of ecclesial existence. It would, however, be shortsighted to assume that the Fourth Gospel is lacking with regard to the church's mission and its ritual. As always, however, the evangelist treats these ecclesial realities differently from the way in which the Synoptics and the Pauline literature describe them.

With regard to mission, it is to be noted that in the Fourth Gospel the call to discipleship typically culminates in evangelization. According to the Johannine pattern, the disciple is one who has come to Jesus through the witness of someone else, who has an encounter with Jesus, and then bears witness to Jesus to yet another person. The pattern of discipleship is a chain of witness.

The motif is graphically described in John 1:29-51. Andrew heard the testimony of John, goes to meet Jesus, and then testifies about Jesus to Simon Peter, his brother (John 1:35-42). Jesus finds Philip, who follows Jesus; then Philip testifies to Nathanael (John 1:43-46). Similarly, Jesus meets the Samaritan woman. After the engaging conversation that the woman had with Jesus, the woman abandons her water jug—a sign of discipleship comparable to Peter, Andrew, James, and John leaving their nets and Levi leaving the tax collector's table. Then she bears witness to the inhabitants of the city (John 4:7-42). In all these examples, those who accepted the testimony about Jesus from someone else then came to Jesus, thus experiencing their own personal encounter with him.

A conversation between Jesus and his disciples (John 4:31-38), one interlude in the long episode of the Samaritan woman, focuses on the idea of mission.[48] Jesus invites the disciples to share in his mission: "But I tell you, look around you and see how the fields are ripe for harvesting" (John 4:35). This proverb is an invitation to mission. "The sending of the disciples," writes J. Eugene Botha, "is de facto included in their association with Jesus."[49]

The Gospel narratives recounting Jesus' resurrection appearances typically feature (1) the recognition of Jesus (thus, Luke 24:13-35), (2) a sending into mission (thus, Matt 28:16-20; cf. Mark 16:14-18), or (3) both motifs (thus, Luke 24:36-49; John 20:11-18). The two motifs appear in the twin accounts of Jesus' appearance to his disciples cowering behind locked doors for fear of "the Jews" (John 20:19-23). The account of the appearance to the disciples in the absence of Thomas (John 20:19-23) focuses on the mission of the disciples: "As the Father has sent me, so I send you"

(John 20:21). The parallel story features the recognition of Jesus by Thomas, the epitome of the disciples' doubt (John 20:26-29). His confessional recognition of the risen Jesus is summed up in the words "My Lord and my God" (John 20:28).

Each of the two narratives has something to say about the mission of the disciples. The first states that the risen Jesus sent the disciples into mission and gave them the gift of the Spirit[50] as he had promised during the farewell discourse. The Spirit empowers the disciples to bear witness to Jesus, thus continuing his mission. The account of the appearance of the risen Jesus to the disciples with Thomas present concludes with a beatitude: "Blessed are those who have not seen and yet have come to believe" (John 20:29). The beatitude implicitly suggests a mission of the disciples: there are those who come to faith when Jesus is no longer physically present in a way that he can be seen.

The Johannine beatitude hearkens back to John 20:23.[51] Through baptism the gift of the Spirit "is given in turn to all believers, so the power to forgive sins is meant to affect all believers."[52] The gift of the Spirit to the disciples speaks of baptism allusively.[53] The meaning of the baptismal ritual was also elucidated during Jesus' conversation with Nicodemus (John 3:1-10). Jesus told this leader of the Jews: "I tell you, no one can enter the Kingdom of God without being born of water and the Spirit" (John 3:5). Baptism, as the narrative suggests, brings about entrance into the Kingdom. It entails being born from above, being born of the Spirit (John 3:3, 6).

Just as the Fourth Gospel does not speak about church organization[54] but rather ponders the profound meaning of discipleship; so the Fourth Gospel does not speak about church ritual. Rather, it focuses on the significance of the ritual. As this is the case with baptism, so it is the case with the eucharist. The meaning of the eucharist appears in an account of Jesus' discourse in the synagogue of Capernaum. The discourse takes the form of a midrash on Ps 78:24, "He gave them bread from heaven to eat" (John 6:31). Commenting on the scripture, Jesus explains: "Those who eat my flesh and drink my blood have eternal life, and I will raise them up on the last day; for my flesh is true food and my blood is true drink. Those who eat my flesh and drink my blood abide in me, and I in them" (John 6:54-56).

The Fourth Gospel has still less to say about forms of ritual and worship apart from baptism and eucharist. Jesus' comment to the Samaritan woman remains, nonetheless, generally apropos: "The hour is coming, and is now here, when the true worshipers will worship the Father in spirit and truth" (John 4:23).

Division within the Community

The Fourth Gospel evinces a notion of the church as a community whose members were one with one another, one with Jesus, and one with the Father. The Johannine Epistles give evidence that the unity of the community did not, however, long endure. Some people left the community (1 John 2:19). A man named Diotrephes, "God-nurtured," was at odds with the elder. He prevented people from welcoming other Christians and was able to expel some people from the assembly (*ekklēsia*, 3 John 10).[55] "These Epistles," writes Raymond Brown, are "the record of a theological life-and-death struggle within a Community at the end of the first century."[56] The principal areas of conflict were Christology,[57] ethics, eschatology, and pneumatology, but they included no little personal conflict.

The existence of different Johannine house churches, perhaps even in one city, may have been a contributing factor in these conflicts,[58] especially since the conflicts were manifest in the way that Johannine Christians extended or refused to extend hospitality.[59] Thus, the author of 2 John warns those to whom he is writing to keep the commandments of the Father and to be on their guard against deceivers (2 John 4-9). He concludes his exhortation by saying: "Do not receive into the house (*eis oikian*) or welcome anyone who comes to you and does not bring this teaching; for to welcome is to participate in the evil deeds of such a person" (2 John 10-11).[60] In contrast with Diotrephes, however, who refuses to welcome other Christians and does everything within his power to prevent others from doing so, the author 3 John commends the beloved Gaius: "You do well faithfully whatever you do for the friends (*tous adelphous*), even though they are strangers (*xenous*) to you" (3 John 5).

The domestic setting of the Johannine house churches is apparent in the two short letters known as 2 John and 3 John. The former speaks of the house and of hospitality; the latter speaks of hospitality and of "the church" (3 John 6, 9, 10). Both texts make use of kinship language, "children" (*tekna*) in 2 John 1, 4; "brothers and sisters" (*adelphoi*) in 3 John 5, 10.[61]

In 3 John, the elder praises Gaius, who is commended for his hospitality to strangers, particularly missionaries whom he is to send on their way with supplies for their journey. These traveling missionaries are to be supported by the community in their journey on behalf of Christ. By supporting the missionaries the members become "coworkers with the truth" (*synergoi tē alētheia*, 3 John 8), a uniquely Johannine description of those who physically support the proclamation of the truth.

The author of these short letters designates himself as the elder (*ho presbyteros*,[62] 2 John 1; 3 John 1). Writing the letters, he has assumed responsibility for addressing problems in the fractured community. Scholars have debated as to whether the term that he used to describe himself has the same connotations as does the use of the word in Acts and the Pastoral Epistles. Using Irenaeus, *Against Heresies* 4.27.1, as an argument, Raymond Brown opined that in these Johannine texts, the "elder" designated a second-generation figure who served as a transmitter of the tradition that came down from the first generation. His influence was that of a prophetic witness rather than that of an authority based on organizational structure.[63]

> "The marriage of the Lamb has come, and his bride has made herself ready" (Rev 19:7-8).

A Vision

In a visionary description of the new Jerusalem,[64] the Johannine seer portrayed the holy city as a large walled city (Rev 21:10-14).[65] The "twelve names of the twelve apostles of the Lamb" are inscribed on the twelve foundations of the wall. The author's apocalyptic imagery unites several important elements of early Christian ecclesiology, especially the notions of the importance of the Twelve, the apostolic foundation of the church, and the idea of the church as a unit of construction. Wilfred Harrington suggests that the image offers "an important and essential balance to Matt 16:17-19—the 'Petrine text.' Peter may be the 'rock'; the Twelve are the *foundation*."[66]

The construction imagery in the seer's vision contrasts with the immediately preceding image of the new Jerusalem as a "bride prepared for her husband" (Rev 21:2). "Come," the angel said to the seer, "I will show you the bride, the wife of the Lamb" (Rev 21:9). The marriage, announced with the cry of a heavenly alleluia, has already taken place. The multitudes have proclaimed: "Let us rejoice and exult and give him the glory, for the marriage of the Lamb has come, and his bride has made herself ready; to her it has been granted to be clothed with fine linen, bright and pure" (Rev 19:7-8).[67]

The double image of the city of God and bride of the Lamb has antecedents in the biblical tradition. Prophetic literature often portrayed Jerusalem or Zion as a woman (Isa 1:8; Jer 4:31; 4 Ezra 9:38-47). In the tradition the city is an ambivalent image. Sometimes a city serves as a symbolic representation of evil; at other times a city is a symbolic representation of divine blessing.[68] The Book of Revelation uses the imagery of cities to contrast Babylon, the city and the great harlot (Rev 17:1-6), with the holy city and bride of the Lamb. A similar contrast between these two cities appears elsewhere in apocalyptic literature.[69]

The double image of the woman/city enabled the author of the Book of Revelation not only to contrast the two cities but also to describe the end-time community in its relationship with God and Christ. The holy city and bride is the center of God's new world and fully united with its Lord. In this book the number twelve is a symbol of the perfection of God's people in the end-time. Those who are sealed out of the twelve tribes of the people of Israel number 144,000 (Rev 7:4-8). These 144,000[70] belong to God and Christ; the names of the Lamb and his Father are written on their foreheads (Rev 14:1). The 144,000 redeemed people sing a new song to the Lord in the presence of the Lamb (Rev 14:1, 3). In sum, Roloff notes, the church is "the people of the twelve tribes, renewed at the end of time, for whom the promises of Israel apply."[71]

Discussion and Study Questions

1. What is the real theological significance of the Fourth Gospel's radically new and different ecclesiology?

2. What does the Johannine love command, "Love one another as I have loved you," mean for the members of the church at the present time?

3. Does the church continue to experience a tension between its ideal self and its real self?

4. Division within the church is as much a reality now as it was at the time of the Johannine community. How can the church realistically deal with division in its midst?

Epilogue

Little more need be said about the vision of the church that arises from a reading of those early Christian texts which the Christian churches consider to be formative and normative. The texts give evidence of the earliest roots of the church in Jesus' ministry, his call to discipleship, and the selection of the Twelve, among whom Simon emerges as spokesperson and eventual leader. These texts show how some of the oldest churches came into being as a response to the preaching of the risen Lord by Paul and the other apostles.

The more recent of those normative documents show that the early Christian communities were concerned about their roots. They portray Peter continuing the ministry of Jesus among the Jews, the church in Jerusalem devoted to the teaching of the apostles, Timothy and Titus succeeding in the Pauline kerygma, and those endowed with the Spirit–Paraclete continuing the mission after the return of Jesus to the Father whence he came.

Sometimes the texts of the New Testament evince practical concerns. Adequate leadership within the church was a matter of concern from the very beginning. Even in the smallest assemblies of those who gathered as church in a home, there were those who presided, those who were in charge and those who admonished. Spirit-endowed prophets proclaimed the word. Within the Pauline tradition, alongside the traditional Jewish notions of elder and shepherd, a different terminology developed to speak of those who led and served the church. They were called overseers and servants. Appropriate qualities were eventually identified as qualities or qualifications which leaders and helpers were expected to possess. The

147

Pastoral Epistles show signs of a process of scrutiny and of a commissioning ritual for those who would serve the church as its leaders.

The church had its characteristic activities, the ritual washing as an entrance rite and a memorial meal as a celebration of fellowship. Those who came together were joined by bonds that united them as brothers and sisters, united in a shared faith and outreaching love. Conscious of their identity as God's holy people, the call to sanctity, these communities recalled the kerygma and were devoted to the scriptures.

On the whole, as the communities of believers developed from various localized movements to groups that had to find their place and establish their niche within the Greco-Roman world, they patterned themselves after existing social structures. The model that is most widely attested in the New Testament is the model of the church as a household gathering. From the pages of Matthew, however, emerges a view of church patterned after the Jewish synagogue with emphasis on catechesis under the aegis of a legendary principal rabbi.

In different ways the New Testament texts emphasize the unity of the local church, yet they also manifest the local church's need to be in union with other communities of believers. On the micro-level there were occasions when various household gatherings came together. On the meso-level there was some interaction among communities of believers, evidenced in phrases such as "the churches that are in Judea" or the "churches of Galatia" as well as in the significance of hospitality as a Christian virtue. On the macro-level, the union between the Gentile churches and the mother church in Jerusalem was experienced in the Jerusalem community's Spirit-inspired approbation of the Gentile mission and the collection on behalf of the saints in Jerusalem.

The community is a gathering or assembly, a house or household, a building or temple, a field or body, a flock and a community, a koinōnia. Each of these images says something about the church; yet no one of them says everything about the church.

Reflection on the unity among the communities of believers, particularly insofar as it transcended the ethnic divide between Jew and Gentile, gave rise to a new and different appropriation of Paul's ecclesial images.

The image of a local community as a gathering and a body yielded the idea of a universal "church" and of the "body" of which the cosmic Christ was the head. To these Pauline images can be added the Johannine image of the "one flock and one shepherd."

Earlier strata of the New Testament use a variety of images to speak of believers. The community is a gathering or assembly, a house or household, a building or temple, a field or body, a flock and a community, a *koinōnia*. Each of these images says something about the church; yet no one of them says everything about the church. Each image provides the reader of the New Testament with an angle of vision; none of them provides the complete picture of the transcendent whole.

Ultimately the New Testament is a mosaic of different images of the church, not only in the various metaphors that are used to describe communities of believers but also in the different ways that the inspired authors experienced and spoke of the church. For them the community of believers was the assembly of God, so real and yet to be realized.

Notes

Chapter One

1. Some interpreters hold that Christian communities in Lystra and Derbe were among those churches in Galatia to whom Paul wrote his Letter to the Galatians.

2. For Jerusalem, see Acts 8:1, 3; Antioch, Acts 11:26; 13:1; 14:27, 15:3; Lystra, Acts 14:23; Derbe, Acts 14:23; Ephesus, Acts 20:17, 28; Syria and Cilicia, Acts 15:41; 16:5.

3. The document traditionally known as 2 Thessalonians was not in fact written by Paul. See Raymond F. Collins, *Letters That Paul Did Not Write: The Epistle to the Hebrews and the Pauline Pseudepigrapha* (GNS 28; Wilmington, Del.: Glazier, 1988) 209-41.

4. *IG* 10.2.1.5-7, 11.

5. On the relationship among "holy ones" (*hagioi*), "chosen ones" (*eklektoi*), and "people who are called" (*klētoi*), see Gerhard Delling, "Merkmale der Kirche nach dem Neuen Testament," *NTS* 13 (1966-67) 297-316, 305. In English versions of the New Testament *hagioi* is sometimes translated "holy ones"; at other times it is translated "saints." The differences owe to the Germanic ("holy ones") and Romance ("saints") roots of the English language. The phenomenon can also be observed in other words derived from *hagi-*, thus, "holiness" or "sanctification," "make holy" or "sanctify."

6. See also 2 Thess 1:1.

7. First Thessalonians is the only one of Paul's uncontested letters addressed to a group identified as the *inhabitants* of a place, "Thessalonians," the *nomen gentilicum*, rather than by a prepositional phrase naming the place itself (see Rom 1:7; 1 Cor 1:2; 2 Cor 1:1; Gal 1:2; Phil 1:1; cf. Phlm 1-2).

8. This is the only time in the extant correspondence that Paul refers to a church as being "in God."

9. The pairing recurs in the wish prayer of 3:11 and the references to the parousia in 3:13 and 5:23. See also 2:14, 5:9, 18.

10. Of the four times that Paul identifies God as Father in 1 Thessalonians (1:1, 3; 3:11, 13), 1 Thess 1:1 is the only time that Paul does not add a qualifying "our" (*hēmōn*) to Father. The author of the pseudepigraphic 2 Thessalonians "rectifies" this lacuna (see 2 Thess 1:1).

11. The titular designation "Christ" is an English word formed from a Greek verbal adjective meaning "anointed." "Messiah" is the English word from the similar Hebrew verbal adjective meaning "anointed." As a title for Jesus, "Christ" would have little meaning in

the Greek-speaking world. Among Jewish-Christians, however, the title "Messiah" would have evoked expectations of God's restoration of his people. In Hellenistic Christian usage, the title was represented by "Christ" with the result that "Jesus Christ" virtually served as a two-word name for Jesus.

12. Paul also uses the term in Rom 9:11; 11:5, 7, 28. See also 2 Pet 1:10.

13. The Greek text has the noun rather than the readable paraphrase of the NRSV, "that he has chosen you."

14. See Karl P. Donfried, *Paul, Thessalonica, and Early Christianity* (Grand Rapids: Eerdmans, 2002) 146-47.

15. On the importance of "the gospel" in 1 Thessalonians, see Donfried, *Early Christianity*, 148-50.

16. See 1 Thess 1:14; 3:5.

17. Paul uses the term elsewhere only in Rom 12:10. See also Heb 13:1; 1 Pet 1:22; 2 Pet 1:7.

18. See Wayne A. Meeks, *The First Urban Christians: The Social World of the Apostle Paul* (New Haven: Yale University Press, 1983) 85-86.

19. See Mikael Tellbe, *Paul Between Synagogue and State: Christians, Jews, and Civic Authorities in 1 Thessalonians, Romans, and Philippians* (ConBNT 34; Stockholm: Almqvist & Wiksell, 2001) 133.

20. See 1 Thess 1:4; 2:1, 9, 14, 17; 3:7; 4:1, 10, 13; 5:1, 4, 12, 14, 25.

21. 1 Corinthians contains twenty-one such uses of "brothers and sisters" (*adelphoi*). See 1 Cor 1:10, 11, 26; 2:1; 3:1; 4:6; 7:24, 29; 10:1; 11:33; 12:1; 14:6, 20, 26, 39; 15:1, 31, 50, 58; 16:15, 20. On the significance of this language, see Mary Kate Birge, *The Language of Belonging: A Rhetorical Analysis of Kinship Language in First Corinthians* (CBET 31; Louvain: Peeters, 2002).

22. See Abraham J. Malherbe, "God's New Family in Thessalonica," in L. M. White and O. L. Yarbrough, eds., *The Social World of the First Christians: Essays in Honor of W. A. Meeks* (Minneapolis: Fortress, 1995) 116-25, 125.

23. In the opinion of some commentators, the third member of Paul's triad, "with full conviction" (*plērophoria*, 1 Thess 1:5), suggests that Paul's preaching of the gospel was convincing. In my judgment it is preferable to take the Greek word, a rare word (Col 2:2; Heb 6:11; 10:22) which first appears in Greek literature in this letter, as parallel with "power" and "Spirit." On my reading of the text, the Greek might be better rendered as "in full force" or "with full certainty" (cf. LSJ). See the discussion in Raymond F. Collins, *The Birth of the New Testament: The Origin and Development of the First Christian Generation* (New York: Crossroad, 1993) 41, 235-36.

24. In the biblical tradition Israel is God's holy people because it has been chosen by God. See A. Asting, *Die Heiligkeit im Urchristentum* (FRLANT 46; Göttingen: Vandenhoeck & Ruprecht, 1930) 133-51.

25. See LSJ and *TLNT* 3:242-43.

26. The charism of the discernment of spirits follows immediately after the gift of prophecy in the list of charismatic gifts in 1 Cor 12:10.

27. See 1 Corinthians 12–14.

28. The expression comes from the subtitle of Abraham J. Malherbe's *Paul and the Thessalonians: The Philosophic Tradition of Pastoral Care* (Philadelphia: Fortress, 1987). The idea echoes throughout his commentary on the Thessalonian correspondence, *The Letters to the Thessalonians* (AB 32B; New York: Doubleday, 2000).

29. The Greek verb is *eidenai*, literally, "to know."

30. The number of polytarchs (*polytarchai*; see Acts 17:6) varied from three to seven, though five may have been the usual complement.

31. Paul does not give any specific indication as to how these people emerged as leaders of the assembly. It is unlikely that they were chosen by Paul or that they had been elected. It is more likely that they were leaders of the household which hosted the gathering.

32. C. Schuler, "The Macedonian Politarchs," *CP* 55 (1990) 90-100, 90, 98-99, n. 9.

33. Perhaps Jason, whose house had been attacked by the mob that was looking for Paul, was a leader of the Thessalonian community. Some commentators opine that Jason is presented as a Christian in Luke's account, Acts 17:6-9.

34. Earlier Paul had used words with the same root to speak of the Thessalonians' labor of love (1 Thess 1:3) and of his own manual labor (1 Thess 2:9).

35. See Herodotus, *Histories* 3.82; Thucydides, *History of the Peloponnesian War* 2.65; 3.70; Lysias 13.7; cf. Aristophanes, *Wasps* 5.419; Josephus, *Ant.* 8.12,3 §300; Justin, *Apology* 1.67.

36. See Joseph A. Fitzmyer, *Romans* (AB 33; New York: Doubleday, 1993) 649.

37. *Epistolary Types* 7. See Abraham J. Malherbe, *Ancient Epistolary Theorists* (SBLSBS 19; Atlanta: Scholars Press, 1988) 35.

38. On the influence of the liturgy in 1 Thessalonians, see my "1 Thess and the Liturgy of the Early Church," *BTB* 10 (1980) 51-64, reprinted in *Studies on the First Letter to the Thessalonians* (BETL 66; Louvain: University Press/Peeters, 1984) 136-53.

Chapter Two

1. De Vos suggests that the home at Thessalonica would have been of the small *insula*-apartment type. See Craig Steven de Vos, *Church and Community Conflicts: The Relationships of the Thessalonian, Corinthian, and Philipppian Churches with Their Civic Communities* (SBLDS 168; Atlanta: Scholars Press, 1999) 148-50.

2. One of the rare contexts in which the two Greek terms are distinguished from one another is Attic law, where *oikos* was used to designate a person's estate or property while *oikia* was restricted to the building in which one lived.

3. See the discussions in Joseph A. Fitzmyer, *The Letter to Philemon* (AB 34C; New York: Doubleday, 2000) 9-11; Raymond E. Brown, *An Introduction to the New Testament* (ABRL; New York: Doubleday, 1997) 507-8.

4. Cf. 2 Tim 4:19.

5. The NRSV renders the Greek *aspasasthe* as "give my greetings." The Greek verb is translated by a simple "greet" in Rom 16:3, 5.

6. See Raymond F. Collins, *Letters That Paul Did Not Write: The Epistle to the Hebrews and the Pauline Pseudepigrapha* (GNS 28; Wilmington, Del.: Glazier, 1988) 171-89; Brown, *Introduction*, 610-17; Margaret Y. MacDonald, *Colossians, Ephesians* (SP 17; Collegeville, Minn.: Liturgical Press, 2000) 6-9.

7. Nympha is not otherwise mentioned in the New Testament. She was probably a widow. With regard to her and the church in her house, see Florence M. Gillman, "Nympha," *ABD* 4:1162; MacDonald, *Colossians*, 182-83, 188.

8. In the Acts of the Apostles Luke uses her diminutive name, Priscilla (Acts 18:2, 18, 26).

9. See Suetonius, *Lives of the Caesars: Claudius* 25.4 and the discussion in Mikael Tellbe, *Paul Between Synagogue and State: Christians, Jews, and Civic Authorities in 1 Thes-*

salonians, Romans, and Philippians (ConBNT 34; Stockholm: Almqvist & Wiksell, 2001) 152-56. For the opinion that the expulsion took place in 41 C.E., rather than in 49 C.E. as is commonly thought, see Jerome Murphy-O'Connor, *St. Paul's Corinth: Texts and Archaeology* (GNS 6; Wilmington, Del.: Glazier, 1983) 130-39.

10. See Acts 18; Rom 16:3-5; 1 Cor 16:19.

11. It may be that the task assigned to Phoebe (Rom 16:1-2) was to gather provisions for Paul's anticipated trip to Spain. See Robert Jewett, "Paul, Phoebe and the Spanish Mission," in Jacob Neusner et al., eds., *The Social World of Formative Christianity and Judaism: Essays in Tribute to Howard Clark Kee* (Philadelphia: Fortress, 1988) 142-61; see further the discussion of the role of Phoebe in Florence M. Gillman, *Women Who Knew Paul* (Zacchaeus Studies: New Testament; Collegeville, Minn.: Liturgical Press, 1992) 59-66; Joseph A. Fitzmyer, *Romans* (AB 33; New York: Doubleday, 1993) 731.

12. See Ronald F. Hock, *The Social Context of Paul's Ministry: Tentmaking and Apostleship* (Philadelphia: Fortress, 1980).

13. Fitzmyer renders the Greek *proselabonto auton* ("they took him aside," NRSV) as "they took him home." See Joseph A. Fitzmyer, *The Acts of the Apostles* (AB 31; New York: Doubleday, 1998) 636 and note, p. 639.

14. See also Acts 16:40.

15. In the mid-twentieth century there was an important discussion, especially among German interpreters, as to whether the baptism of a whole household implied that small children were also baptized. Among others, Joachim Jeremias and Kurt Aland came down on different sides of the debate. See, for example, Joachim Jeremias, *Infant Baptism in the First Four Centuries* (Library of History and Doctrine; Philadelphia: Westminster, 1962), 19-24; and *The Origins of Infant Baptism: A Further Study in Reply to Kurt Aland* (Studies in Historical Theology; London: SCM, 1963). The issue of infant baptism is a moot question; what is more important is that entire household units were baptized when the head of the household embraced the Christian faith.

16. See Murphy-O'Connor, *St. Paul's Corinth*, 153-56.

17. See Fitzmyer, *Romans*, 742.

18. Robert Banks makes the point that the adjective would have been superfluous if the church at Corinth regularly came together in that configuration. See Robert Banks, *Paul's Idea of Community: The Early House Churches in Their Historical Setting* (Exeter: Paternoster; Grand Rapids: Eerdmans, 1980) 38.

19. See Murphy-O'Connor, *St. Paul's Corinth*, 156-58.

20. The Greek text of 1 Cor 11:20 is very clear that the gathering occurs in a single place (*epi to auto*). Many English translations omit an explicit translation of the prepositional phrase, including the RSV, NRSV, JB, and NJB. The Authorized Version (King James Version) translates it literally, "into one place." Today's English Version renders the phrase dynamically, "as a group." The NEB and REB give "as a congregation" as the translation of the phrase.

21. Note that Paul uses the compound verb "come together," *syn-erchomenein*, three times, that is, in verses 17, 18, and 20. Twice the verb recurs in the pericope's peroration (vv. 33-34a). In his writings Paul uses a number of compound words with the prefix *syn-*, "with." In nouns, the prefix often occurs as "co-" as in "coworker." Thus, the NRSV renders *synergē* as "coworker" in Phlm 1 but translates the plural, *synergoi* as "fellow workers" in Phlm 24. These compounds reflect the solidarity of Christians with Paul, with one another, and/or with Jesus. On coworker, see Rom 16:3, 9, 21; 1 Cor 3:9; 2 Cor 1:24; 8:23; Phil 2:25; 4:3; 1 Thess 3:2; Phlm 1, 24. Apart from Paul's use of the term, "coworker" appears

in the New Testament only in Col 4:11 and 3 John 8. See also the use of the cognate verb in 1 Cor 16:16 and 2 Cor 6:1. See W. H. Ollrog, *Paulus und seine Mitarbeiter: Untersuchungen zu Theorie und Praxis der paulinischen Mission* (WMANT 50; Neukirchen-Vluyn: Neukirchener, 1979) 63-72.

22. See especially Panayotis Coutsoumpos, "Paul's Teaching of the Lord's Supper: A Socio-Historical Study of the Pauline Account of the Last Supper and Its Graeco-Roman Background," Ph.D. thesis, University of Sheffield, 1996. See also Dennis E. Smith, *From Symposium to Eucharist: The Banquet in the Early Christian World* (Minneapolis: Fortress, 2003).

23. See Plutarch, "Table Talk," *Moralia* 613F.

24. Luke 22:20 speaks of "the new covenant in my blood" and omits the eschatological reference.

25. Note the explanatory *gar*, "for."

26. Some of the church's early credal formulas focused only on the death of Jesus; others only on the resurrection; still others on both the death and resurrection. All three forms are found in the credal formulas of 1 Thessalonians, respectively 1 Thess 5:10, 1 Thess 1:10, and 1 Thess 4:14. In 1 Cor 11:26 Jesus' resurrection is evoked by Paul's use of the title "Lord." This, the most frequently used christological title in Paul's letters, was used by him in reference to the resurrection or the parousia. In Pauline theology the resurrection and the parousia are closely related to one another.

27. Note that the first two verbal forms are intensive compounds of the verb *krinein*, from which the third verb is derived.

28. See especially Gerd Theissen, *The Social Setting of Pauline Christianity: Essays on Corinth* (Philadelphia: Fortress, 1982), esp. 69-120, 145-74. The latter section, the fourth chapter of the book, originally appeared in German as "Soziale Integration und sakramentales Handeln: Eine Analyse von 1 Cor. 11:17-24," *NovT* 16 (1974) 179-206.

29. See 1 Cor 11:33.

30. Pliny described those who gave different qualities of wine to different kinds of people as acting in "a sordid manner" (*Epistles* 2.6).

31. Jude 12 refers to these Christian meals as "love feasts" (*agapais*). This terminology also appears in Ign. *Smyrn.* 8:2: "It is not permissible apart from the bishop either to baptize or to celebrate the love feast (*agapēn poiein*)." Some commentators have taken the appearance of the cognate verb in Ign. *Rom.* 7:3 and *Smyrn.* 7:1 as a reference to this celebration but the verb does not otherwise have this meaning.

Commenting on Ign. *Smyrn.* 7:1, Schoedel notes: "A possible key to this problem is the fact that the ancient love-feast (which must often have included the eucharist) served as an important agency for taking care of the needs of the poor including especially widows and orphans. In a very obvious way, then, to avoid the common meal was to avoid doing the works of love" (William R. Schoedel, *Ignatius of Antioch* [Hermeneia; Philadelphia: Fortress, 1985] 241-42.

32. See Benjamin Fiore, "'Covert Allusion' in 1 Corinthians 1-4," *CBQ* 47 (1985) 85-102.

33. See also the remark of Raymond E. Brown: "In a given town or city there may have been several house churches of Johannine Christians. It is a serious possibility, then, that the Gaius and Diotrephes of III John, although living in the same town, belonged to different Johannine churches" (*The Community of the Beloved Disciple: The Life, Loves, and Hates of an Individual Church in New Testament Times* [New York: Paulist, 1979] 98.

34. See also 1 Cor 1:2, "to the church of God that is in Corinth . . . together with all

those who in every place call on the name of our Lord Jesus Christ," and 2 Cor 1:1, "to the church of God that is in Corinth, including (*syn*) all the saints throughout Achaia." Commentators correctly indicate that the preposition is properly translated "with." Thus, for example, Victor P. Furnish, *II Corinthians* (AB 32A; Garden City: Doubleday, 1984) 100; and Jan Lambrecht, *Second Corinthians* (SP; Collegeville, Minn.: Liturgical Press, 1999) 18.

35. The issue of the meaning of "Galatia" in Paul's letter is treated in virtually all of the commentaries. See, for example, Frank J. Matera, *Galatians* (SP 9; Collegeville, Minn.: Liturgical Press, 1992) 19-26.

36. So F. F. Bruce, *The Epistle to the Galatians* (NICNT; Grand Rapids: Eerdmans, 1982) 74; Richard N. Longenecker, *Galatians* (WBC 41; Dallas: Word, 1990) 6; Matera, *Galatians*, 38.

37. See 1 Thess 4:9-10.

38. So, Hans Dieter Betz, *Galatians* (Hermeneia; Philadelphia: Fortress, 1979) 40.

39. See Wayne A. Meeks, *The First Urban Christians: The Social World of the Apostle Paul* (New Haven and London: Yale University Press, 1983) 63-72.

40. Paul does not explicitly state when the gathering in which men and women prayed and prophesied and the potluck during which the institution of the eucharist was recalled took place. 1 Cor 16:2 suggests that it took place on the first day of the week, the collection being a third activity that occurred during the gathering. See also Acts 20:7.

41. See Hans Dieter Betz, *2 Corinthians 8 and 9: A Commentary on Two Administrative Letters of the Apostle Paul* (Hermeneia; Philadelphia: Fortress, 1985).

Chapter Three

1. The introductory and stage-setting functions were continued in Paul's thanksgivings. The thanksgiving section of 1 Corinthians, 1 Cor 1:4-9, draws attention both to the gifts that were given to the Corinthians (see 1 Corinthians 12–14) and to the parousia (see 1 Corinthians 15).

2. The construction of the phrase "the church that is in Corinth" resembles an expression in Rom 16:1, "the church at Cenchreae" (*tēs ekklēsias tēs en Kenchreias*), but this phrase from Romans lacks the verb. The verb is used in 1 Thess 2:14, "the churches of God . . . that are in Judea."

3. See Lucien Cerfaux, *The Church in the Theology of St. Paul* (New York: Herder, 1959) 95-117; Peter Stuhlmacher, *Gottes Gerechtigkeit bei Paulus* (FRLANT 87; Göttingen: Vandenhoeck & Ruprecht, 1965) 211 n. 2.

4. See Deut 4:10; 9:10; 18:16; 31:30; and especially Deut 23:2, 3 [LXX] where *ekklēsia tou kyriou*, "assembly of the LORD" occurs as a translation of the Hebrew *qahal YHWH*. Note, however, that the term *qahal* is rendered as *synagōgē* in Deut 5:22; 33:4.

5. The Greek phrase *klētoi hagioi* without the verb "to be" designates a quality of the members of the community. Designated saints by God, sanctification is their vocation (see 1 Thess 4:3). Similarly Paul is "called to be an apostle" (*klētos apostolos*). Being an apostle is both his status and his vocation.

6. Often in Paul's letters, the title "Christ" appears to have all but lost its formal significance. For all practical purposes "Jesus Christ" functions as a proper name.

7. See also Seneca, *Epistles* 59.6, who speaks of the necessity of metaphors. The philosopher used them to develop moral arguments in much the same manner as did Paul. See *Epistles* 12.1-3; 59.6; 78.16.

8. See, for example, Deut 20:5-6; Jer 1:10; 18:7-10; 24:6; 31:28; 42:10; Sir 49:7; cf. Luke 17:28.

9. See, for example, Plato, *Laws* 1.643B; Dio Chrysostom, *Orations* 71.5; Philo, *Allegorical Interpretation* 3.48; *Cherubim* 100-102.

10. A major exception is the image of the grafted olive branch in Rom 11:17-24.

11. The interrogative pronouns, *ti* ("what?"), are neuter.

12. Compare 1 Cor 12:7, 11.

13. The Greek *synergoi* literally means "coworkers" or "fellow workers" (see p. 154 n. 21). The literal meaning is found in the RSV, "fellow workers," and in JB, NJB, NEB, NIV, and the AV as well. The REB renders the phrase "fellow-workers in God's service" to emphasize the cooperative endeavor of the farmers and to subordinate them to God, thereby avoiding any hint of theological synergism. The NRSV's "God's servants" is far more cautious. Totally avoiding a theological synergetic interpretation, the version obliterates the idea of cooperation — Paul's major point! — seemingly implying that Paul used the word "servants" (*diakonoi*) with which he began in verse 5.

14. Paul's real point was that the leaders of the church in Corinth must work with one another if they are to do God's work. See above, pp. 58-60, 162 n. 54.

15. Note the presence of the root *oiko-*. See above p. 16.

16. In Greek the two epithets immediately follow one another; a single verb "to be" is reserved until the final emphatic place at the end of the sentence.

17. There is some irony in Paul's use of the adjective *sophos*. Applied to a tradesman, the adjective means "master," "experienced," "skillful." Its basic meaning, however, is "wise." Some of the Corinthians thought themselves wise, but their wisdom was not God's wisdom (1 Cor 3:18-21; cf. 1 Cor 1:26).

18. See Euripides, *Alcestis* 348; Maximus Tyrius (6.4d); and Philo, *Dreams* 2.8.

19. See 1 Cor 1:1, "called apostle."

20. The apostolate is listed as the first of the charisms in 1 Cor 12:28.

21. See Beverly Roberts Gaventa, "Mother's Milk and Ministry in 1 Corinthians 3," in *Theology and Ethics in Paul and His Interpreters: Essays in Honor of Victor Paul Furnish*, ed. E. H. Lovering, Jr., and J. L. Sumney (Nashville, Tenn.: Abingdon, 1996) 101-13.

22. See C. D. Buck, *Greek Dialects* (Chicago: University of Chicago Press, 1955) 201-3; Jay Y. Shanor, "Paul as Master Builder: Construction Terms in First Corinthians," *NTS* 34 (1988) 461-71.

23. See 1 Cor 3:8.

24. See, for example, Num 31:22-23; Wis 3:4-6; 1 Pet 1:7; 4:12; Rev 3:18; Philo, *Sacrifices* 80; *Decalogue* 48. Paul writes about testing with fire (*pyr auto dokmasei*). The verb that he used had a technical meaning with regard to assaying metals. Isocrates (12.39), for example, used the verb to describe the assaying of porphyry and gold.

25. An example is offered by Diodorus Siculus, who wrote: "Since the huts [= the homes of the poor] were made of reeds and straw and the fire was forcibly fanned by the breeze, the aid brought by the soldiers came too late" (*Library of History* 20.65.1).

26. Each significant element in an allegory has a specific referent. Occasionally the specificity of the referents adds peculiar details to the image.

27. Since Diodorus Siculus and Josephus use "precious stones" (*lithoi timioi*) to refer to costly stone, for example, marble, used in the construction of major edifices, it is not impossible that Paul's similar reference (1 Cor 3:12) may have had the same connotation.

28. See 2 Cor 6:16 where Paul uses an emphatic "we" to say "we are the temple of the living God." At the time of Second Temple Judaism the only other group so identified were

the sectarians of the Dead Sea Scrolls: "When these things exist in Israel the Community council shall be founded on truth [. . .] to be an everlasting plantation [see *Jub.* 16:26], a holy house for Israel and the foundation of the holy of holies for Aaron. . . . This is the tested rampart, the precious cornerstone that does not [. . .] whose foundations shake or tremble from their place. [. . .] the most holy dwelling for Aaron . . . a house of perfection and truth in Israel . . ." (1QS 8:4-9).

29. See Ernst Käsemann, "Sentences of Holy Law in the New Testament," in *New Testament Questions of Today* (NTL; Philadelphia: Fortress, 1969) 66-81.

30. Thus, Paul J. Achtemeier, *1 Peter* (Hermeneia; Minneapolis: Fortress, 1996) 152.

31. Achtemeier correctly notes that the verse should not be understood in terms of the individual priesthood of each believer. See Achtemeier, *1 Peter*, 156-57, 165. Similarly, John H. Elliott, *1 Peter* (AB 37B; New York: Doubleday, 2000) 451.

32. Cf. 1 Tim 3:15.

33. Paul frequently used a chiastic A-B-A' pattern to develop an argument. Typically, the first section (A) dealt generally with the topic; the second (B) was a rhetorical aside in which Paul strengthened his argument with a basic reflection; the third (A') returned to the original topic, specifically addressing the issue at hand. 1 Corinthians 12–14 follows the chiastic pattern.

34. See above, p. 155 n. 26.

35. See vv. 4, 7, 8 [2x], 9 [2x], 10, 11.

36. The literary device of ring construction (*inclusio*) consists of the repetition of key words or phrases at the beginning and at the end of a passage. In this way, the passage is identified as a discrete literary unit within the author's composition.

37. The term appeared in the *Rhetorica ad Alexandrum* 2.503 (cf. Aristotle, *Rhetorica* 1.3.5), the only extant pre-Aristotelian manual of rhetoric, probably written by Anaximenes of Lampascus (c. 380-320 B.C.E.). On the use of the term in deliberative rhetoric, see Margaret M. Mitchell, *Paul and the Rhetoric of Reconciliation: An Exegetical Investigation of the Language and Composition of 1 Corinthians* (Louisville, Ky.: Westminster/John Knox, 1991) 25-39, esp. 25-32.

38. Note the use of the root *oiko-*. The same root appears in the verb *oikodomeō* ("to build up") in verses 4 [2x] and 17 of chapter 14. The noun also appears in verses 3, 5, and 12.

39. See Richard J. Sklba, "Body of Christ," *TBT* 40 (2002) 219-23.

40. Thus Aristotle wrote, "examples (*paradeigmata*) are most suitable for deliberative speakers" (*Rhetoric* 1.9.40), and again, "If we have no enthymemes, we must employ examples as demonstrative proofs, for conviction is produced by these" (*Rhetoric* 2.20.9).

41. In Greek, "suffer together with it" and "rejoice together with it" are two compound verb forms, *sym-paschei* and *syn-chairei*. For "arranged," Paul used the compound verb *syn-ekerasen*, with the same prefix (cf. v. 18 where the NRSV's "arranged" renders the Greek *etheto*, "placed"). On the use of the prefix, see above, p. 154 n. 21.

42. See the comment in Raymond F. Collins, *First Corinthians* (SP 7; Collegeville, Minn.: Liturgical Press, 1999) 463.

43. See Robin Scroggs, "Woman in the NT," *IDBSup* 966; Bruce, *Galatians*, 187; J. Louis Martyn, *Galatians* (AB 33A; New York: Doubleday, 1997) 375-76. Longenecker (*Galatians*, 157) suggests that Gal 3:27-28 may be a pre-Pauline Christian confession. Its ultimate origins may lie in an old Hellenistic adage, going back as far as Thales of Miletus, one of the Seven Sages of Antiquity (6th c. B.C.E.). Thales is reputed to have said that he was thankful that he was born a human being not a beast, a man and not a woman, a Greek and not a

barbarian. See Diogenes Laertius, *Lives of Eminent Philosophers* 1.33, who attributes a similar saying to Socrates and Plato (on Plato, see also Plutarch, *Marius* 46.1). Gal 3:27-29 is the only passage in the Letter to the Galatians that speaks of baptism.

44. The fact that the second and third couplets of the formula, slave or free, male and female (see Gen 1:27), are extraneous to Paul's rhetorical argument confirm the formulaic nature of Paul's wording.

45. See James D. G. Dunn, *The Epistle to the Galatians* (BNTC; London: A & C Black, 1993) 207.

46. On Paul's possession of the gift of tongues, see 1 Cor 13:1; 14:6a, 14, 18; for the gift of prophecy, see 1 Cor 13:2; 14:6b.

47. The gift of speaking in tongues was obviously problematic. The abuse of this gift prompted Paul to write about the charisms. The gift of healing may have been a problem. The gift does not appear in the list of gifts in Rom 12:4-8, but it does appear in all three lists in 1 Corinthians 12. Paul's emphasis on the gift of healing as a gift given by the Spirit of God may have been his response to the cult of Serapion. The cult of this god, the god of healing, was spread throughout the regions in which Paul preached. Among the pagan temples in Corinth was an important one in honor of Serapion. Archaeological excavations in the city have unearthed a whole collection of ex-votos, life-sized reproductions of various parts of the body, in the Serapion. This ancient phenomenon is comparable to the presence of similar ex-votos in the grotto at Lourdes. See Collins, *First Corinthians*, 461-62; G. G. Garner, "The Temple of Asklepius at Corinth and Paul's Teaching," *Buried History* 18 (1982) 52-58.

48. See 1 Cor 14:23.

49. It is to be noted that the passage does not use the Greek word properly translated as "veil."

50. See Collins, *First Corinthians*, 393-416.

51. So problematic in fact that some commentators, on the basis of very meager evidence, claim that the passage was not an authentic part of Paul's letter. They hold it to be an interpolation placed in the letter a couple of generations later. See the discussion of this claim and other issues in Collins, *First Corinthians*, 511-25.

52. In this passage the word *ekklēsia* (vv. 33, 34, 35) maintains its original meaning, "assembly." It is synonymous with the term *synagōgē*. Today, however, the word "church" is used for a Christian assembly, "synagogue" for a Jewish assembly.

Chapter Four

1. On these debates, see Brendan Byrne, "The Letter to the Philippians," *NJBC* 791-92; Peter T. O'Brien, *The Epistle to the Philippians: A Commentary on the Greek Text* (NIGTC; Grand Rapids: Eerdmans, 1991) 10-26; Raymond E. Brown, *An Introduction to the New Testament* (ABRL; New York: Doubleday, 1997) 493-98.

2. The designation "European" was not used in Paul's own time.

3. On the hospitality of Lydia and the anonymous jailer, see John Gillman, "Hospitality in Acts 16," *LS* 17 (1992) 181-96.

4. Luke employs a rarely used adverb, *panoikei*, which means "with the whole house."

5. Paul did not again use language of holiness in Philippians until the end of the letter. The second and third person greetings in Phil 4:21-22 again mention the saints in Christ Jesus. The mention of saints in Phil 1:1 and again in 4:21-22 constitutes a literary inclusion.

6. See also Rom 1:7; 16:16; 1 Cor 1:2; 16:20; 2 Cor 1:1; 13:12.

7. Since these words are missing from the oldest corpus of Paul's letters, P⁴⁶, Skeat has observed that we cannot be sure that they were part of the original text. See T. C. Skeat, "Did Paul Write to 'Bishops and Deacons' at Philippi? A Note on Philippians 1:1," *NovT* 37 (1995) 12-15. The observation is a possibility; the manuscript has been damaged at the bottom of that particular sheet of papyrus.

8. This translation is found in a footnote of the NRSV. In my commentary on the Pastoral Epistles, I translated *diakonoi* as "servers." See *1 & 2 Timothy and Titus* (NTL; Louisville, Ky.: Westminster John Knox, 2002) 86.

9. The abstract noun *episkopē* ("oversight") appears in Luke 19:44 and Acts 1:20. Acts 1:20 contains a citation of Ps 109:8, which is used to describe the selection of Matthias as a replacement for Judas Iscariot in the Twelve's ministry of "oversight."

10. The term *episkopos* ("overseer") is masculine in form, as is the term *diakonos* ("helper"). Plato used the masculine form *episkopos* to describe these women just as Paul used the masculine form *diakonos* to describe Phoebe (Rom 16:1).

11. Texts of some fifty or so farewell discourses are to be found in Jewish and Christian literature, dating from approximately 100 B.C.E. to 100 C.E. The *Testaments of the Twelve Patriarchs* represents some of the best-known examples; some are found in biblical literature (e.g., Gen 49:1-17, Deuteronomy, John 14–17).

12. Fitzmyer, *Acts*, 675.

13. Succession in ministry or responsibility is one of the typical features of the genre.

14. See LSJ *s.v. tithēmi*. Thus, the term is used of matchmakers and those who get married. Both matchmakers and men who marry make some woman a wife. The term was also used of those who adopt a child, that is, who make someone their son or daughter.

15. On *tēn ekklēsian tou theou*, see above pp. 32-33.

16. See 4 Ezra 5:18; *1 Enoch* 89:13; Matt 7:15; 1 Pet 5:8; cf. John 10:12.

17. See also Matt 26:31; Mark 14:27 (= Zech 13:7); 1 Pet 2:25; Heb 13:20.

18. See 1QS 6:12, 20; CD 9:18, 19, 22; 13:6, 7, 13, 16; 14:8, 11, 13; 15:9, 11, 14. *Episkopos*, *měbaqqēr*, and "overseer" have similar etymologies in their respective language groups.

19. In the Martinez-Tigchelaar edition, *měbaqqēr* is translated as "inspector." For consistency's sake, I have rendered the term as "overseer."

20. See Pol. *Phil.* 6:1.

21. See also Titus 1:5-7; *1 Clem.* 44:1-6; Pol. *Phil.* 6:1

22. Several ancient Greek manuscripts, including Sinaiticus and Vaticanus, lack this word. See the discussion of its authenticity in Bruce M. Metzger, *A Textual Commentary on the Greek New Testament* (2nd ed.; Stuttgart: Deutsche Bibelgesellschaft, 1994) 625-26.

23. For a good discussion of this passage with particular reference to shepherding and oversight, see John H. Elliott, *1 Peter* (AB 37B; New York: Doubleday, 2000) 824-28.

24. The image of the flock as a description of God's holy people is biblical. See Ps 77:20, etc.

25. In contrast, the term does not appear at all in Acts.

26. A NRSV footnote gives "minister" as an alternative translation of *diakonos*. "Minister" is the translation given in Fitzmyer, *Romans*, 728. In both 2 Cor 3:6 and 11:23, the NRSV gives "ministers" as the translation of *diakonoi* when it is used in reference to Paul and his coworkers.

27. The two verses have all the traits and quite closely follow the example of a letter of commendation described by Pseudo Demetrius in "Epistolary Types." See Malherbe, *Ancient Epistolary Theorists*, 32-33.

28. See *IG*$_9$ (1).486; *IGRom* 4.474.12; 4.824.6; Otto Kern, ed., *Die Inschriften von Magnesia am Maeander* (Berlin, 1900; reprinted: Berlin: de Gruyter, 1967) 109, 217.

29. See *CIG* 3037.

30. See *NewDocs* 4 §122.3-4. A sixth-century Cappadocian epigraph uses the term "deacon" in its masculine form to describe a married woman named Maria (*NewDocs* 2 §109.4) During the Patristic era the term *diakonissa* was sometimes used to describe women deacons in the Christian church. See *Apostolic Constitutions* 3.7.

31. The NRSV translation of *diakonia* in Rom 12:7 is "ministry." Fitzmyer compromises, rendering Paul's phrase as "ministry, let it be used in service" (*Romans*, 645, 648).

32. See Fitzmyer, *Romans*, 648.

33. See Brendan Byrne, *Romans* (SP 6; Collegeville, Minn.: Liturgical Press, 1996) 373.

34. Etymologically, the participle means "presider." The RSV translated it as "he who contributes," but most of the modern English versions render it as "leader."

35. Note that 1 Cor 11:5 indicates that some women at Corinth enjoyed the gift of prophecy.

36. The JB, NEB, and REB translate the Greek *diakonian* as "administration." The NJB reads "the gift of practical service."

37. See Byrne, *Romans*, 453.

38. Ibid., 42.

39. Note that *Did.* 11.3-6 distinguishes apostles from false prophets and gives some examples. The *Didache,* like *The Shepherd of Hermas,* considers "apostles" to be a larger group than the twelve of later Christian tradition. The *Shepherd* speaks of forty apostles and teachers (*Herm. Vis.* 3.5.1; *Herm. Sim.* 9.15.4; 9.16.5; 9.25.2). Note that Paul used "apostles" to designate an unnamed group of people in 1 Cor 9:5; 12:28; 2 Cor 8:23; 11:13. See also Eph 4:11.

40. Note that in 1 Thess 2:7 (Greek text; 1 Thess 2:6 in NRSV) Paul refers to himself, Silvanus, and Timothy as apostles of Christ.

41. The noun is derived from the verb *apostellō,* "to send." The term was commonly used as a nautical term with meanings such as "naval expedition" or "cargo that has been sent." Herodotus (5th cent. B.C.E.) used the term to designate a messenger or envoy (*Histories* 1.21). Its first attested Christian usage is in 1 Thess 2:7.

42. "Junias" appears in the RSV, NAB, JB, NJB, NEB, NIV, but "Junia" is the name that appears in more recent translations, NRSV, NABRNT, and REB. The unaccented Greek noun *Iounian* could refer to either a man named Junias or a woman named Junia. Ninth-century minuscules accent the name in such a way as to imply that it is the name of a man. In the twelfth century, Giles of Rome referred to the person as a man (*Aegidii Columnae Romani in epistulam Pauli ad Romanos commentaria,* 97). Patristic and early medieval commentators, however, universally thought the person to be a woman, generally suggesting that she was Andronicus's wife (see also C. E. B. Cranfield, *The Epistle to the Romans* [ICC; Edinburgh: T & T Clark, 1979] 2:788; Byrne, *Romans,* 453). In the Eastern Church the feast of Junias and Andronicus was celebrated on May 17.

43. The Greek *syngeneis,* "relatives," is used of Paul's fellow Jewish Christians in Rom 9:3, where Paul cites the privileges of Israel.

44. James D. G. Dunn, *Romans* (WBC 38; Dallas: Word, 1988) 2:895.

45. See *In epistolam ad Romanos* 31.2 (PG 60.669-70).

46. See Stefan Schreiber, "Arbeit mit der Gemeinde (Röm 16.6, 12): Zur versunkenen Möglichkeit der Gemeindeleitung durch Frauen," *NTS* 46 (2000) 204-26.

47. Etymologically, the Greek term means "yokefellow," as the term was translated in

the RSV. It was often used of those who were "yoked together" in marriage. Euripides, for example, used the term to mean "wife" (*Alcestis* 314, 342). This has led to occasional speculation that Paul used "loyal companion" in reference to Lydia (so, Clement of Alexandria) and that she was his wife (so, Renan in the 19th century), though she remained behind in Philippi. See the discussion of several different possibilities in Peter T. O'Brien, *The Epistle to the Philippians* (NIGTC; Grand Rapids: Eerdmans, 1991) 480-81.

48. See p. 154 n. 21. Note, also, that "loyal companion" (*sy-zyge*) and "help" (*syl-lambanou*) also have the prefix *syn* ("with").

49. See Rom 16:3, 9, 21; 1 Cor 3:9; 2 Cor 1:24; 8:23; Phil 2:25; 4:3; 1 Thess 3:2; Phlm 1, 24.

50. One of my students, Kathleen McGlynn, has suggested "be a teammate with" as a translation of the verb *syn-athleō* to render adequately the athletic imagery of the metaphor.

51. See, among other examples, 1 Cor 9:24-27. See Victor C. Pfitzner, *Paul and the Agon Motif* (Leiden: Brill, 1967) esp. 119-20 in reference to Phil 4:3.

52. Epaphroditus is mentioned in the New Testament only in Phil 2:25 and 4:18. He shares the relative anonymity of Euodia, Syntyche, and Clement, whose names are cited only once in this letter and nowhere else in the New Testament. His name is derived from that of the goddess Aphrodite, an indication that at some time in the past his family had been devotees of the goddess.

53. On the significance of Paul's use of kinship language, see pp. 8-9, 16-17.

54. The first three terms used to describe Epaphroditus appear in the salutation of the Letter to Philemon, probably written more or less at the same time during Paul's imprisonment in Ephesus. It is to be noted that "fellow soldier" is a compound noun with the prefix *syn*. Paul used the term only of Epaphroditus (Phil 2:25) and Archippus (Phlm 2).

55. Military metaphors were often used by Paul. See 1 Thess 5:8; 1 Cor 9:7; 2 Cor 10:3-6. Paul's practice of using military images was imitated by the author of the Pastoral Epistles. See 2 Tim 2:3-5; 4:7.

56. The NRSV notes an alternate possibility of translation, "apostle."

57. Thus O'Brien, *Philippians*, 331.

58. See also Phil 4:18; cf. Rom 12:1.

59. See Victor Paul Furnish, *II Corinthians* (AB 32A; Garden City: Doubleday, 1984) 425, 437-38.

60. See John Gillman, "Epaphroditus," *ABD* 2:533.

Chapter Five

1. Some authors have gone so far as to suggest that Ephesians replaces Christology with ecclesiology.

2. On the authenticity of these two texts, see Collins, *Letters That Paul Did Not Write*, 132-208; Raymond E. Brown, *An Introduction to the New Testament* (ABRL; New York: Doubleday, 1997) 610-15, 627-30. With particular regard to the church, see Collins, *Letters*, 144-49, Brown, *Introduction*, 625-26, 633.

3. See above, pp. 18, 153 n. 7. Aletti notes that by itself the expression "the church in her house" does not allow the reader to judge whether the church that gathered in Nympha's house was the only such gathering in Colossae or whether the author was extending greetings to just one of several house churches in Colossae, namely the one that

met in Nympha's house. See Jean-Noël Aletti, *Saint Paul: Épitre aux Colossiens* (EBib; Paris: Gabalda, 1993) 269.

4. Dunn opines that "the church" (*tēs ekklēsias*) has been added to an earlier hymn in pre-Colossians Christian usage or by the author of Colossians himself. See James D. G. Dunn, *The Epistles to the Colossians and to Philemon* (NIGTC; Grand Rapids: Eerdmans; Carlisle: Paternoster, 1996) 94-95; cf. Aletti, *Colossiens*, 104.

5. Cf. Rom 11:36b; 16:25-27; Gal 1:5; Phil 4:20; 1 Tim 1:17; 6:16d; 2 Tim 4:18; Heb 13:21; 1 Pet 4:11; 2 Pet 3:18; Rev 1:5b-6; 5:13b; 7:12.

6. Cf. Phil 3:20.

7. Achtemeier, however, suggests that "Eph 2:19-22 look like a further reworking (and summarizing) of material contained in 1 Pet 2:1-22" (Achtemeier, *1 Peter*, 156 n. 88).

8. That is, "people outside the house." The term was used to designate people living in a place that was not their own home.

9. Technically, the repeated *oiko-* is an example of paronomasia. The passage employs six different words derived from this root. Among them, *synoikodomeisthe* ("built together") is used only here in the New Testament. The prefix *syn* implies that the construction project is a joint effort. On the importance of the use of words with the root *oiko-*, see above, p. 16.

10. See R. J. McKelvey, *The New Temple: The Church in the New Testament* (London: Oxford University Press, 1969) 108-20.

11. That is, Christian prophets, not the prophets of the Jewish scriptures. On the importance of prophecy in the church, see above, pp. 43-45.

12. The Greek has an emphatic *autou*, "himself." So, Christ himself is the cornerstone.

13. Apart from 1 Pet 2:6, where the term "cornerstone" (*akrogōniaios*, keystone or cornerstone) appears in a citation of Isa 28:16, Eph 2:20 contains the only other use of the word in the New Testament. Stig Hanson (*The Unity of the Church: Colossians and Ephesians* [ASNU 14; Uppsala: Almqvist & Wiksells, 1946] 131) argued that the proper translation of the term is "keystone" rather than "cornerstone." Some authors discern an allusion to Isaiah in the author's use of the metaphor in 1 Peter.

14. The unity of Jews and Gentiles in the church is indicated by the author's use of verbs with the prefix *syn*: "structure is joined together" (*syn-armologoumenē*) . . . "you also are built together" (*syn-oikodomeisthe*).

15. For the temple, see 1 Kgs 8:10; for heaven, see 1 Kgs 8:39, 43, 49.

16. Notwithstanding Peter T. O'Brien (*The Letter to the Ephesians* [Pillar New Testament Commentary; Grand Rapids: Eerdmans; Leicester: Apollos, 1999] 221-22), who claims that the temple is a "*heavenly*" entity." See Andrew T. Lincoln, *Ephesians* (WBC 42; Dallas: Word, 1990) 158-65; Margaret Y. MacDonald, *Colossians, Ephesians* (SP 17; Collegeville, Minn.: Liturgical Press, 2000) 250, 254-55.

17. See 1 Cor 3:16; 6:19-20. On access to God made possible because of Christ Jesus, see Eph 3:12.

18. See Isa 56:6-8; cf. Isa 2:2-3; 25:6-9; Mic 4:3; Zech 8:20-23.

19. Note the use of words with the root *syn* in this passage: "fellow heirs" (*syn-klēronoma*), "members of the same body" (*sys-sōma*), and "sharers" (*sym-metocha*). The author's use of the root to indicate the unity of Jew and Gentile represents a divergence from Paul's own use of the prefix. See above, p. 154 n. 21.

20. The Greek term translated as "plan" is *oikonomia*, with the root *oiko-*. The primary meaning of the term is "household management."

21. According to O'Brien, the "church" in Eph 3:10 should be taken "as the heavenly

gathering that is assembled around Christ *and* as a local congregation of Christians in which Jews and Gentiles are fellow-members of the body of Christ" (his emphasis; see O'Brien, *Ephesians*, 246).

22. This term was often used in common parlance to mean "favor" or "grant [in legal form]." See LSJ, *s.v.* To render the term as "grace" runs the risk of encouraging the reader to introduce theological connotations that are foreign to the author's meaning.

23. Apostles and prophets are also mentioned in Eph 2:20 and 3:5, where they appear as the foundation of the house of God.

24. On the image of the shepherd, see above, pp. 52-54.

25. Note that Colossians' household code is totally lacking in ecclesiological accommodation. A similar three-part scheme, though from the male's point of view, is found in Pseudo-Procylides, 175-227 (see *OTP*, 580-82), which spells out the obligations of the husband, father, and master in turn.

26. See Jer 3:6; Isa 50:1; cf. Exod 34:15-16; Lev 17:7.

27. See Matt 22:1-4; 25:1-3; Mark 2:18-20; John 2:1-11; 3:29; Rev 19:6-9.

28. The Greek *mysterion* ("mystery") of Eph 5:32 was rendered *sacramentum* in Jerome's Vulgate. This Latin translation contributed to the Roman Catholic understanding of Christian marriage as a sacrament. The primary meaning of the Greek *legō* is "say" or "speak."

29. Paul uses the title "savior" in regard to Christ in Phil 3:20, but the expression "savior of the body" occurs in no other place in the New Testament.

30. The title "savior" is unique in this epistle in 5:23, but the cognate verb "to save" (*sōzō*) has a theological sense in Eph 2:5, 8. MacDonald rejects the idea that a Gnostic myth lies behind Eph 5:23's use of the title (*Colossians, Ephesians*, 327), an idea proposed by Heinrich Schlier (*Der Brief an die Epheser* [Dusseldorf: Patmos, 1957] 266-76; and Karl Martin Fischer, *Tendenz und Absicht der Epheserbriefs* (FRLANT 111; Göttingen: Vandenhoeck & Ruprecht, 1973) 186-94.

31. See Judg 11:37-38.

32. Note the use of *kathōs*, "just as," in verses 25 and 29.

33. See *TLNT* 3:21-23; Wiard Popkes, "*paradidōmi*," *EDNT* 2:18-20.

34. See Lev 15:21-33; 17:15-16; 22:6; Isa 1:16; Ezek 36:25; Ps 51:2.

35. Schlier, *Epheser*, 257.

36. See Acts 22:16; Heb 10:22. Cf. Eph 4:5. The baptismal allusion is, however, disparaged by O'Brien, *Ephesians*, 422-23.

37. MacDonald considers these two qualities as attributes of the church (*Colossians, Ephesians*, 199).

38. The description may contain an allusion to Ezek 16:10-14 with its description of Yahweh clothing his covenanted bride. See Rev 19:7-8.

39. This Greek word appears in Eph 5:26, where the NRSV renders it as "washing." On *loutron*, see *TLNT* 2:410-16.

40. Aristophanes, *Lysistrata* 378; *Peace* 843ff.; Euripides, *Phoenician Maidens* 347; Aeschylus, *Prometheus Bound* 556; Thucydides, *Peloponnesian War* 2.15.5. MacDonald, however, considers the bath not as a reference to Hellenistic practices; rather she affirms that it is an allusion "to the ritual bath of purification taken by Jewish women before marriage" (*Colossians, Ephesians*, 76).

41. See the explanatory *gar*, "for," in verse 29.

42. See also Jan Lambrecht, "Christ and the Church, Husband and Wife in Ephesians

5,21-33," in *Collected Studies on Pauline Literature and on the Book of Revelation* (AnBib 147; Rome: Pontifical Biblical Institute, 2001) 295-308, especially 301-3.

43. See Joachim Gnilka, *Die Epheserbrief* (HTKNT 10/2; Freiburg/Vienna: Herder, 1971) 264.

44. *P.Cair.Masp.* 6 B, 132 (see Jean Maspero, ed., *Papyrus grecs d'époque byzantine: Catalogue général des antiquités égyptiennes du Musée du Caire* (3 vols.; Cairo: Zeller Osnabrück, 1911-1916). The Greek reads: *thalpein kai trephein kai himatizein autēn*. Eph 5:29 uses similar vocabulary: *ek-trephei kai thalpei*.

45. *Corpus Papyrorum Raineri Archeducis Austriae*, ed. Carl Wessely et al. (8 vols.; Vienna: Kaiserlich königlich Hof- und Staatsdruckerei, 1895-1983) 1.30.20. The Greek reads: *agapan kai thalpein kai therapeuein*. Ephesians uses the first two verbs to speak of a husband's love for his wife and of Christ's love for the church.

46. Since the Greek verb *ektrephō* and the simple form *trephō* frequently connote feeding, providing nourishment, it would not be excessive to suggest that in the author's choice of vocabulary there is an allusion to the eucharist.

47. The literal meaning of the verb *thalpō* is "to keep warm." Thus, it was used of birds sitting on their eggs until the birth of their young. Used as a metaphor, it came to connote tender affection. See *TLNT* 2:184-85.

48. Note, however, that Eph 4:16 reads: "as each part (*merous*) is working properly." In its stead, a few ancient manuscripts, particularly A, C, Ψ, read *melous*, "members."

Chapter Six

1. See Raymond Collins, *1 & 2 Timothy and Titus* (NTL; Louisville, Ky.: Westminster John Knox, 2002) 102-11.

2. See "The Origins of Church Law," *The Jurist* 61 (2001) 134-56. Qumran's *Manual of Discipline*, which contains rules for the community, has a similar literary form.

3. 2 Timothy can be usefully compared to testaments such as the *Testaments of the Twelve Patriarchs* and the farewell discourses of Luke 22:24-38, John 13–16, and Acts 20:18-35.

4. Normally such catalogues were used to praise a person. Similar catalogues of vices were used to denounce someone. When either of these types of catalogues were used by ancient authors, their cumulative effect was more important than the individual virtues or vices that are cited.

5. Cf. Eph 6:4.

6. On the meaning of each of these qualifications, see Collins, *1 & 2 Timothy and Titus*, 78-86.

7. Since 1 Timothy and Titus offer pastoral directives, it seems appropriate to designate their anonymous author as "the Pastor."

8. The Greek word *oikonomos* is derived from two roots, *oiko-* ("house") and *nomos* ("law"). Thus the *oikonomos* was the slave responsible for the good order of a household.

9. Cf. 1 Pet 2:5. On the meaning of the term *oikos*, see above, p. 16. See also Luke Timothy Johnson, "The Church as God's Household," *TBT* 40 (2002) 224-28.

10. See also *IG* 3.1580.

11. Cf. Rom 9:26; 2 Cor 3:3; 6:16; 1 Thess 1:9 (see Heb 3:12; 9:14; 10:31; 12:22). In biblical times, Jews swore by the living God. See 2 Sam 12:5, etc.

12. Cf. Eph 2:19-22.

13. Possession of "the full knowledge of the truth" (*epignōsis tēs alētheias*) is a hallmark of the church. See 1 Tim 2:4; 4:3; 2 Tim 2:25; 3:7; Titus 1:1. The phrase is a leitmotif in the Pastoral Epistles. It designates the gospel proclaimed by Paul as handed down and understood within the Pastor's church. See Collins, *1 & 2 Timothy and Titus*, 97-98.

14. The imagery may have been derived from Isa 28:16 (cf. 1QS 8:7-10).

15. See 1 Tim 1:3-4, 19-20; 4:1-5; 6:3-5; 2 Tim 2:14; 3:6-9; 4:3-4; Titus 1:10-16; 3:9-11.

16. 1 Tim 1:15; 3:1; 4:9; 2 Tim 2:11; Titus 3:8. See Collins, *1 & 2 Timothy and Titus*, 41-44.

17. See Collins, *1 & 2 Timothy and Titus*, 95-96.

18. Similarly, Raymond E. Brown, *Priest and Bishop* (New York: Paulist, 1970) 34-43, 65-72; idem, *The Critical Meaning of the Bible* (New York: Paulist, 1981) 136-44; idem, *The Churches the Apostles Left Behind* (New York: Paulist, 1984) 32-33. The three-fold distinction among bishops, priests, and deacons, that is, overseers, presbyters, and helpers, first appeared in the writings of Ignatius of Antioch. See Ign., *Magn.* 2; 6:1; *Phld.* 4; 7:1; *Pol.* 6:1; *Smyrn.* 8:1; *Trall.* 2:2–3:1; cf. *Trall.* 12:2; 13:2. In *Trall.* 3:1, having mentioned the bishop, presbyters, and deacons, Ignatius says: "nothing can be called a church without these" (*chōris toutōn ekklēsia ou kaleitai*).

19. See above, pp. 51-54.

20. See above, p. 53.

21. One of the characteristics of the testamentary genre is that it attends to the succession of the person who is about to depart, whether by death or by travel, to another location.

22. Note not only the formal theological presentation of Paul's apostolate in the epistolary prescript, which some authors consider to have been the introduction to the three-letter corpus, but also the way that Paul's apostolic authority is invoked in 1 Tim 1:1; 2:7; 2 Tim 1:1, 11.

23. The verb *proistēmi* appears in 1 Tim 3:4, 5, and 12 in reference to the management of one's own household. Paul himself used the verb to describe those who exercised leadership in the church (1 Thess 5:12) and leadership considered as a charismatic function (Rom 12:8).

24. Note that this bill of rights follows immediately upon a long pericope dealing with the support of widows (1 Tim 5:3-16).

25. The ambiguity arises because the Greek *timē*, whose primary meaning is "honor," was also used to designate compensation or payment.

26. See Collins, *1 & 2 Timothy and Titus*, 144-46.

27. Cf. Matt 18:16.

28. Note the use of the plural in the final farewell greeting (1 Tim 6:21).

29. The division of the New Testament into chapters occurred in the thirteenth century. Accordingly, it is anachronistic to speak of the author writing in the third chapter.

30. The NRSV renders the verb *diakoneitōsan* as "serve as deacons," thereby interpreting and clarifying the author's meaning. The basic meaning of the term was simply "to serve."

31. The Greek juxtaposes the words *prōton, eita*, "first, then."

32. The Greek means "step" or "pedestal."

33. In Greek, *gynē* denotes a mature woman, but only the context allows the reader to determine if she is married or not. Most adult women would have been married.

34. See the discussion on Phoebe above, pp. 55-56.

35. "Husbands of one wife" is the literal translation of *mias gynaikos andres*" which is rendered as "married only once" in the NRSV. See the footnote with regard to this phrase in the NRSV at 1 Tim 3:2.

36. It might be noted that various emperors and imperial authorities required that Jews who enjoyed tolerance within the empire pray for the emperor in lieu of offering sacrifice to the emperor as other people were obliged to do.

37. "Good works" was an important theme in the Pastorals. See also 1 Tim 5:10; 2 Tim 2:21; 3:17; Titus 1:16; 3:1.

38. It should be noted that in the Great Synagogue of Tel Aviv, built in the early part of the twentieth century, there is a balcony for the women who attend the synagogue service. To this day women are separated from men when they come to pray at the base of the western wall of the old temple in Jerusalem, the "wailing wall." Women are denied access to some of the subterranean reaches of the ancient temple. Similarly, the great mosques of Islam have purification and prayer areas for women that are separate from the central hall of the mosque. The area in which men can purify themselves is adjacent to the main hall of the mosque.

39. See Collins, *First Corinthians*, 393-416.

40. "The public reading of scripture" represents the NRSV's translation of a single Greek word, *anagnōsei*, literally, "reading." The translation is a correct interpretation of the Greek.

41. See 1 Cor 15:3-4.

42. For a discussion of the meaning of this gesture and its biblical origins, see Collins, *1 & 2 Timothy and Titus*, 195-97.

43. See *y. Sanh.* 19a.

44. The Greek reads *cheiras tacheōs mēdeni epithei*, literally, "do not impose hands hastily on anyone." The NRSV reads "Do not ordain anyone hastily," a translation that interprets the text as many commentators understand it. The translation, however, neglects the fact that words with the same key roots, *cheir-* and *epitith-*, are rendered with a literal translation in 1 Tim 4:14 and 2 Tim 1:6.

45. See above, p. 113.

46. The epiphany passages contain significant christological and soteriological insights. See Collins, *1 & 2 Timothy and Titus*, 202-9.

47. The reader must note the unique language used by the Pastor in this pericope: "rebirth" (*palingenesia*) does not otherwise appear in the New Testament; "renewal" (*anakainōseōs*) appears elsewhere only in Rom 12:2; "poured out" (*execheen*) and "heirs" (*klēronomoi*) are not otherwise used in the Pastorals; "justified" (*dikaiōthentes*) is not otherwise used in reference to mere humans in these epistles (cf. 1 Tim 3:16).

48. Cf. John 3:3.

49. See Exod 20:12; Deut 5:16.

50. Bonnie Bowman Thurston's significant monograph *The Widows: A Women's Ministry in the Early Church* (Minneapolis: Fortress, 1989) portrays these women as belonging to an order of widows.

51. Many of the Greek manuscripts and ancient versions mention only "the believing woman" (*pistē*). Some ancient manuscripts (D, L, K, Ψ) along with the overwhelming majority of medieval manuscripts read "the believing man or woman" (*pistos ē pistē*). Taken over into the *Textus Receptus*, the expanded reading is reflected in the KJB and Luther's German Bible. It later appeared in the NEB, but not in the REB.

Chapter Seven

1. The evangelist may have had some acquaintance with Paul at the time of the first missionary journey. See Acts 15:38-39.

2. See my short article, "Los Milagros en el Evangelio de Marcos," *Actualidad Pastoral* 132 (1980) 93-95.

3. Thirteen of its forty-four words in Greek, almost 30 percent, express the domestic setting. The primary meaning of the Greek verb *katekeito* (NRSV, "was in bed") is "lie down." Among its specific meanings is "lie in bed" and "lie sick." See Luke 5:25; Herodotus, *Histories* 7.229; Aristophanes, *Women of the Assembly* 313. It may be interesting for the readers of this book to note that the Greek title of Aristophanes' fourth- or fifth-century B.C.E. comedy is *Ecclesiaezusae*. The domestic detail of Peter's mother-in-law lying in bed is absent from the parallel accounts in Matthew and Luke. The later evangelists had less interest in the house than did Mark. See my "The Transformation of a Motif: 'They Entered the House of Simon and Andrew' (Mark 1,29)," *SNTSU* 18 (1993) 5-40.

4. John R. Donahue and Daniel J. Harrington observe: "The house in Mark is often the site of healing, teaching, preaching, or controversy (see 1:29; 2:1, 15; 3:20, 32-33; 5:38; 7:17; 9:33). Since Mark's community gathered as a 'house church' (13:34-37; see Rom 16:5), Mark's readers may have seen these actions of Jesus as proleptic of their community life." See John R. Donahue and Daniel J. Harrington, *The Gospel of Mark* (SP 2; Collegeville, Minn.: Liturgical Press, 2002) 232.

5. Ancient miracle stories, including those narrated in the New Testament, have a three-part structure: (1) the setting of the scene with details highlighting the difficult circumstances; (2) the ritual of the miracle effected by means of ritual gesture or authoritative word; and (3) affirmation of the effect of the miracle through show or tell. Sometimes the narrator shows that the miracle had taken place with a narrative detail that highlights that things are back to normal; sometimes the narrative says that the miracle is effective by using some form of choral response.

6. Contrary to the expectations of much popular piety as well as nineteenth- and twentieth-century apologetics, the miracle stories would not have "proved Jesus' divinity." The Jewish world of Jesus' day knew of exorcists other than Jesus; Hellenists spoke of the cures effected by Serapis/Asklepios and of the wonders brought about by other deities.

7. Cf. Matt 9:2-8; Luke 5:17-26.

8. The Greek *en oikō* means "at home." Presumably the reference is to the home of Simon and Andrew. Many commentators draw attention to the Markan redactional elements in the setting of the story, among them the reference to the house and the crowds "in front of the door" (*pros tēn thyran*, see 1:33).

9. See Matt 9:18-19, 23-26; Luke 8:40-42, 49-56.

10. As Mark tells the story, Jesus took the initiative in putting the mourners who were in the house outside. Only then did he and the chosen group enter where the child was. The verb "went in" (*eisporeuetai*) suggests a room within the house. The ruler of the synagogue had a house larger than the one-room houses in which many people of that time lived.

11. Obviously someone spoke about the story. Otherwise it would not have been preserved and entered into the written Gospel. Similarly, the silence of the women at the tomb was broken (Mark 16:8), despite this being the note on which the Markan Gospel ends.

12. See Matt 15:22-28.

13. Note that different words using the *oiko-* root appear in Mark's Gospel with reference to the temple. See Mark 2:26; 11:17; 13:1, 2; 14:58; 15:29.

14. See above, pp. 21-25.

15. The same sequence—sitting, calling, speaking—appears in the episode of the widow's mite (Mark 12:41-44). On sitting as an official posture for teaching, see Matt 5:1; 23:2; Mark 12:41; Luke 4:20; 5:3. On sitting as a sign of authority, see Matt 19:28; 20:23; 25:31; Mark 10:37, 40.

16. See Matt 12:46-50; Luke 8:19-21.

17. Jesus' saying about the prophet without honor in his own home is the only logion that appears in all four canonical Gospels. See Matt 13:57; Mark 6:4; Luke 4:24; John 4:44. Each of the evangelists uses the prophetic utterance in pursuit of his own redactional interests. Mark strategically placed the saying just before the short missionary discourse.

18. The parallel account in John 6:11 has "took . . . gave thanks . . . distributed" (literally, "gave"). In this account, the Fourth Gospel uses the verb "give thanks" (*eucharistein*) rather than the verb "bless" (*eulogein*). The accounts in Mark 8:6 and Matt 15:36 also have "give thanks" rather than "bless." These two accounts also omit the narrative detail of Jesus' lifting up his eyes to heaven.

19. See among other possible references my "The Eucharist in the New Testament," *Orientale Lumen IV Conference 2000 Proceedings* (Fairfax, Va.: Eastern Christian Journal [2001]) 87-106.

20. See Luke 9:4. The parallel verse in Matt 10:11 does not mention the house. Rather, Matt 10:11 stresses the importance of the missionaries staying with someone who is worthy, a feature that is consistent with Matthew's emphasis on good conduct.

21. On the role of the disciples in Mark, see Jack Dean Kingsbury, *Conflict in Mark: Jesus, Authorities, Disciples* (Minneapolis: Fortress, 1989) 90-117.

22. Cf. Mark 10:28-30.

23. Cf. Mark 10:52.

24. The traditional translation of *alieis anthrōpōn*, "fishers of men," reflects the grammatical syntax of the phrase. The NRSV's attempt to avoid exclusive language has led to the rendering of a noun as if it were a verb.

25. The verb *deute*, "follow," is an aorist imperative form.

26. See the description of the role of Peter in Mark's Gospel given by Pheme Perkins, *Peter: Apostle for the Whole Church* (Studies on Personalities of the New Testament; Columbia, S.C.: University of South Carolina Press, 1994) 57-66.

27. Mark's text is ambiguous. It does not clearly indicate whether the twelve are those whom Jesus summoned or whether Jesus constituted a group of twelve from among those whom he had summoned. See the survey of opinions in Robert A. Guelich, *Mark 1–8:26* (WBC 34A; Dallas: Word, 1989) 157.

28. Among the wide variety of connotations of the Greek verb *poieō*, "do" or "make," is that of making someone something, for example, a wife, a son, a friend. In these cases, the Greek could be rendered "marry," "adopt," "befriend." In Mark 3:14, Jesus "makes" a group of twelve, he constitutes a group of twelve.

29. Luke cites Ps 109:8.

30. See also Mark 10:35-45.

31. Cf. Rev 20:4 and the commentary of Jürgen Roloff, who takes issue with those who see in the thrones, whose number is not given, a reference to either the twenty-four elders or the twelve apostles. See Jürgen Roloff, *Revelation* (CC; Minneapolis: Fortress, 1993) 227.

32. Although the phrase was present in some of the most important ancient manuscripts, including ℵ, B, C, and Θ, it was deleted from C and does not appear in the majority of medieval manuscripts. Its omission is reflected in the *Textus Receptus*, KJB, Luther's Bible, RSV, JB, NJB, NEB, and REB. On the textual discussion, see Metzger, *Textual Commentary*, 69.

33. Moloney notes that this first part of the charge "provides the christological foundation for the disciples' mission." They are to be with Jesus so that they might do what Jesus does. See Francis J. Moloney, *The Gospel of Mark: A Commentary* (Peabody, Mass.: Hendrickson, 2002) 78.

34. Note that the cited verses reprise the vocabulary of Mark 3:13-14: called (*proskaleitai*) the Twelve (*tous dōdeka*) and began to send (*apostellein*).... So they went out and proclaimed (*ekēryxan*).... They cast out many demons... (*daimonia... exeballon*)."

35. With regard to the Greek text, see Metzger, *Textual Commentary*, 69.

36. The Fourth Gospel speaks of the Twelve but does not give a list of their names. See "The Twelve: Another Perspective," in Raymond F. Collins, *These Things Have Been Written: Studies on the Fourth Gospel* (LTPM 2; Louvain: Peeters, 1990; Grand Rapids: Eerdmans, 1991) 68-86.

37. The name Peter appears in Acts 1:13.

38. See below, pp. 102, 106, 111-12.

39. See Mark 14:66-72.

40. The anonymous companion of Jesus who struck off the ear of the high priest's servant (Matt 26:51; Mark 14:47; Luke 22:50) is identified as Simon Peter in John 18:10.

41. Andrew was also in on this conversation. See Mark 13:3.

42. See Brown, *Introduction*, 148-49; Metzger, *Textual Commentary*, 102-6.

43. Jesus' companions are "those who had been with him" (*tois met' autou genomenois*, Mark 16:10). The first part of the charge addressed to the Twelve is "to be with him" (*hina ōsin met' autou*, Mark 3:14).

44. See also the second-century *Gospel of Mary* [Magdalene] and the Ethiopic version of the second-century *Epistula Apostolorum*.

Chapter Eight

1. This kind of utilization of the Gospel according to Matthew came to an end in the Latin church with the development of a three-year cycle of Sunday readings in response to Vatican Council II's call for greater use of the scriptures in the liturgy. Shortly thereafter was published the *Common Lectionary*, whose selection of readings for Sunday liturgy is similar to that of the Latin church.

2. See J. Andrew Overman, *Matthew's Gospel and Formative Judaism: The Social World of the Matthean Community* (Minneapolis: Fortress, 1990).

3. In this regard there is some similarity between the way in which the author of the Epistle to the Ephesians worked with Colossians and the way in which the author of the Gospel according to Matthew worked with Mark.

4. Cf. Matt 10:2; 16:16.

5. Cf. Mark 1:39.

6. See my "Jesus within the Jewish Catechetical Tradition: Matthew's Portrayal of a Teacher at Work," in Catherine Dooley and Mary Collins, eds., *The Echo Within: Emerging*

Issues in Religious Education. A Tribute to Berard L. Marthaler, O.F.M. Conv. (Allen, Tex.: Thomas More, 1997) 89-102.

7. Note the threefold repetition, "began to speak" (literally, "opened his mouth," *anoixas to stoma autou*), "taught," "saying."

8. See Luke 6:47-49. With regard to the saying, see James M. Robinson, Paul Hoffmann, and John S. Kloppenborg, *The Critical Edition of Q* (Hermeneia; Minneapolis: Fortress; Louvain: Peeters, 2000) 96-101; Collins, "The Transformation of a Motif," 31-33.

9. See Matt 14:28, 29; 15:15; 16:16, 18, 22, 23; 17:1, 4, 24; 18:21; 19:27; 26:33, 35, 37, 40, 58, 69, 73, 75.

10. Mark 6:7 and Luke 9:1 simply mention "the Twelve."

11. Jeannine K. Brown describes them as a "character group," noting that in Matt 16:21–20:28 they are almost always Jesus' primary dialogue partner. See Jeannine K. Brown, *The Disciples in Narrative Perspective: The Portrayal and Function of the Matthean Disciples* (Academica Biblica 9; Atlanta: Scholars Press, 2002) 41, 47.

12. Note the tone that is set for the missionary discourse by Matt 9:38.

13. See 2 Cor 12:12 and above, p. 57.

14. The Greek preposition is *hōste*, implying purpose, so, "in order to," "so that they might."

15. On the "I-sayings" in the Synoptic tradition see Rudolf Bultmann, *The History of the Synoptic Tradition* (Oxford: Basil Blackwell, 1963) 150-63, with particular attention to Matt 15:24 on pp. 153, 155, 163.

16. See Num 27:17; 2 Chr 18:16; Jdt 11:19.

17. See above, pp. 95-96.

18. Cf. Acts 1:13.

19. The conjunction *kai*, "and," is used eleven times in Mark's compilation of the names (Mark 3:16-19). Matthew uses the conjunction just six times. An extra *kai* links the two pairs of brothers, reflecting the call narratives in Matt 4:18-22.

20. Note that Mark 3:18, Luke 6:15, and Acts 1:13 do not identify Matthew as the tax collector.

21. See above, pp. 94-95.

22. Rudolf Pesch, "Levi-Matthäus (Mc. 2.14/Mt. 9.9; 10.3): Ein Beitrag zur Lösung eines alten Problems," *ZNW* 59 (1968) 40-56.

23. A consequence is that the name Matthew would be used in the church as the name of the anonymous author of this Gospel.

24. The scene was omitted by Luke, most likely a casualty of his de-eschatologizing the story of Jesus. Luke then transposed the lecture on authority so that it became part of his farewell discourse (Luke 22:24-27).

25. See Brown, *Disciples*, 101-7.

26. See Luke 12:28 and Robinson, *Critical Edition of Q*, 346-47. Apart from Matthew, Luke 12:28 represents the only instance of the use of *oligopistos* or the cognate noun, *oligopistia*, in the New Testament.

27. A parallel address is lacking in Mark's version of the story. See Mark 8:17.

28. See Daniel J. Harrington, *Matthew* (SP 1; Collegeville, Minn.: Liturgical Press, 1991) 258.

29. Cf. John 6:15-21.

30. Ulrich Luz has observed that the closest literary parallel to the episode is a Buddhist text, *Jataka*, 190. The text, cited in English translation in Luz, *Matthew 8–20*

(Hermeneia; Minneapolis: Fortress, 2001) 321-22, is taken from Johannes B. Aufhauser, *Buddha und Jesus in ihren Paralleltexten* (KIT 157; Bonn: Marcus und Weber, 1926) 12.

31. Brown minimalizes the role of Simon Peter, viewing him "as basically a representative of the disciples," with the result that the characteristics assigned to Peter can be assigned to the disciples in general. See Brown, *Disciples*, 42-43.

32. On this motif as an element in a theophany, see Matt 17:7; 28:5, 10; Luke 1:13, 30; 2:10; Acts 18:9; 27:24; Rev 1:17; *2 Enoch* 1:8.

33. Daniel Harrington describes Peter's walking on water as trying "to share in Jesus' power." See Harrington, *Matthew*, 227.

34. With reference to Psalms 18 and 144, W. D. Davies and Dale C. Allison note: "The pattern, theophany + deliverance from water, would have been familiar to readers of the psalms." See W. D. Davies and Dale C. Allison, Jr., *The Gospel According to Saint Matthew*, 2: *Commentary on Matthew VIII–XVIII* (ICC; London: T & T Clark, 1991) 509.

35. Luz notes: "faith is 'little faith,' that is, that mixture of courage and fear . . . of trust and doubt that according to Matthew remains a fundamental characteristic of Christian existence." See Luz, *Matthew 8–20*, 321. Cf. Matt 28:17.

36. See Matt 15:15; 16:16; 17:4; 18:21; 19:27; 26:33, 35.

37. Note that Matthew had established the link between Peter and the church in Matt 16:18.

38. See Mark 9:30-32; Luke 9:43-45.

39. Luz notes that the question directed to Peter "speaks compellingly for concluding that the entire apophthegm is a creation of the church." See Luz, *Matthew 8–20*, 415. For a contrary opinion, see Davies and Allison, *Matthew*, 2:737-38.

40. The qualifying personal pronoun is in the plural, *ho didaskolos hymōn*.

41. Luz, *Matthew 8–10*, offers a good summary of the *Traditions- und Wirkungsgeschichte* of the text. See also Davies and Allison, *Matthew*, 2:738-42.

42. The narrative specifically mentions the collection of the double drachma (*didrachma*). This amount was roughly equivalent to the biblical half-shekel that every free adult Jewish man was required to pay annually for the support of the Temple. The double drachma had been used as the form of payment for more than a century before Matthew's composition of the Gospel.

43. Note that despite the appearance of the adjective in such passages as John 8:31-38; Romans 8; and Gal 3:23–5:1, "free" (*eleutheroi*) is a Synoptic *hapax legomenon*. But the disciples of Jesus will be called "children of God" (*huioi theou*, Matt 5:9; cf. Matt 5:49), an epithet of Jesus in Matt 3:17; 4:3, 6; 8:29; 14:33; 16:16; 17:5; 26:63; 27:40, 43, 54; cf. Matt 2:15; 21:37-38; 28:19.

44. Tellbe considers the payment of this tax to have been one of the four major Jewish identity markers. The others are circumcision, the dietary laws, and observance of the Sabbath and festivals. See Tellbe, *Paul Between Synagogue and State*, 44-45, 182-88.

45. With regard to the historicity of the tradition, see Davies and Allison, *Matthew*, 2:603-15.

46. See Mark 8:27-30; Luke 9:18-21.

47. This is the only time that the name and the nickname appear together in this fashion.

48. On "living" as the primary trait of God, see above, pp. 78, 165 n. 11.

49. See Matt 5:16, 45; 6:1, 9; 7:21; 10:32, 33; 12:50; 18:10, 14, 19.

50. That the Greek *Bariōna*, a *hapax legomenon* in the New Testament (cf. John 1:42), is a transcription from the Aramaic is a sign of the antiquity and provenance of the logion.

51. Cf. Isa 38:10; Wis 16:13; *Pss. Sol.* 16:2; 3 Macc 5:51; 1QH 6:24.

52. Cf. Matt 18:17.

53. Strictly speaking, the narrative does not describe Jesus giving Simon a new name; the burden of the narrative is the interpretation of a name previously given. It is somewhat erroneous to speak of a name change, even though Simon is commonly called Cephas or Peter in early Christian texts, including the New Testament. The new name is a nickname used in addition to or in place of Simon's given name.

54. See 1 Cor 1:12; 3:22; 9:5; 15:5; Gal 1:18; 2:9, 11, 14. Cf. John 1:42.

55. See Richard Bauckham, "Hades, Hell," *ABD* 3:14-15.

56. The mixture of the two metaphors has led some scholars to think that verses 18 and 19 circulated independently from each other in Palestinian Jewish-Christian communities.

57. See Ulrich Luz, *Matthew 8–20*, 364: "Whoever has the keys is either the gatekeeper or—what is more probable with several keys—the manager who has authority over his Lord's rooms and buildings."

58. That is, the Matthean *Sondergut* (M).

59. See, for example, *m. Giṭ.* 9:10.

60. Two texts in the Book of Revelation help to shed some light on the image of the keys. In a vision of the heavenly Christ, Jesus says: "I have the keys of Death and Hades" (Rev 1:18). Later, the seer affirms: "These are the words of the holy one, the true one, who has the key of David, who opens and no one will shut, who shuts and no one opens" (Rev 3:7).

61. See Str-B, 1:739-41; CD 13:9-10; Josephus, *J.W.*, 1.111; Luz, *Matthew 8–20*, 364-65; Overman, *Matthew's Gospel*, 104-6.

62. See Robinson, *Critical Edition of Q*, 280-81. The saying also appears in *Gos. Thom.* 39:1-2 and in a similar version of this text in P. Oxy. 655.

63. Cf. Gal 2:7-10. Note, also, the discussion of limits in 2 Cor 10:13-18.

64. See 1 Tim 3:15 and above, pp. 78-79.

65. It is to be noted that the singular is used in Matt 16:19 of both the person and the object; in Matt 18:18 the plural is used of the subject and of the object. Matt 16:19 uses the Semitizing *en tois ouranois*, literally, "in the heavens," whereas Matt 18:18 uses a simple *en ouranō*, "in heaven." Otherwise, the two sayings are fully parallel with each other.

66. The mention of "two or three witnesses" is taken from Deut 19:15.

67. In the context of Matthew's Jewish-Christian community, *adelphos* is most likely better rendered as "brother" than as "brother and sister." "Brother" occurs in Matthew's Q-source. See Robinson, *Critical Edition of Q*, 488-99. Unlike Luke (Luke 17:3), Matthew has made of the traditional logion the first step in a three-step process.

68. Cf. Matt 5:23-24.

69. Note that in Matt 16:18 "church," *ekklēsia*, refers to a local Jewish-Christian community.

70. Michael Wise et al. render the phrase as "so that he does not continue in sin" (Michael Wise, Martin Abegg, Jr., and Edward Cook, *The Dead Sea Scrolls: A New Translation* [San Francisco: Harper, 1996] 133).

71. 1 Cor 5:3-5 also addresses the community's responsibility to excommunicate a sinner. In this case, the offense is adultery with one's own father's wife—conduct so egregious that it would not be found even among Gentiles. See also 2 Thess 3:6; 2 John 10-11.

72. See above, p. 112.

73. Davies and Allison describe it as "a Christified bit of rabbinism." See Davies and Allison, *Matthew*, 2:790.

74. Two verses contained in the longer conclusion to Mark, Mark 16:15-16, appear to have been based on Matt 28:19.

75. The scene and its language are somewhat similar to the description of the vision of the Son of Man in Dan 7:14.

76. B. J. Hubbard's study, *The Matthean Redaction of a Primitive Apostolic Commissioning: An Exegesis of Matthew 28:16-20* (SBLDS 19; Missoula, Mont.: Scholars Press, 1974), draws attention to the elements of biblical commissioning stories that are found in Matthew's composition.

77. See, however, *Did.* 7:1, 3.

78. Cf. Matt 7:24.

79. Cf. Deut 31:23.

Chapter Nine

1. In a departure from its usual rendition of the Greek text, the NRSV translation of Luke 10:1 reads "seventy." A footnote indicates that some ancient authorities read "seventy-two." These ancient authorities are the source of the reading *ebdomēkonta [duo]*, "seventy [two]," adopted in *GNT*[4] [=N-A[27]]. With its use of brackets the editorial committee indicated some uncertainty, but one of its leading members, the late Kurt Aland, pleaded that the evidence of the textual tradition was such that "seventy-two" should be read without any qualification. See Metzger, *Textual Commentary*, 126-27.

2. The collection and eventual canonization of the New Testament texts had as an unfortunate result the separation of Acts from the Gospel according to Luke. This separation of the two parts of Luke's work has obscured from the sight of many readers Luke's vision of the close link between Jesus and the church.

3. The Greek text reads *eōs eschatou tēs gēs*, "to the end of the earth," in the singular. "To the ends of the earth" (NRSV, together with most English versions) is good English but obscures the point. The phrase "the end of the earth" suggests the capital of the empire, Rome, where Luke ended his story of early Christian evangelization. See Joseph A. Fitzmyer, *The Acts of the Apostles* (AB 31; New York: Doubleday, 1998) 206-7; Luke Timothy Johnson, *The Acts of the Apostles* (SP 5; Collegeville, Minn.: Liturgical Press, 1992) 26-27.

4. Note that in addition to his nineteen "ecclesial" uses of the word *ekklēsia*, Luke used the term once to describe the assembly of God's people during the Exodus (Acts 7:38) and three times to describe a public assembly in Ephesus (Acts 19:32, 39, 40).

5. The story of Peter and Cornelius in Acts 10 has a similar anticipatory function. It prepares the way for and validates the mission to the Gentiles to be carried out by Paul and his companions.

6. Luke mentions Peter some twenty-nine times in the Gospel narrative. In comparison, Peter is named only twenty-three times in Mark and twenty-five times in Matthew. On the role of Peter in the Gospel according to Luke, see Raymond F. Collins, "The Primacy of Peter: A Lukan Perspective," *LS* 26 (2001) 268-81.

7. This terminology is frequently used to describe material from the sayings source that appears in Matthew and Luke. In comparison, the triple tradition contains Markan material subsequently used by Matthew and Mark. A scholarly dispute exists among source critics on the question of the dependence of Luke 12:35-36 (Matt 24:42-51) on Q. Opposing positions are given by Frans Neirynck and by James Robinson et al. See Frans Neirynck,

Q-Synopsis: The Double Tradition Passages in Greek (rev. ed.; Leuven: University Press/Peeters, 1995) 45, and Robinson, *Critical Edition of Q*, 356-75.

8. Cf. Matt 24:42-51.

9. Cf. 1 Tim 3:15.

10. Simon responds in the name of the group. Luke has used both a plural participle (*kopiasantes*, "worked") and a plural verb (*elabomen*, "have caught") in formulating Peter's retort.

11. The only mention of Andrew, Simon's brother, in Luke is to be found in the list of the names of the apostles (Luke 6:14).

12. See above, p. 172 n. 32.

13. See Acts 3:1, 3, 4, 11; 4:13, 19; 8:14.

14. The discourse incorporates material appropriated from the Markan and Matthean narrative sequence (cf. Mark 10:41-45; 14:29-30; Matt 19:28; 20:24-28; 26:33-34), a saying taken over from the sayings source (22:28-30; par. Matt 19:28), and some material that is proper to Luke (22:27a-b, 31-32; 35-38).

15. Cf. Mark 10:42-44; Matt 20:25-27.

16. Cf. John 13:1-11.

17. See Peter K. Nelson, *Leadership and Discipleship: A Study of Luke 22:24-30* (SBLDS 138; Atlanta: Scholars Press, 1994), especially the summary, pp. 256-64.

18. The third unit is 22:35-38. This hearkens back to the missionary discourse in Luke 10. Luke 22:35 reprises the motif found in 10:4. After a reference to the fulfillment of a scripture, namely, Isa 53:12, a short dialogue takes place between "them" [the apostles] and Jesus about a pair of swords. From a narrative point of view, this dialogue anticipates 22:50 when "one of them struck the slave of the high priest and cut off his ear" (22:49-51, v. 50). The name of the swordsman is not given by Luke nor by the other two Synoptists (cf. Mark 14:47; Matt 26:51-54).

19. This short prayer has a function similar to that of the high priestly prayer of Jesus in the farewell discourse of the Fourth Gospel (John 17).

20. The contrast between the emphatic "I" (*egō*) and "you" (*sou*) in Luke's rendition of this prayer report is striking.

21. Neither Luke nor either of the Synoptists identifies the swordsman. The Johannine narrative identifies him as Simon Peter (see John 18:10-11).

22. The text is found in P[75] and in many other ancient manuscripts; it is, however, lacking in some manuscripts of the Western text type and some modern translations, including the RSV.

23. See also John 21:4-14 (23).

24. The three thousand "were added" to the original group of one hundred and twenty believers (Acts 1:15). On Luke's use of numerical summaries, see Fitzmyer, *Acts of the Apostles*, 98.

25. Luke himself always uses the term *ekklēsia* to designate a local assembly.

26. See p. 160 n. 9.

27. Note the emphasis on the number in verse 17, "he [Judas] was numbered among us" (*katērithēmenos ēn en hēmin*), and verse 26, "and he [Matthias] was added to the eleven apostles" (*meta tōn endeka apostolōn*).

28. See above, p. 57.

29. See Richard F. Zehnle, *Peter's Pentecost Discourse: Tradition and Lukan Reinterpretation in Peter's Speeches of Acts 2 and 3* (SBLMS 15; Nashville, Tenn.: Abingdon, 1971).

30. The verses are cited according to the versification found in the NRSV. The first

passage appears as Joel 3:1-5 in the Hebrew Bible [MT]. The second passage appears as Ps 15:8-11 in the Greek Bible [LXX]. See Gert J. Steyn, *Septuagint Quotations in the Context of the Petrine and Pauline Speeches of the Acta Apostolorum* (CBET 12; Kampen: Kok, 1995) 38-63.

31. See Robrecht Michiels, "The 'Model of Church' in the First Christian Community of Jerusalem: Ideal and Reality," *LS* 10 (1985) 303-23.

32. Fitzmyer, *Acts of the Apostles*, 268. Johnson notes that Luke's description is "the sort of 'foundation story' that was rather widespread in Hellenistic literature." See Johnson, *Acts*, 62.

33. Cf. 5:28; 13:12; 17:19. It is also to be noted that in Acts 6:1, the disciples are called *mathētai*, those who are taught.

34. See Schuyler Brown, "Koinonia as the Basis of New Testament Ecclesiology," *One in Christ* 12 (1976) 157-67.

35. Thus, Fitzmyer, *Acts*, 269.

36. Cf. 1 Tim 2:1.

37. See the positive example in 4:36-37 and the negative examples in 5:1-11.

38. See Deut 15:4, 11.

39. See 1QS 1:1, 11-16; 5:1, 2, 16; 6:17, 21-25; 7:20; 1QSa 1:36, 27). On common possessions within the community, see 1QS 5:1-3, 14-16, 20; 6:17-22, 24-25; 7:24-25; 8:22-23; 9:3-11; CD 9:10-15; 10:18-20; 12:6-7; 13:14-15; 14:20; 20:7.

40. Thus, Plato, *Republic* 449C; Aristotle, *Nichomachean Ethics* 1168B; *Politics* 1263A; Plutarch, *Dialogue on Love* 21 [*Moralia* 767E]; Philo, *Abraham* 235.

41. See Johnson, *Acts*, 86.

42. See the discussions in Fitzmyer, *Acts*, 272, 313, 314.

43. This is also Pauline usage. See 1 Thess 2:13, etc.

44. Note, however, that it is Peter who speaks when a problem arises (Acts 5:1-11).

45. See P. W. van der Horst, "Peter's Shadow: The Religio-Historical Background of Acts 5:15," *NTS* 23 (1976-1977) 204-12.

46. The complaint is an indication that the ideal of *koinōnia* portrayed by Luke in the first and second summaries was not always realized in practice.

47. See Leland Ryken et al., *Dictionary of Biblical Imagery: An Encyclopedic Exploration of the Images, Symbols, Motifs, Metaphors, Figures of Speech and Literary Patterns of the Bible* (Downers Grove, Ill.; Leicester, UK: Intervarsity, 1998) 774.

48. See Raymond F. Collins, "Paul's Damascus Experience: Reflections on the Lukan Account," *LS* 11 (1986) 99-118.

49. On the apparent tension between Acts 9:28 and Gal 1:22, see Fitzmyer, *Acts*, 440.

50. Fitzmyer, *Acts*, 538.

51. Ibid.

52. See, for example, Hervé Ponsot, "Peut-on encore parler de 'Concile' de Jérusalem? À propos d'Ac 15 et de la chronologie paulinienne," *RB* 109 (2002) 556-86.

53. Cf. Acts 14:23.

54. Acts 15:20, 29. The four conditions, sometimes identified as Noachic regulations, are derived from the Holiness Code in Leviticus 17–18. They are comparable to the expectations that were set down for aliens living in Israel. See Fitzmyer, *Acts*, 556-58.

55. See John Painter, *Just James: The Brother of Jesus in History and Tradition* (Studies on Personalities in the New Testament; Columbia, S.C.: University of South Carolina Press, 1997), especially pp. 48-56; also, Perkins, *Peter*, 88-95.

56. See Acts 15:30; 16:4-5.

57. At this point in the history of early Christianity, the apostolic letter was already recognized as an authoritative expression of the gospel. The *intitulatio* of the letter expresses the authority on the basis of which the decision was promulgated, namely, that of "apostles and elders." Fitzmyer's translation (*Acts*, 561) is more faithful to the demands of Hellenistic epistolary style than is the version given in the NRSV.

58. Luke typically uses the word "apostles" with reference to the Twelve. In Acts 14:4, 14, however, he uses the designation of Paul and Barnabas.

59. See above, pp. 28-29.

Chapter Ten

1. "The Community of the Beloved Disciple" is the title of his book published in 1979.

2. Paul S. Minear, "Logos Ecclesiology in John's Gospel," in R. Berkey and S. Edwards, eds., *Christological Perspectives: Festschrift for H. K. MacArthur* (New York: Pilgrim, 1982).

3. Johan Ferreira, *Johannine Ecclesiology* (JSNTSup 160; Sheffield, UK: Sheffield Academic Press, 1998) 203.

4. See Raymond F. Collins, "The Twelve: Another Perspective. John 6,67-71," *MelT* 90 (1989) 95-109; reprinted in *These Things Have Been Written: Studies on the Fourth Gospel* (LTPM 2; Louvain: Peeters, 1990; Grand Rapids: Eerdmans, 1991) 68-86.

5. The only use of the word *apostolos* in the Fourth Gospel is in John 13:16. Cf. Rev 21:14.

6. Andrew in John 1:40, 44; 6:8; and 12:22; Philip in John 1:43-46, 48; 6:5-7; 12:21-22; 14:8-9; the sons of Zebedee in the epilogue, John 21:2.

7. Mark 8:29, 31; cf. Matt 16:16, 21; Luke 9:20, 22. There are, however, reasons to question whether "passion" is the correct vocabulary with which to describe the events leading up to Jesus' death as they are narrated in the Fourth Gospel. See Raymond F. Collins, "John's Gospel: A Passion Narrative?" *TBT* 24 (1986) 181-86; reprinted in *These Things Have Been Written*, 87-93.

8. See Gilbert van Belle, *Les parenthèses dans l'Évangile de Jean: Aperçu historique et classification; Texte grec de Jean* (SNTA 11; Louvain: University Press/Peeters, 1985) 78.

9. See Raymond F. Collins, "The Representative Figures of the Fourth Gospel — II," *DRev* 94 (1976) 118-32, 124-26; reprinted in *These Things Have Been Written*, 35-38; "Thomas (Person)," *ABD* 6:528-29.

10. On the identity of this enigmatic figure, see the excellent survey in James H. Charlesworth, *The Beloved Disciple: Whose Witness Validates the Gospel of John?* (Valley Forge, Pa.: Trinity Press International, 1995).

11. Pheme Perkins notes that in John 21:15 and Luke 22:31 Jesus addresses Peter by his given name, Simon. She observes: "This formulation supports the suggestion that the two variants may go back to a single account of the commissioning of Peter by the risen Lord. Luke refers to that tradition in his account of the Easter appearances (Luke 24:34)" (*Peter*, 81).

12. See Raymond Brown, *Community of the Beloved Disciple*, 81: "The Johannine choice of Peter and the Twelve to represent a group of Christians suggests that this group was Jewish Christian in origin, but not necessarily so in constituency." Brown calls them "Christians of Apostolic Churches."

13. Perkins sees in the "other sheep" of John 10:16 a reference to churches which derive their tradition from Peter. She makes reference to Brown, *Community of the Beloved Disci-*

ple, 81-88. See Perkins, *Peter*, 83, 104. Brown himself saw the image as a reference to the Gentile mission. See Brown, *The Gospel According to John: I-XII* (AB 29; Garden City, N.Y.: Doubleday , 1966) 396.

14. See also Acts 20:28-29; 1 Pet 5:1-4; and above, pp. 51-54.

15. Cf. Luke 5:1-11.

16. See Brown, *Community of the Beloved Disciple*, 81.

17. See Raymond F. Collins, *John and His Witness* (Zacchaeus Studies: New Testament; Collegeville, Minn.: Liturgical Press, 1991). Reprinted: Manila: St. Pauls, 1996.

18. Thus, J. Louis Martyn and Brown. See Brown, *The Community of the Beloved Disciple*, 27.

19. See John 13:1; 18:1. The unity of John 13–17 is an exegetical crux. The debate about the relationship of John 13–14 with John 15–16 and John 17 is ongoing. Some authors consider that the narrative setting for the farewell discourse(s), John 13:1-11, should not be included within the material that is assigned to the farewell discourse(s). The purpose of the present work obviates the need for an extensive discussion of these debatable issues. In this work "farewell discourse" simply designates the material found in John 13–17.

20. See above, pp. 51-52, 121-23.

21. Cf. Luke 22:24-38.

22. Misunderstanding is one of the principal themes of the Fourth Gospel. See, for example, R. Alan Culpepper, *Anatomy of the Fourth Gospel: A Study in Literary Design* (FF; Philadelphia: Fortress, 1983), 152-65.

23. The editors of the NRSV have rightly considered that the word *apostolos* must be taken in the nontechnical sense. See also Brown, *Community of the Beloved Disciple*, 81 n. 150. In Greek, *apostolos* is singular, as is *doulos*.

24. The fact that all of the nouns in verse 16 are in the singular suggests that the logion is of a proverbial nature (cf. Matt 10:24b). On proverbial sayings in the Fourth Gospel, see Raymond F. Collins, "Proverbial Sayings in St. John's Gospel," *MelT* 37 (1986) 42-58, 42-58; reprinted as "Proverbial Sayings in John's Gospel," in *These Things Have Been Written*, 128-50, 137.

25. See also John 20:22, apropos of which Moloney (*The Gospel of John* [SP 4; Collegeville, Minn.: Liturgical Press, 1998] 533) comments: "The gift of the Spirit-Paraclete will render the absent Jesus present within the worshipping community (cf. 14:18-21), sharing their experience so that the world might know and believe that Jesus is the Sent One of the Father (cf. 17:21-23)."

26. See also John 16:7. Within the New Testament the word *paraklētos*, "Advocate," appears only in the Johannine corpus (John 14:16, 26; 15:26; 16:7; 1 John 2:1). A substantivized form of a verbal adjective, the word designates someone who is called to another's side in order to help. Thus it can mean "consoler," "intercessor," or, in a legal setting, an "advocate" or legal counsel. LSJ offers "intercessor" as an appropriate meaning for its use in the New Testament. Existing English language translations reflect the wide range of the meaning of the term. Some versions merely transliterate the Greek as Paraclete, thus trying to respect the uniqueness of the Johannine "profile" of the *paraklētos*.

27. On the notion of truth in the Fourth Gospel, see the comprehensive study by Ignace de la Potterie, *La vérité dans Saint Jean* (AnBib 73-74; Rome: Pontifical Biblical Institute Press, 1977).

28. The Fourth Gospel uses "the world" (*kosmos*) as a cipher for opposition to Jesus. The meaning of the term is much more symbolic than it is descriptive of a physical reality. The Fourth Gospel's understanding of "the world" is uniquely Johannine. The term occurs

seventy-eight times in the Fourth Gospel, twenty-four times in the Johannine letters. It occurs only fourteen times in the three Synoptics combined.

29. The formulation of this verse reflects the judicial role of the Advocate. The role is similar to that of a contemporary defense counsel, confronting the prosecutor and the prosecutor's witnesses.

30. See Raymond F. Collins, "'A New Commandment I Give to You, That You Love One Another . . .' (Jn 13:34)," *LTP* 35 (1979) 235-61; reprinted in *These Things Have Been Written*, 217-56.

31. See Collins, "A New Commandment," 238-42; idem, *These Things Have Been Written*, 221-27. On the centrality of the new commandment within the structure of the entire farewell discourse, see Moloney, *John*, 478.

32. See 1 John 2:7; 2 John 5-6. The adjective *kainē*, "new," suggests a qualitative difference.

33. See Fernando F. Segovia, *The Farewell of the Word: The Johannine Call to Abide* (Minneapolis: Fortress, 1991) 148-63.

34. Cf. John 10:16.

35. See 1QS 5:2-3; 6:21; 7:24; 8:16; 9:5-6; CD 20:33.

36. In this context, "Law" (Torah) is the study of the Torah, the characteristic activity of the community.

37. See Ferreira, *Johannine Ecclesiology*, 127. He devotes the entire fourth chapter of his work (pp. 80-137) to an exegesis of John 17 from an ecclesiological perspective.

38. Ibid., 85-86.

39. With regard to their election, see John 15:16: "You did not choose me, but I chose you."

40. This is the import of the neuter singular *pan*, "all." See Moloney, *John*, 463. C. K. Barrett (*The Gospel According to St John* [2nd. ed.; Philadelphia: Westminster, 1978] 502) observes that *pan* designates "the whole."

41. Note also that Jesus' love is the foundation of the disciples' love for one another and is linked to his death. The departing Jesus identifies death on behalf of those who are loved as a love exceeded by no other (John 15:13). Jesus' washing the disciples feet is a symbol of his death. See the several references in Moloney, *John*, 379.

42. *Sic*, and his emphasis. The quotation comes from Ferreira, *Johannine Ecclesiology*, 124.

43. E. Käsemann, *The Testament of Jesus: A Study of the Gospel of John in the Light of Chapter 17* (NTL; London: SCM, 1968) 40.

44. The image is used with negative implications in Jer 2:21 and Ezek 19:12-14. See also the Isaian Song of the Vineyard (Isa 5:1-7), the inspiration of the Synoptic Parable of the Wicked Tenants (Matt 21:33-41; Mark 12:1-12; Luke 20:9-19).

45. See John 14:2.

46. I owe this insight to Mary Coloe's paper on "Anointing the Temple of God: John 12:1-8," presented at the Toronto meeting of the Society of Biblical Literature, November 26, 2002. She drew attention to the death and resurrection motifs in the narrative as well as to the idea that the fragrance of the perfume pervaded the entire house/household.

47. Cf. John 1:12-13.

48. See, especially, Teresa Okure, *The Johannine Approach to Mission: A Contextual Study of John 4:1-42* (WUNT 2nd. ser. 32; Tübingen: Mohr-Siebeck, 1988) 133-68.

49. He draws the conclusion that from this it follows that "the association of others, like the readers, with Jesus can also possibly imply the same." See J. Eugene Botha, *Jesus &*

the Samaritan Woman: A Speech Act Reading of John 4:1-42 (NovTSup 65; Leiden: Brill, 1991) 180.

50. Many authors describe this account as the Johannine Pentecost. As such it would be comparable to the Lukan account of Pentecost in Acts 2:1-12.

51. See Raymond E. Brown, *The Gospel according to John* (AB 29A; Garden City, N.Y.: Doubleday, 1970) 1044.

52. Ibid.

53. Cf. Matt 28:19.

54. So, explicitly, Käsemann, *The Testament of Jesus*, 40.

55. Among the Johannine epistles, only 3 John mentions "the church." It is interesting, however, that the letters to the seven churches of Asia in the Book of Revelation mention "the church" in the introduction to each of the individual letters. See Rev 2:1, 8, 12, 18; 3:1, 7, 14; cf. 2:7, 11, 17, [23], 29; 3:6, 13, 22. This usage may reflect continuing Pauline influence in the churches of Asia Minor. On the discussion as to whether 3 John 10 refers to an excommunication from the church or to Diotrephes exercising his prerogative as a householder, see John Painter, *1, 2, and 3 John* (SP 18; Collegeville, Minn.: Liturgical Press, 2002) 373-74.

56. Raymond E. Brown, *The Epistles of John* (AB 30; Garden City, N.Y.: Doubleday, 1982) xv.

57. See, for example, 1 John 1:1-4. This preface of the letter is more of a confession of common faith than it is an epistolary salutation, of which there is no trace in this "epistle."

58. See p. 155 n. 33.

59. On the importance of hospitality, see above, pp. 18, 29, 79-80.

60. Cf. *Did.* 11:1-2.

61. In a departure from its usual practice, the NRSV has rendered *adelphoi* as friends, consigning "brothers" to a footnote.

62. See above, pp. 51-54, 79-81.

63. See Brown, *Epistles of John*, 647-51, esp. 650-51. The pertinent quotation from Irenaeus is: "I heard it from a certain presbyter who had heard it from those who had seen the apostles and from those who had taught." See also a statement attributed to Papias, a second-century bishop of Hierapolis, by Eusebius (*Ecclesiastical History* 3.39.4).

64. Apropos of Rev 21:9–22:5, the final vision in the book, Jürgen Roloff writes: "In spite of the confusing multitude of visual details, at stake here is not, finally, cosmology, or statements regarding the form and essence of the new creation, but rather ecclesiology, that is, the image of the future that is promised to the church." See Roloff, *Revelation*, 240-41.

65. Cf. Ezek 48:31-34.

66. His emphasis. See Wilfred J. Harrington, *Revelation* (SP 16; Collegeville, Minn.: Liturgical Press, 1993) 213. Harrington sees Eph 2:20 as having a similar function. According to Roloff, the idea of "twelve apostles" excludes Paul. See Roloff, *Revelation*, 243.

67. Rev 19:9 speaks of the invitation to the wedding banquet.

68. See "City," in Ryken, *Dictionary of Biblical Imagery*, 150-54, 152-53.

69. See, for example, 4 Ezra 3:28-36.

70. G. K. Beale correctly observes that "the number 144,000 emphasizes figuratively that this is a picture of the church in its entirety." With reference to such passages as Rev 5:9, 7:9; and 14:6, he notes that it is a "multiracial Christian church" that is redeemed. See G. K. Beale, *The Book of Revelation* (NIGTC; Grand Rapids: Eerdmans; Carlisle: Paternoster, 1999) 413, 1070.

71. Roloff, *Revelation*, 243.

Index of Scripture Passages

Index of Subjects